Electoral Systems

Also by David M. Farrell

Comparing Electoral Systems
Electoral Strategies and Political Marketing (co-edited)
British Elections and Parties Yearbook 1994 (co-edited)
British Elections and Parties Yearbook 1995 (co-edited)
British Elections and Parties Yearbook 1996 (co-edited)
Party Discipline and Parliamentary Government (co-edited)

Electoral Systems

A Comparative Introduction

David M. Farrell

palgrave

This book is a direct replacement for the author's
earlier work *Comparing Electoral Systems* (1997)

The author has asserted his right to be identified
as the author of this work in accordance with the
Copyright, Designs and Patents Act 1988.

First published 2001 by
PALGRAVE
Houndmills, Basingstoke, Hampshire RG21 6XS and
175 Fifth Avenue, New York, N.Y. 10010
Companies and representatives throughout the world

PALGRAVE is the new global academic imprint of St. Martin's Press LLC
Scholarly and Reference Division and Palgrave Publishers Ltd (formerly
Macmillan Press Ltd).

ISBN 0–333–80161–X hardcover
ISBN 0–333–80162–8 paperback

This book is printed on paper suitable for recycling and
made from fully managed and sustained forest sources.

A catalogue record for this book is available
from the British Library.

Library of Congress Cataloging-in-Publication Data
Farrell, David M., 1960–
    Electoral systems : a comparative introduction/David M. Farrell.
        p.   cm.
    Includes bibliographical references and index.
    ISBN 0–333–80161–X – ISBN 0–333–80162–8 (paper)
    1. Elections.   2. Representative government and representation.
I. Title.

JF1001 .F35 2000
324.6'3 – dc21

00–055694

10 9 8 7 6 5
10 09 08 07 06 05 04

Printed in China

Contents

List of Tables and Figures

Tables

Figures

Preface and Acknowledgements

Like my earlier book, *Comparing Electoral Systems*, this book has the aim of making current research and debates on electoral systems accessible to a wider student and general interest readership. While sections draw substantially on the earlier book, its scope is much broader, especially in terms of the themes and countries covered. The amount of updating and new material added throughout convinced me that what was required was a new book, rather than a new edition. As well as taking account of a spate of new elections and important new research on electoral systems, requiring substantial extending and updating of chapters in my previous work, in two new chapters this book gives much more attention to the question of electoral reform and the criteria for choosing electoral systems (Chapter 8), and, in addition, to the question of the supposed trade-off between stability and proportionality (Chapter 9).

The World Wide Web has proved to be a gold mine, making it possible to provide more extensive coverage of trends in a wider range of countries than in my previous book. The richness of material available at such sites as those provided by the International Foundation for Election Systems, the Inter-Parliamentary Union, the International IDEA, or, indeed, Wilfried Derksen's Electoral Web Sites, or the Lijphart Elections Archive, provide the electoral systems researcher with invaluable sources of free data simply unavailable a few years ago.

The scholarly community, particularly in the USA, has also been very active since the publication of *Comparing Electoral Systems*. In the Preface to that book I made reference to the recent publication of important theoretical and comparative studies by Matthew S. Shugart and Rein Taagepera and by Arend Lijphart. The Californian freight train of electoral systems books has continued, most notably exemplified by Gary Cox's *Making Votes Count* (1997), but also represented by a series of edited volumes produced as a result of conferences held at the University of California, Irvine (with books edited by Shaun Bowler, Bernard Grofman, Matthew S. Shugart and Martin P. Wattenberg). Not all the traffic has been from the American west coast. The timely publication of Richard S. Katz's *Democracy and Elections* (1997) has provided a further wealth of new material.

One of the factors causing the rush of new studies on electoral systems has been the emergence of new democracies, providing a heady mix of new cases to survey, as well as the recent fashion for electoral reform in some established democracies. Such developments have contributed to two relatively new trends in the study of electoral systems, both of which are dealt with in this book. First, particularly with the fashion for designing more complex 'mixed' electoral systems, and their attendant effects on how voters and parties make use of them, the focus has shifted to considering the strategic (as opposed to the systemic) consequences of electoral systems. Work in this area by authors like Shaun Bowler or Gary Cox needs to be included in any review of the study of electoral systems; the second half of Chapter 7 has been reworked to take account of this. In addition, Chapter 5 has been substantially re-written to take account of new approaches to conceptualizing and analysing mixed electoral systems.

Second, there has been a growing interest in exploring the factors behind, and the patterns in, the selection of particular electoral systems, especially in the rich tapestry of new democracies (Chapter 8). Among the scholars to be singled out here are Shaheen Mozaffar, Ben Reilly and Andrew Reynolds.

Most of the work on this book was done in Manchester. Its final editing was completed, in early 2000, in the beautiful surroundings of the Australian National University in Canberra, where I enjoyed a brief fellowship. I am grateful to the Research School of Social Sciences for providing me the time and space, and more particularly to my colleagues at the Department of Government at Manchester, for allowing me to take it.

There are a number of people I should thank for their helpful comments on, and corrections to, *Comparing Electoral Systems*, many of which have been incorporated into this book: David Broughton, Michael Dyer, Justin Fisher, Glyn Ford, Wolfgang Hirczy de Mino, Lauri Karvonen, Simon Hix, Alan McRobie, Rick Pildes, Ben Reilly, Geoffrey K. Roberts, Wilma Rule and Martin P. Wattenberg. My publisher, Steven Kennedy, was supportive and encouraging throughout, Keith Povey was his usual thoroughly professional self, and my wife, Arlene McCarthy, continued with her peripatetic lifestyle, allowing me plenty of long evenings to get on with this.

Among the other people who provided useful information and help are (and I apologize to any I may have forgotten): Elisabeth Carter, David Denver, Robert Elgie, Brian Farrell, Rachel Gibson, Jeffrey Karp, Ray Kennedy, Richard S. Katz, Ian McAllister, Pippa Norris, Andrew Reynolds, Geoffrey K. Roberts, Marian Sawyer and Jack Vowles. As always, the McDougall Trust's Paul Wilder was an invaluable source of information; Shaun Bowler guided me through the interpretation of some of the data; and Ken Janda provided wise counsel on my conclusions. Three people I must single out for special thanks for having put up with repeated requests for advice and suggestions, and who always graciously and generously gave them, are Michael Gallagher, Arend Lijphart and Matthew S. Shugart. Doubtless they, and many of the others who have helped me over the past 12 months, will find errors and misinterpretations. I can only hope that these are not too numerous; of course, any that occur are entirely my responsibility.

Given the relationship between this book and *Comparing Electoral Systems*, I want to take the opportunity of once again thanking those people who helped me in my writing of the earlier study. Among those not already mentioned are: Luciano Bardi, Yoram Gorlizki, Paul Harris, Sergei Kondrashov, Malcolm Mackerras, J. P. Pomeroy, Thomas Poguntke, Christopher Siddal and Elizabeth Winship. Finally, as with the previous volume, I wish to dedicate this book to the late Enid Lakeman, who played a very important role in first kindling my interest in electoral systems.

DAVID M. FARRELL

1

The Study of Electoral Systems

1.1 Why Study Electoral Systems?

For people who do not specialize in this area, electoral systems are usually seen as a big 'turn-off'. It can be difficult to instil much interest in the subject of counting rules; to enthuse about the details of how one electoral system varies from another. After all how many wars were fought over whether the electoral formula was 'largest remainder' or 'highest average'; how many politicians have been assassinated over the issue of 'single transferable vote' versus 'single member plurality'? Pity the student on a hot Friday afternoon who has to struggle through the niceties of the 'Droop quota'. Pity the teacher who has to burn midnight oil getting to grips with the issue of 'monotonicity'. It does seem fair to pose the question: why bother? What is the point of spending time examining electoral systems?

Several reasons can be given. First, a very large and growing number of people specialize in electoral systems, so *somebody* must think these systems are important. In actual fact, the interest in studying electoral systems is quite new. As recently as the 1980s, scholars drew attention to how undeveloped was this branch of the political science literature (Lijphart 1985; Taagepera and Shugart 1989). But even then it was already clear that this was likely to become a major field of interest. In his *International Bibliography on Electoral Systems*, Richard S. Katz (1989) listed some 1,500 works 'dealing with the forms and effects of representation and electoral systems'. By 1992 this list had grown to 2,500 works (Katz 1992).[1] These have included some very significant developments in the

1

methodology of studying electoral systems. For more than thirty years one name has dominated over all treatments of electoral systems. The seminal work by Douglas Rae (1967) set the trend on how to study electoral systems and their political consequences. It is only in recent times that Rae's work has come under closer scrutiny as scholars such as Gary Cox, Michael Gallagher, Richard Katz, Arend Lijphart, Matthew Shugart and Rein Taagepera have sought to develop and improve on some of his ideas. Their work (and the work of others) needs to be incorporated into the textbook treatment of electoral systems. This is one of the major functions of this book.

Second, electoral systems are worth examining because they have become politically interesting. With the process of democratization, in Mediterranean Europe in the 1970s, across Latin America and parts of Africa more recently, and perhaps most dramatically towards the end of the 1980s in Central and Eastern Europe and the former Soviet Union, important decisions had to be taken on which electoral systems to adopt in the fledgeling representative democracies. As we shall see in later chapters, in none of these cases was the single member plurality system chosen; in only one case (and only briefly) was the single transferable vote system selected. It is interesting to speculate on the reasoning behind these particular decisions, which we shall do in Chapter 8. Of even greater interest is the recent trend towards reform of existing electoral systems, notably in Italy, Japan and New Zealand – all during the 1990s – and also in a host of other countries where electoral reform has been placed high on the political agenda. This contradicts the impression that electoral reform is rare, occurring only 'in extraordinary historical situations' (Nohlen 1984: 218). These reforms also indicate a growing sympathy for 'mixed' electoral systems (for a long time associated almost solely with postwar Germany), as we see in Chapter 5. Suddenly electoral reform actually looks possible; it is more than some theoretical notion of unrealistic, out-of-touch academics.

There is a third reason why it is important to study electoral systems and that is because they are important: they define how the political system will function. Metaphorically, electoral systems are the cogs that keep the wheels of democracy properly functioning. In almost any course on politics the following themes generally feature as important topics for consideration: elections and representation; parties and party systems; government formation and the politics of coalitions. In each of these areas, the electoral system plays a key role. Depending on how the system is designed it may be easier or harder for particular politicians to win seats; it may be easier or harder for particular parties to gain representation in parliament; it may be more or less likely that one party can form a government on its own. In short, there are important questions about the functioning of political systems which are influenced, at least in part, by the design of the electoral system.

Apart from their primary function of ensuring the smooth running and accepted legitimacy of the system, electoral systems are designed to fulfil a number of other – often conflicting – functions, such as reflecting the wishes of voters, producing strong and stable governments, electing qualified representatives and so on. In selecting a particular design of electoral system, the 'electoral engineers' have to take important decisions about which function to stress most. As a result, no two countries have the same electoral system.

It is important to distinguish between electoral *laws* and electoral *systems*. Electoral laws are the family of rules governing the process of elections: from the calling of the election, through the stages of candidate nomination, party campaigning and voting, and right up to the stage of counting votes and determining the actual election result. There can be any number of rules governing how to run an election. For instance, there are laws on who can vote (citizens, residents, people over seventeen years of age, the financially solvent and so on); there can even be laws, such as in Australia or Belgium, obliging citizens to turn out to vote. Then there is usually a set of rules setting down the procedures for candidate nomination (for example, a minimum number of signatures or a deposit). The campaign process can also be subject to a number of rules: whether polling, television advertising or the use of campaign cars is permitted; the size of billboards; the location of posters; balance in broadcasting coverage, and so on.

Among this panoply of electoral laws there is one set of rules which deal with the process of election itself: how citizens vote, the style of the ballot paper, the method of counting, the final determination of who is elected. It is this aspect of electoral laws with which this book is concerned. This is the electoral system, the mechanism of determining victors and losers, which clicks into action once the campaign has ended. This is the stage where the political pundits take over from the politicians; where the television companies dust off their 'pendulums' and 'swingometers' and wheel out their latest computer graphic wizardry. Campaign slogans and electoral re-criminations have ended. All attention is focused on thousands of people shuffling ballot papers in 'counting centres' throughout the country. (At least, this is the situation in Britain. In other countries, the counting and even the voting is done by computer.) Politicians, journalists and (some) voters wait with bated breath for the return-ing officer to announce 'the result'. TV presenters work long into the night, probing with their panellists the meaning of the results and assessing the voters' 'verdict'.

This scenario of 'election night coverage' is common to most po-litical systems. There may be some variation in detail, but the basic theme is similar: we the voters have voted, and now we are waiting to see the result of our votes, in terms of who wins or loses, in terms of the number of seats won by each of the parties. It is the function of the electoral system to work this transformation of votes into seats. To put this in the form of a definition: *Electoral systems deter-mine the means by which votes are translated into seats in the process of electing politicians into office.*

1.2   Classifying Electoral Systems

Inevitably, the world of electoral systems is crowded and complex: one country's electoral system is never the same as another's (although in some cases the differences are quite small). Given the range of variations among the different electoral systems, this makes life quite difficult for the analyst seeking to produce an acceptable typology. One option might be to simply base a classification of the systems in terms of their *outputs*, that is, with reference to the process of translating votes into seats where one distinguishes between those systems which have 'proportional' outcomes and those with 'non-proportional' outcomes. The essence of proportional systems is to ensure that the number of seats each party wins reflects as closely as possible the number of votes it has received. In non-proportional systems, by contrast, greater importance is attached to ensuring that one party has a clear majority of seats over its com-petitors, thereby (hopefully) increasing the prospect of strong and stable government.

At first glance, a classification based on the outputs of electoral

Table 1.1   Proportional and non-proportional results: two 1983 elections

	Vote (%)	Seats (%)	Diff. (%)
Britain			
Conservative	42.4	61.1	+18.7
Labour	27.6	32.2	+4.6
SDP/Liberal Alliance	25.4	3.5	−21.9
Germany			
Christian Democrats	38.2	38.4	+0.2
Social Democrats	38.2	38.8	+0.6
Free Democrats	7.0	6.8	−0.2

Source: Electoral returns.

systems would seem eminently sensible. Take two diametrically opposite cases, such as Germany and Britain. Table 1.1 provides a useful demonstration from 1983 of how the two systems varied in terms of the number of seats awarded to the third party. Despite polling a quarter of the national vote, the British SDP/Liberal Alliance (a precursor to the Liberal Democrats) was awarded less than 4 per cent of the seats. By contrast, the German Free Democrats' proportion of seats reflected very closely the party's share of the vote. It would seem to make perfect sense, therefore, to have a classification that places Britain and Germany in distinct categories.

But, as ever, reality is never quite so simple. There are different degrees of proportionality; indeed, most authors go so far as to talk of an in-between category of semi-proportional systems (Bogdanor 1983; Lakeman 1974; Reynolds and Reilly 1997). The question then becomes one of deciding on where to locate the different electoral systems. As we shall see in Chapter 6, this focus on 'outputs' has led some scholars, for instance, to locate the single transferable vote in the semi-proportional category, based largely on a review of its performance in one country (Katz 1984). More generally, there is the problem of supposedly proportional systems (such as the list systems used in Greece or Spain) frequently producing less proportional results than supposedly non-proportional systems (such as the single member plurality systems used in the USA or Britain).

An alternative approach to classifying electoral systems – and the basis for most of the existing typologies – entails breaking the electoral system down into its component parts and focusing on the *mechanics* of how votes are translated into seats. Douglas Rae (1969) was the first to distinguish three main components of an electoral system: 'district magnitude', 'electoral formula' and 'ballot structure'. While these terms may sound grandiose, in fact their meaning is quite simple, and they will be used throughout the following chapters to structure our examination of the different electoral systems covered in this book. District magnitude (DM) refers to the size of the constituency ('district' in American parlance; 'electorate' in Australian parlance), measured in terms of the number of seats to be filled. For example, in the USA and the UK, which both use the single member plurality system, each constituency elects just one legislator (DM = 1); by contrast, in Spain, which uses a list system of proportional representation, on average each constituency (or region) elects seven legislators (DM = 7).

The ballot structure determines how voters cast their votes. Here the common distinction is between *categorical* ballots, such as used in the USA or the UK (see Figure 2.1), where voters are given a simple either/or choice between the various candidates on the ballot paper, and *ordinal* ballots, such as in Ireland (see Figure 6.1) or Malta, where voters can vote for all the candidates, ranking them in order of preference. Finally, the electoral formula manages the translation of votes into seats. As we shall see in later chapters, there is a large range of electoral formulas currently in operation (and theoretically a limitless supply of alternatives), but in essence they break down into three main families: plurality, majority and proportional.

Having outlined the three main components of electoral systems, the next stage is to determine exactly how to use them in developing an appropriate classification of electoral systems. As we shall see in the following chapters (and particularly in Chapter 7), there has been a lot of discussion about the precise effects of the three components on the performance of electoral systems. The general consensus is that district magnitude has the greatest effect on the overall proportionality of the result: the larger the district magnitude the more proportional the translation of votes to seats. This might lead us to expect that a classification of electoral systems should base itself first and foremost on this component. The fact is, however, that most of the existing classifications tend to be based on the electoral formula first, only taking secondary account of the other features of electoral systems (Blais and Massicotte 1996; Bogdanor 1983; Lakeman 1974). More sophisticated classifications are available which give equal attention to all three components of electoral systems (Blais 1988; Taylor and Johnston 1979), but while these may produce more theoretically appropriate typologies they also tend to be somewhat unwieldy.

By way of compromise, this book will adopt a mix of several approaches. In this introductory chapter, the electoral systems used in most of the world's existing democracies will be classified on the basis of electoral formula. This is no more than an administrative convenience, helping to group the following five chapters. In each of these chapters the classification will then be refined in terms of all three electoral system components. Finally, in Chapters 7–9 the electoral systems will be reassessed in terms of their outputs, paying particular attention in Chapter 7 to questions of proportionality as well as to their strategic effects.

Table 1.2 provides some preliminary information on the world of electoral systems. Fifty-nine democracies are grouped according to the four main electoral formulas in use. For the most part, these are the same countries identified by Lawrence LeDuc and his colleagues (1996) in their survey of democracies in the mid-1990s, and by Arend Lijphart (1999a) in his more recent survey of *Patterns of Democracy*. These countries were selected on the basis of size (only countries with a population of 2 million or greater are included) and measures of 'political freedom'. The latter is based on the most recent (1998–9) Freedom House annual survey of 'freedom country scores', selecting those countries which achieve a score of 4.0 or less.

Of the main families of electoral systems dealt with in this book, the plurality system (called 'single member plurality' in Chapter 2, often referred to as 'first past the post') predominates in Anglo-Saxon democracies. Eleven (of our sample of 59) countries use it, included among them some of the largest democracies in the world. Indeed, the case of India, with an estimated population just short of one billion, is singularly responsible for the fact that the plurality system is used by a plurality of the world's voters (53 per cent of our sample; for similar trends, see Reynolds and Reilly 1997: 20). In Chapter 3 we will examine the majority systems, which, though less popular (only used by 3 per cent of the population in our sample

Table 1.2   The world of electoral systems in 1999

	Freedom score[a]	Population[b]
Plurality systems		
Bangladesh	3.0	127.6
Canada	1.0	30.7
India	2.5	984.0
Jamaica	2.0	2.5
Malawi	2.5	9.8
Mongolia	2.5	2.5
Nepal	3.5	23.7
Papua New Guinea	2.5	4.4
Thailand	2.5	60.0
United Kingdom	1.5	59.0
USA	1.0	270.3
Majority systems		
Australia	1.0	18.6
France	1.5	58.8
Mali	3.0	10.1
Proportional systems		
Argentina	3.0	36.3
Austria	1.0	8.1
Belgium	1.5	10.2
Benin	2.0	5.6
Brazil	3.5	169.8
Bulgaria	2.5	8.2
Chile	2.5	14.8
Colombia	3.5	38.6
Costa Rica	1.5	3.6
Czech Republic	1.5	10.3
Denmark	1.0	5.3
Finland	1.0	5.2
Greece	2.0	10.7
Ireland	1.0	3.6
Israel	2.0	5.6
Latvia	1.5	2.5
Madagascar	3.0	14.5
Mozambique	3.5	18.6
Netherlands	1.0	15.7
Norway	1.0	4.4
Poland	1.5	38.6
Portugal	1.0	9.9
Slovakia	2.0	5.3

Plurality systems: 11 countries (18.6%), 1,574.5 m (52.8%)

Majority systems: 3 countries (5.1%), 87.5 m (2.9%)

Proportional systems: 29 countries (49.2%), 548.8 m (18.4%)

Table 1.2 *Continued*

	Freedom score[a]	Population[b]	
Slovenia	1.5	2.0	
South Africa	1.5	42.8	
Spain	1.5	39.1	29 countries (49.2%)
Sweden	1.0	8.9	548.8 m (18.4%)
Switzerland	1.0	7.3	
Uruguay	1.5	3.3	
Mixed systems			
Bolivia	2.0	7.8	
Ecuador	2.5	12.3	
Germany	1.5	82.1	
Hungary	1.5	10.2	
Italy	1.5	56.8	
Japan	1.5	125.9	
Lithuania	1.5	3.7	
Mexico	3.5	98.6	16 countries (27.1%)
New Zealand	1.0	3.6	769.4 m (25.8%)
Panama	2.5	2.6	
Philippines	2.5	77.7	
Russia	4.0	146.9	
South Korea	2.0	46.4	
Taiwan	2.0	21.9	
Ukraine	3.4	50.1	
Venezuela	2.5	22.8	

[a] Freedom House combined average ratings 1998–99, where countries ranked 1.0–2.5 are designated 'free', those ranked 3.0–5.5 are 'partly free', and those ranked 5.5–7.0 are 'not free'. Only those countries with a score of 4.0 or less have been included.
[b] In millions. 1998 estimates. Only those countries with a population of 2 million or greater have been included.
Sources: LeDuc *et al.* (1996); Massicotte and Blais (1999); Reynolds and Reilly (1997); Wilfried Derksen's Electoral Web Sites (http://www.agora.stm.it/elections/election.htm); CIA World Factbook 1998 (http://www.odci.gov/cia/publications/factbook/index.html); Freedom House, Annual Survey of Freedom Country Scores (1999) (http://www.freedomhouse.org/).

countries), are used by two leading democracies – Australia and France.[2] The proportional systems come in two main forms: the single transferable vote (used in Ireland and Malta and dealt with in Chapter 6), and the far more popular list systems (dealt with in Chapter 4). As Table 1.2 shows, proportional systems are used by the plurality of countries in our sample; however, in many cases these are quite small countries, so that in total just 18 per cent of the population (of our sample countries) use proportional systems.

The final group of mixed electoral systems, which are dealt with in Chapter 5, have only recently come into their own as a distinct category. The principal defining characteristic of these systems is that they involve the combination of different electoral formulas (plurality and proportional) in one election. For a long time, mixed systems were 'dismissed as eccentricities, transitional formulas, or instances of sheer manipulation doomed to disappear' (Blais and Massicotte 1996: 65). This was not without good reason for they were only used by a handful of countries which, with the exception of postwar Germany (where the system is generally referred to as 'additional member'), were not noted for their democratic longevity. Since the early 1990s, with the new 'wave' of democratization, mixed systems have become quite fashionable, in our sample eclipsing proportional systems for the status of second most commonly used systems (based on population size). According to Massicotte and Blais (1999), a total of 29 countries currently use some form of mixed system.

Chapters 2–6 deal with the operation of each of the systems in turn, in each case describing how the system works, how it has adapted (if at all), and the political context in which it has operated. Having dealt with each of the systems in some detail, the book concludes, in Chapters 7–9, with an assessment of the political consequences of electoral systems, dealing with such questions as: proportionality versus stability; the role of representatives; party campaigns; and the potential for strategic voting.

As pointed out earlier, central to any discussion about electoral systems and their reform are questions of stability and the representation of minority interests. One is often seen as, at least partially, a trade-off against the other. A main contention of this book is that this argument is fallacious, that an electoral system can allow for maximum representation of minority interests without necessarily threatening the stability of government. We will return to this point in the concluding chapter, having reviewed the comparative evidence in Chapters 2–6.

Before proceeding to an analysis of the different electoral systems, however, it is necessary to deal with two issues central to the study of electoral systems: (1) the issue of representation, and (2) the attempts to, as it were, 'artificially' influence the effects of electoral systems.

1.3 Conflicting Views on the Meaning of 'Representation'

The precise meaning of the term 'representation' can vary markedly. The basic distinction is between a 'microcosm' and a 'principal–agent' conception of representation (McLean 1991; Reeve and Ware 1992). The first of these is associated with proponents of proportional electoral systems, the second with supporters of non-proportional systems. A classical exponent of the microcosm view was John Adams, one of the founding fathers of the USA, who said that parliament 'should be an exact portrait, in miniature, of the people at large, as it should think, feel, reason, and act like them' (quoted in McLean 1991: 173). Taken literally this perspective is similar to the governing principle behind public opinion polls: that is, the notion of a representative sample. In other words a society which is made up of the following sorts of ratios – men : women 50 : 50; urban : rural 70 : 30; middle class : working class 40 : 60; black : white 20 : 80 – should elect a parliament which reflects these ratios in microcosm. To put it another way, parliament should be a 'representative sample' of the population. Obviously it is impossible to achieve a perfect representative sample, but the aim should be to get as close as possible to it. On this view, as Raymond Plant (1991: 16) explains, 'the representativeness of a parliament is accounted for by its proportionality'. It is a sociological mirroring of society.

According to the microcosm conception of representation, therefore, it is the pattern of composition of the parliament that matters; but, according to the principal–agent conception, it is the decisions of the parliament that matters. The basis of the principal–agent conception is the notion of one person acting on behalf of another. The representative is elected by the people to represent their interests. In this case, even if the parliament comprises a preponderance of 50-year-old, white, middle-class males, it is representative providing it is seen to be taking decisions on behalf of the voters. It is less important that the parliament is statistically representative of voters, and more important that it acts properly in the interests of the citizens; composition is less important than decisions.

In his excellent summary of these two positions, Iain McLean (1991: 172) observes that each 'seems entirely reasonable, but they are inconsistent'. There is no reconciliation; either you support one perspective or you support the other. Either you are in favour of a parliament that is a microcosm of society, or, instead, you have a view of parliament that stresses its ability to act properly in the interests of all citizens. Ultimately it is a normative judgement call: 'The PR school looks at the composition of a parliament; majoritarians look at its decisions' (McLean 1991: 175). On this basis therefore we can see that it is not possible to draw firm conclusions as to which is better, a proportional or a non-proportional electoral system. Nor, indeed, can any firm conclusions be drawn over *which* particular electoral system is best. This latter point is demonstrated very clearly by Richard S. Katz in his magisterial study, *Democracy and Elections* (1997a). On the basis of his review of 14 models of democracy and their potential fit with alternative electoral systems, Katz's conclusion is deliberately and unapologetically non-committal: 'there is no universally correct, most democratic electoral system, notwithstanding a variety of "one size fits all" prescriptions offered by committed advocates of particular systems' (1997a: 308; see also pp. 181–3 below).

Once we delve more deeply into the question of specific electoral system consequences, however, it is possible to find other more empirical areas where conclusions can be drawn. Some systems are apparently associated with greater degrees of governmental stability; some systems promote smaller parties better than others; there are effects on the nature of parliamentary representation (for example, 'delegate' versus 'trustee' roles) and on the organization and campaign styles of political parties; and there are effects on the representation of women and ethnic minorities. It is possible to be far more definitive in assessing such individual themes, and we will return to them in Chapters 7–9.

1.4   Built-in Distortions to Electoral Systems

As will become all too readily apparent in due course, no single electoral system achieves full proportionality: all electoral systems distort the election result, with some parties benefiting more than others. The best a proportional electoral system can hope to achieve is to minimize the degree of distortion.

Quite apart from the 'natural' distorting effects of electoral systems (which is the subject of Chapter 7), there are instances where electoral engineers resort to added 'artificial' measures, seeking to direct the distorting effects in their favour. There are four such measures which merit discussion here: two of which are most common in (though by no means exclusive to) non-proportional systems, characterized as they are by constituency representation, and two of which are generally found in proportional systems, in which efforts are made to minimize the explosion of minor (and especially extremist) parties. Let us deal with each in turn.

First, there is the practice of *malapportionment*. This refers to a situation in which there are imbalances in the population densities of constituencies that favour some parties over others. This can happen as a matter of course, by population shifts not being compensated for by a redrawing of constituency boundaries. But it can also be engineered on purpose. Take, for example, the case of a governing party reliant on rural votes which fails to redraw the constituency boundaries to take account of rural depopulation. Malapportionment was a serious problem in the USA prior to the 1960s when the Supreme Court (most notably in *Baker* v. *Carr* 1962) started to play a more active role in ordering the regular reapportionment of district boundaries. By the end of the decade the problem of malapportionment had been largely removed (Baker 1986; Peacock 1998).

It is possible to build in measures in the country's electoral laws to protect against such practices. The Irish constitution, for example, contains a clause which ensures that each MP must represent between 20,000 and 30,000 voters. If the government does not meet this requirement it faces a constitutional challenge. In 1968 the governing Fianna Fáil party (whose traditional electoral base is rural) sought to have this clause diluted in a constitutional referendum, but was resoundly defeated.

In his review of comparative trends, Katz (1998) shows how malapportionment can be caused by a range of different factors. For instance, a requirement that certain regions retain a minimum number of parliamentary constituencies regardless of population movements prevents any allowance being taken of population shifts over time: examples of this include Scotland, Wales and Northern Ireland which have fixed numbers of UK parliamentary constituencies set by law. Similar issues arise wherever laws are enacted (such as in the Canadian province of Alberta or parts of Australia) to limit the physical size of constituencies in sparsely populated rural areas. In general, malapportionment is found to occur wherever 'criteria other than the exact equality of population are also to be taken into account in defining constituencies' (Katz 1998: 252). As Rossiter and his colleagues (1999a) demonstrate, the requirements set by British law – such as, for instance, those relating to the City of London, or regarding the treatment of county boundaries – have over time set limitations on the efforts of successive (independent) boundary commissions to achieve a degree of population equality in constituency representation.

A second strategy commonly employed in non-proportional electoral systems (though also found in some proportional systems) is *gerrymandering*. This refers to the practice in which constituency boundaries are redrawn with the intention of producing an inflated number of seats for a party, usually the governing party. There are two ways of achieving this. The first method is to divide one party's supporters into smaller pockets across a range of constituencies so as to ensure that they are kept in a permanent minority in each of the constituencies formed, thereby preventing this party from winning any seats. Wherever the party is too large to allow such a method to work, an alternative tack is to try to minimize the number of seats it can win by designing the constituency boundaries in such a way that where the governing party's vote is high it stands to win a lot of seats and where it is low it stands to lose a few seats.

The term 'gerrymander' came from the shape of a constituency designed by Governor Elbridge Gerry of Massachusetts in 1812. It was so long, narrow and wiggly that one journalist thought it looked like a salamander, and it was accordingly dubbed a 'gerrymander'.

Gerrymandering is generally seen as a common phenomenon in the USA, especially since the onset of computer cartography, and the parties have perfected systems of 'redistricting' to their advantage in those areas where they are in power. For instance, Douglas Amy (1993: 44) refers to a case in the 1990 House of Representatives election in Texas where the Democrats won the bulk of the congressional seats despite the fact that the Republicans had virtually the same vote: the vote tally was Democrats 1,083,351, Republicans 1,080,788. He argues that, at least in part, this reflected a successful gerrymander. A more famous example was in California in 1982 where one constituency (or district) 'designed to protect the incumbent Democrat . . . was an incredible 385-sided figure' (Amy 1993: 46). (For some wonderful examples of recent winners of the Elbridge

Gerry Memorial Award for Creative Cartography, see Baker 1986: 272–3.)

While there may be many apparent examples of gerrymandering, it is necessary to introduce a degree of caution to these interpretations, however. A bad result for one party may have as much to do with an unusual constituency shape as it has to do with the naturally distorting effects of the plurality electoral system. Furthermore, there is always the possibility that a swathe of voters may have switched parties. Mark Rush stresses the need to treat some of the examples of supposed gerrymandering with a pinch of salt. As he comments: 'The contention that a gerrymander results in the actual denial or impairment of a group's representational opportunity presupposes the existence of durable, identifiable groups of voters. But not all groups are so durable or identifiable' (Rush 1993: 5).

Clearly the more identifiable the group, such as on the basis of racial or ethnic characteristics, the more certain we can be about whether we are dealing with gerrymandering. Although there has been much debate over this (for a review, see Whyte 1983), the former devolved government in Northern Ireland (in existence from 1920 to 1972) is often seen as a good example. The Unionist-dominated system was accused of practising a comprehensive system of gerrymandering to protect the interests of the majority Protestant population. A much-cited example is the case of Derry City in the 1960s. As Table 1.3 shows, despite the fact that Catholic voters outflanked

Table 1.3   Gerrymandering in Northern Ireland? Derry City in the 1960s

	Total seats	Nationalist seats	Unionist seats	Catholic votes	Protestant votes	Total votes
South Ward	8	8	0	10,047	1,138	11,185
North Ward	8	0	8	2,530	3,946	6,476
Waterside Ward	4	0	4	1,852	3,697	5,549
Total	20	8	12	14,429	8,781	23,210

Source: O'Hearn (1983: 441).

Protestant voters by a ratio of 1.6:1 (that is, 14,429 as against 8,781), the Nationalists (predominantly supported by Catholic voters) won just 8 of the 12 seats in the Council, so that Unionist councillors out-flanked Nationalist councillors by a ratio of 1.5:1.

In the USA, in the wake of the 1965 Voting Rights Act (VRA; and its subsequent amendments), affirmative racial gerrymandering, involving the creation of 'majority–minority districts', became a prominent means of trying to increase the representation of black (and other) minorities, particularly in the southern states. Such moves have been put in jeopardy, however, as a result of recent Supreme Court decisions (most notably *Shaw* v. *Reno* in 1993), which have judged racial gerrymandering as unconstitutional on the grounds that it flouts the 14th Amendment Equal Protection Clause. This has left the people involved in redrawing district boundaries in a no-win situation: 'their districting plans must somehow comply with the VRA's remedial requirements without being unduly con-scious of race and thereby offending the Court's interpretation of the Equal Protection Clause' (Cain and Miller 1998: 144–5; Karlan 1998). In the light of these new restrictions, attention has now turned to the possibility of switching to more proportional electoral systems as an alternative means of improving minority representation (Engstrom 1998; and see below, pp. 43–4).

Gerrymandering is generally associated with non-proportional electoral systems which have single-member constituencies. However, there are instances of its use in proportional systems, particularly in the case of the single transferable vote electoral system, which is characterized by multi-member constituencies (Mair 1986). The most notorious example in recent Irish history was in the mid-1970s when the minister responsible for boundary revision, James Tully, sought to redesign the constituency boundaries to benefit the gov-erning coalition of Fine Gael and Labour. In the subsequent 1977 election the plan backfired badly, largely due to the fact that the swing against the governing parties was much higher than antici-pated. As a result, the loss for the governing parties was exaggerated by the effects of the attempted gerrymander. As Richard Sinnott (1993: 79) noted, this 'incident has contributed a new term to the political lexicon. The minister responsible was James Tully, and a tul-lymander is a gerrymander that has an effect opposite to that intended.'

For established, mainstream politicians, one of the drawbacks of proportional systems is that they tend to produce proportional results. It is easier for smaller parties and for independents to win seats. There is a danger that counted among these will be political extremists, who in the eyes of the established politicians threaten democracy and give Proportional Representation (PR) a bad name. To try to minimize the risk of too many minor (and especially extremist) parties, it is common for PR systems to include *minimum electoral thresholds* (usually a minimum vote percentage, or minimum number of seats won) which a party must pass in order to be granted any seats in the parliament. Therefore even if under the electoral rules a party could actually win some seats, if it fails to surpass the threshold it is not awarded any seats. The most famous of these electoral thresholds operates in Germany. After the unstable experiences of PR under the Weimar Republic (1919–33) where successive governments were held hostage to the vagaries of minor parties, the German system operates a rule that a party must win either 5 per cent of the vote or three constituency seats in order to pass the electoral threshold (for further discussion, see Chapter 5).

As we shall see in Chapter 4, electoral thresholds are quite a common feature of PR systems, though they can vary greatly in size and method of operation. The lowest threshold in use is in the Netherlands where a party must win at least 0.67 per cent of the national vote to gain parliamentary representation. In Denmark the threshold is set at 2 per cent; in Poland it is 7 per cent. In Sweden a party must win either 4 per cent of the national vote, or else 12 per cent of the vote in one constituency, to be eligible for seats. In some systems a party which fails to pass a minimum electoral threshold is allowed to keep the seats it wins, but it is prevented from receiving what are known as 'top-up' seats, thereby ensuring an in-built advantage to the larger parties. Such top-up advantages are enjoyed, for instance, by larger parties in Austria, Greece, Iceland and Norway (for more details and discussion, see Chapter 4).

A final means of distorting the translation of votes to seats is to introduce a range of *party laws* to restrict the activities of certain categories of parties. The most controversial of these laws are the ones which seek to ban parties from running in elections, or, at least, to make it difficult for them. Again Germany offers the best example with its party law banning 'anti-system' parties, although this has been used very infrequently (Poguntke 1994). Less explicit are the various legal restrictions on the operation of certain types of parties. For instance, in the 1980s in Northern Ireland a full panoply of legal restrictions were brought into play which made life very difficult for the Sinn Féin party. Its candidates were banned from the airwaves (until 1995), except during the final three weeks or so of the formal election campaign. (A similar ban in the Irish Republic from 1973 to 1995 was even more restrictive in that it included the election campaign.) Also a matter of some controversy for Sinn Féin candidates was the non-violence declaration which all Northern Ireland candidates were required to sign.

1.5 Conclusion

In general, however, there is relatively little the established politicians can do to try to influence the effects of electoral systems on the political process. Ultimately the main factor determining the influence an electoral system can bring to bear on a polity is the way in which it has been designed, whether in terms of the degree of electoral proportionality it produces, the type of party system it engenders, the degree of choice it offers to the voter, or other such factors.

These issues can only be assessed through an examination of the different electoral systems on offer, exploring how they operate and with what consequences. This is the function of the remainder of this book, which examines each of the five main families of electoral systems in operation starting, in Chapter 2, with the oldest and simplest single member plurality system. Chapter 3 deals with the two main types of majoritarian system. List systems are dealt with in Chapter 4. Chapter 5 reviews the main types of 'mixed' systems, paying particular attention to the long-established German variant. Finally, the single transferable vote system is dealt with in Chapter 6. The last three chapters deal with comparative themes in the study of electoral systems. Chapter 7 considers their systemic and strategic consequences. Chapter 8 turns things on their head, this time looking at electoral systems in terms of their causes rather than their consequences. The book concludes, in Chapter 9, with a review of the debate over electoral systems and stability.

2

The Single Member Plurality System and its Cousins

This electoral system has been given a range of different titles, such as 'relative majority', 'simple majority', 'single member simple plurality' and the more colloquial 'first past the post'. In this chapter we will refer to it as single member plurality (SMP) as this best reflects the essence of the system. For its supporters the beauty of this system is its simplicity: to get elected a candidate must win a 'plurality' of the vote. This does not mean that the candidate has more votes than all the other candidates combined. It is not necessary to win an overall majority of the vote: providing the candidate has at least one vote more than each of the other candidates, then he or she is declared the victor.

SMP is used for elections in the USA, the UK, Canada and India. Among the other countries using it are Bangladesh, Malawi, Nepal, Pakistan, Thailand, Zambia, and a host of other smaller countries, many of them former British colonies. Since the early 1990s the trend has been away from plurality and towards proportional systems (as will be evident in later chapters), although as we saw in the previous chapter, in population terms SMP remains the most commonly used system (thanks in large part to India's vast population which tends to skew the figures). In the 1990s, SMP was replaced by a mixed system in New Zealand, and by list PR in South Africa. In this context, it is also worth noting that none of the newly emerging democracies, in Mediterranean Europe (that is, in Greece, Portugal and Spain) in the 1970s or in East and Central Europe and the former Soviet Union in the 1980s, adopted SMP as the new electoral system. Without exception they have all opted for list systems, or some form of mixed system (more on this in later chapters).

In discussions about SMP and its possible reform, three main themes resonate: simplicity, stability and constituency representation. First, the system is undoubtedly easy to understand; it is simple and straightforward. In the polling booth, all the voters have to do is mark an 'X' (or in some countries, pull a lever) next to their preferred candidate. The result is also simple to understand: whoever gets the most votes – that is, whoever gets a plurality of the votes, or is, as they say, 'first past the post' – wins. This point about simplicity is particularly apt when, as we see later, comparisons are drawn with the ordinal ballots used in single transferable vote elections, or the 'Droop quota', or the concepts of largest remainders or highest averages.

Second, the argument is usually made that SMP produces stable government and, by extension, a stable political system. For instance, British governments generally enjoy large parliamentary majorities. Indeed, for some time, this distortive tendency in SMP was said to have law-like status, referred to as the 'cube law' on how votes are translated into seats. Coalition government is virtually unknown, unlike under PR systems where the norm is coalition governments. Under SMP the government, so the argument goes, is not hostage to the vagaries of relying on small (often extremist) parties for legislative support. The voters know that the party with the most seats forms the next government, unlike the situation common, say, in the rest of Western Europe where governments are formed as a result of agreements struck between party leaders in smoke-filled rooms after the election. The 'result' (that is, the determination of who forms the government) is more democratic and fairer.

Third, a central feature of political life under SMP is constituency representation. (Note that here 'representation' is taken in its 'principal–agent' conception rather than the 'microcosmic' conception.) Each member of the parliament represents a constituency. Each voter has a constituency MP who can be approached. This is in stark contrast to the situation in, say, Israel where the entire country is one vast constituency, where there may be a concentration of MPs from certain parts of the country, and where certain areas (especially rural, underpopulated areas) are essentially 'unrepresented' (in the sense that there is no single recognizable MP serving the area).

The practice which is being followed in this and subsequent chapters is to focus predominantly on one case as the main source for examples – and in this case the focus will be on Britain. We start, in section 2.1, with a description of how SMP works there, and with what consequences for the nature of British electoral politics. Section 2.2 provides a historical review of the debate over electoral reform in the United Kingdom, a debate which achieved considerable prominence over the 1990s. Section 2.3 extends the coverage to include four additional countries: Canada, India and the USA, which have always used SMP, and New Zealand – formerly seen as the preeminent example of the 'Westminster model of democracy' (Lijphart 1984) – which abandoned SMP in 1993. What have been the experiences of these countries with the system, and what evidence, if any, is there of a rise in demand for electoral reform in Canada, India or the USA? Needless to say, of course, SMP does have its variants. There are versions of it which incorporate multi-member constituencies; there are also versions – such as the limited vote and cumulative vote – that provide greater scope for small parties to win seats. These will be dealt with in section 2.4.

2.1 The Single Member Plurality System in Practice

This is such an easy system to understand that it requires little explanation – and certainly nothing like the detailed explanations required for the other systems in later chapters. To aid comparison with the other systems dealt with in this book, SMP's main points will be described according to the three main features of electoral systems which were outlined in Chapter 1: *district magnitude, ballot structure* and *electoral formula*.

First, the principal characteristic of SMP is that it incorporates single-member constituencies (that is, a district magnitude of one, or DM = 1). For instance, the United Kingdom is divided into 659 constituencies each electing one MP. This is *the* central feature distinguishing proportional and non-proportional systems. Single-seat constituencies do not produce proportional results, as shown by the fact that there are large numbers of voters who do not support the winning candidate. Proportional results require multi-seat constituencies as well as a proportional electoral formula. Basically – as we see in later chapters – the larger the district magnitude (that is, the more seats, or MPs, per constituency), the more proportional the result. It is important to note, however, that this rule only applies in PR systems. In plurality and majoritarian electoral systems the relationship can actually be reversed: the more seats per constituency the less proportional the result.

Second, the election contest in each constituency is between candidates, not (as happens in list systems) between parties. The voting act consists of a voter placing an 'X' (in some countries, colouring in a box, or even pulling a lever) next to the name of their preferred candidate (usually representing their preferred party). The voter can place only one 'X': they can declare a preference for just one candidate. In Figure 2.1 we see an example of a British ballot paper. The

VOTE FOR ONE CANDIDATE ONLY

1	**GRIFFIN** Theresa Griffin of 16 Dovedale Road, Liverpool L18 1DW Labour Party	
2	**MORRIS** Richard James Morris of 46 Croxteth Road, Liverpool L8 3SQ Liverpool Green Party	
3	**MUIES** Gabriel Muies of 26 Loudon Grove, Liverpool L8 8AT Independent	
4	**PRIDDIE** Hulbert Llewelyn Priddie of 10 Lesseps Road, Liverpool L8 0RD Liberal Democrat	
5	**ZSIGMOND** Carol Ann Zsigmond of 43 Rodney Street, Liverpool L1 9EW Conservative Party Candidate	

Figure 2.1   A British SMP ballot paper

act of voting is short and sweet. The voter marks 'X' next to the appropriate candidate and then pops the ballot paper into the ballot box. The whole exercise requires barely a minute to complete. In the jargon of the electoral systems literature the fact that the voter has only one choice means that the SMP *ballot structure* is 'categorical' (an either/or choice), not 'ordinal' (where a preference can be declared for more than one candidate on the ballot paper). Figure 2.2 provides an example of a recent ballot paper from Tulsa county, Oklahoma in the USA.[1] Note how here the voting act consists of 'completing the arrows', and while in this case the process of voting may be as simple as in British parliamentary elections, there is one very important difference – Oklahoma voters are voting for more than twenty different offices at the same time (from governor down to county treasurer), which puts a much greater burden on Oklahoma voters than on British voters. At the heart of the matter is the meaning of a 'general election'. In the UK (as in many other countries) it means that all parliamentary seats are up for election. In the USA, it means that all (or mostly all) of the national, state and local offices are up for election. That difference has an enormous consequence for the nature of US politics, not least in terms of the numbers of voters who bother to turn out (as we shall see in Chapter 9).

The third main feature of SMP relates to how a candidate wins: the successful candidate is the one who receives most votes. Note that the candidate does not have to win an overall majority of votes, they must only have more votes than anybody else, or a plurality of support. Therefore the *electoral formula* is a plurality election. The 1992 British election provides one of the most fascinating recent examples of the difference between 'plurality' and 'majority'. As Table 2.1 shows, in the constituency of Inverness, Nairn and Lochaber, Sir Russell Johnston was elected despite having only 26 per cent of the total vote in the constituency (when we allow for those who did not vote, this represents just 19 per cent of the electorate). He had a plurality of support, but not by any means an overall majority. In fact, he had just 458 votes (0.9 per cent) more than his nearest rival. To look at this from another angle, 74 per cent of those who voted in Inverness, Nairn and Lochaber did not vote for the 'winning' candidate; 81 per cent of the electorate (that is, including those who did not vote) did not show support for him. In the 1992 British general election as a whole, 40 per cent of MPs were

OFFICIAL ABSENTEE BALLOT
GENERAL ELECTION
NOVEMBER 8, 1994
TULSA COUNTY, OKLAHOMA

0

26

TO VOTE: COMPLETE THE ARROW(S) ⬅ ◀ POINTING TO YOUR CHOICE(S), LIKE THIS ⬅◀

USE A #2 PENCIL (NO INK)

STATE OFFICERS

STRAIGHT PARTY VOTING
(Vote for One)

DEMOCRAT ⬅ ◀
REPUBLICAN ⬅ ◀

FOR GOVERNOR
(Vote for One)

JACK MILDREN, Democrat ⬅ ◀
FRANK KEATING, Republican ⬅ ◀
WES WATKINS, Independent ⬅ ◀

FOR LIEUTENANT GOVERNOR
(Vote for One)

NANCE DIAMOND, Democrat ⬅ ◀
MARY FALLIN, Republican ⬅ ◀
BRUCE D. HARTNITT, Independent ⬅ ◀

FOR STATE AUDITOR AND INSPECTOR
(Vote for One)

CLIFTON H. SCOTT, Democrat ⬅ ◀
JERRY GERALD PAUL DULANEY, Republican ⬅ ◀

FOR ATTORNEY GENERAL
(Vote for One)

DREW EDMONDSON, Democrat ⬅ ◀
MIKE HUNTER, Republican ⬅ ◀

FOR STATE TREASURER
(Vote for One)

ROBERT BUTKIN, Democrat ⬅ ◀
BOB KEASLER, Republican ⬅ ◀

FOR SUPERINTENDENT OF PUBLIC INSTRUCTION
(Vote for One)

SANDY GARRETT, Democrat ⬅ ◀
LINDA MURPHY, Republican ⬅ ◀

FOR COMMISSIONER OF LABOR
(Vote for One)

DAVE RENFRO, Democrat ⬅ ◀
BRENDA RENEAU, Republican ⬅ ◀

FOR STATE INSURANCE COMMISSIONER
(Vote for One)

CARROLL FISHER, Democrat ⬅ ◀
JOHN P. CRAWFORD, Republican ⬅ ◀

FOR CORPORATION COMMISSIONER
(Vote for One)

CHARLES NESBITT, Democrat ⬅ ◀
BOB ANTHONY, Republican ⬅ ◀

CONGRESSIONAL OFFICERS

STRAIGHT PARTY VOTING
(Vote for One)

DEMOCRAT ⬅ ◀
REPUBLICAN ⬅ ◀

FOR U.S. SENATOR
(Unexpired Term)
(Vote for One)

DAVE McCURDY, Democrat ⬅ ◀
JAMES M. INHOFE, Republican ⬅ ◀
DANNY CORN, Independent ⬅ ◀

FOR U.S. REPRESENTATIVE DISTRICT NO. 1
(Vote for One)

STUART PRICE, Democrat ⬅ ◀
STEVE LARGENT, Republican ⬅ ◀

JUDICIAL OFFICERS

FOR DISTRICT JUDGE DISTRICT NO. 14, OFFICE NO. 11 ELECTORAL DIVISION NO. 1
(Vote for One)

ART PRICE ⬅ ◀
THOMAS S. CREWSON ⬅ ◀

FOR DISTRICT JUDGE DISTRICT NO. 14, OFFICE NO. 1
(Vote for One)

ALVIN HAYES, JR. ⬅ ◀
RONALD L. SHAFFER ⬅ ◀

FOR DISTRICT JUDGE DISTRICT NO. 14, OFFICE NO. 7
(Vote for One)

GAIL HARRIS ⬅ ◀
TOM GILLERT ⬅ ◀

FOR DISTRICT JUDGE DISTRICT NO. 14, OFFICE NO. 9
(Vote for One)

JAY DALTON ⬅ ◀
NED TURNBULL ⬅ ◀

FOR DISTRICT JUDGE DISTRICT NO. 14, OFFICE NO. 10
(Vote for One)

JAMES A. HOGUE, SR. ⬅ ◀
DONALD CLINTON LANE ⬅ ◀

FOR DISTRICT JUDGE DISTRICT NO. 14, OFFICE NO. 12
(Vote for One)

DAVID E. WINSLOW ⬅ ◀
DAVID K. HOEL ⬅ ◀

LEGISLATIVE, DISTRICT & COUNTY OFFICERS

STRAIGHT PARTY VOTING
(Vote for One)

DEMOCRAT ⬅ ◀
REPUBLICAN ⬅ ◀

FOR STATE REPRESENTATIVE DISTRICT NO. 77
(Vote for One)

GARY A. STOTTLEMYRE, Democrat ⬅ ◀
MARK LIOTTA, Republican ⬅ ◀

FOR DISTRICT ATTORNEY DISTRICT NO. 14
(Vote for One)

DAVID MOSS, Democrat ⬅ ◀
WILLIAM J. MUSSEMAN, Republican ⬅ ◀

FOR COUNTY ASSESSOR
(Vote for One)

JAMES R. DUVALL, Democrat ⬅ ◀
CHERYL CLAY, Republican ⬅ ◀

FOR COUNTY TREASURER
(Vote for One)

J. R. MASLANKA, Democrat ⬅ ◀
ROBERT NELSON, Republican ⬅ ◀

VOTE BOTH SIDES

Figure 2.2   A US SMP ballot paper

Table 2.1   Winning with a bare quarter of the vote: the British
constituency of Inverness, Nairn and Lochaber in 1992

	Number of votes	Per cent vote
Johnston, Sir Russell (Liberal Democrat)	13,258	26.0
Stewart, D. (Labour)	12,800	25.1
Ewing, F. S. (SNP)	12,562	24.7
Scott, J. (Conservative)	11,517	22.6
Martin, J. (Green)	766	1.5
Total vote	50,903	
Turnout		73.3%

Source: Electoral returns.

elected without having an overall majority of the votes in their constituency. In the subsequent 1997 election, this figure rose to 47 per
cent. Such an outcome is quite normal in Britain, as evidenced by
the trends over time shown in Table 2.2. Here we see that the most
striking results were in the two 1974 elections when almost two-
thirds of MPs were elected with less than half the total vote in their
constituencies.

When the figures are aggregated across the country as a whole, it
is possible to see the levels of distortion that can be produced under
SMP. Table 2.3 gives the percentage of votes and seats for the three
main parties in postwar British elections. The trend to follow is the
percentage difference between the share of votes received and
the share of seats won by each of the parties. A plus sign implies the
party gained a greater share of seats than its share of the vote; a
minus sign implies it received a lesser share of seats.

Clearly the most striking trend is that for the Liberals/Liberal
Democrats. This party has consistently won fewer seats relative to its
total vote. The starkest example, as we saw in Table 1.1, was in the
supposedly 'mould-breaking' election of 1983, when despite having
almost as many votes as Labour (25.4 per cent compared with 27.6
per cent), the SDP/Liberal Alliance won a far smaller share of seats
(3.5 per cent compared with 32.2 per cent): a vote–seat difference of
21.9 per cent. To show this discrepancy in another way, in 1983 on
average each Conservative MP represented 32,777 voters; each

Table 2.2   British MPs elected with less than 50 per cent of the vote,
1918–97

	MPs elected with a minority of votes	Minority MPs as % of all MPs
1918	97	14.5
1922	173	30.0
1923	203	35.2
1924	124	21.5
1929	310	53.8
1931	34	5.9
1935	58	10.1
1945	174	29.0
1950	187	29.9
1951	39	6.2
1955	37	5.9
1959	80	12.7
1964	232	36.8
1966	185	29.4
1970	124	19.7
February 1974	408	64.3
October 1974	380	59.8
1979	207	32.6
1983	334	51.4
1987	283	43.5
1992	258	39.6
1997	310	47.0

Sources: Punnett (1991); election returns.

Labour MP represented 40,464 voters; while each Alliance MP
represented a grand total of 338,302 voters.

The large discrepancy in Liberal Democrat seats and votes is
caused by the fact that the party's support is spread thinly across the
country; it does not have the same levels of concentrated support
in particular parts of the country that the two larger parties enjoy.
The Conservative Party's electoral base is in the South of England;
Labour's electoral base is in the North, and in Scotland and Wales.[2]
Similarly the small regional parties in Scotland, Wales and Northern Ireland benefit from a strong local focus in support and, on the
whole, they tend to win an appropriate share of seats relative to their
share of the vote.

Table 2.3   British election results, 1945–97: vote and seat percentages

	Conservatives			Labour			Liberals/Liberal Democrats[a]		
	Vote (%)	Seat (%)	Diff. (%)	Vote (%)	Seat (%)	Diff. (%)	Vote (%)	Seat (%)	Diff. (%)
1945	36.8	31.1	−5.7	48.0	61.4	+13.4	9.0	1.9	−7.1
1950	43.4	47.7	+4.3	46.1	50.4	+4.3	9.1	1.4	−7.7
1951	48.0	51.4	+3.4	48.8	47.2	−1.6	2.6	1.0	−1.6
1955	49.7	54.8	+5.1	46.4	44.0	−2.4	2.7	1.0	−1.7
1959	49.4	57.9	+8.5	43.8	41.0	−2.8	5.9	1.0	−4.9
1964	43.4	48.3	+4.9	44.1	50.3	+6.2	11.2	1.4	−9.8
1966	41.9	40.2	−1.7	48.0	57.8	+9.8	8.5	1.9	−6.6
1970	46.4	52.4	+6.0	43.1	45.7	+2.6	7.5	1.0	−6.5
Feb. 1974	37.9	46.8	+8.9	37.2	47.4	+10.2	19.3	2.2	−17.1
Oct. 1974	35.8	43.6	+7.8	39.3	50.2	+10.9	18.3	2.0	−16.3
1979	43.9	53.4	+9.5	36.9	42.4	+5.5	13.8	1.7	−12.1
1983	42.4	61.1	+18.7	27.6	32.2	+4.6	25.4	3.5	−21.9
1987	42.3	57.8	+15.5	30.8	35.2	+4.4	22.6	3.4	−19.2
1992	41.9	51.6	+9.7	34.4	41.6	+7.2	17.8	3.1	−14.7
1997	30.7	25.0	−5.7	43.2	63.4	+20.2	16.8	7.0	−9.8

Notes: Percentages do not add up to 100 because not all parties are included. In the 'Diff.' columns a positive sign implies that the party gained a greater share of seats than its share of the vote, a negative sign implies it received a lesser share of seats.
[a] Includes the Social Democratic Party in 1983 and 1987.
Sources: Mackie and Rose (1991); election results.

The other point to note about the trends in vote–seat per cent differences in Table 2.3 is that the differences have become larger in recent decades, starting with the elections in the first part of the 1970s. This reflects the fact that the Liberal surge in votes coincided with a decline in the total vote for the two larger parties. What this demonstrates is that SMP works best in a two-party system. In a multi-party system – as the 1983 results indicate – there are bound to be some gross anomalies. Of course, the political parties are well aware of this, and do their level best to try and increase the 'efficiency' of their vote, in particular by focusing their campaign efforts on marginal seats and encouraging voters to vote tactically. In recent elections, the focus of such campaigns has been on trying to unseat electorally vulnerable Conservative MPs (for example, GROTT –

Get Rid of the Tories – in 1997). Media coverage of the 1997 election headlined some prominent cases of where MPs were unseated
in the light of such campaigns. Subsequent analysis of the aggregate
voting trends (and as also is implied by the final entry in Table 2.3)
confirmed the successes of Labour and the Liberal Democrats in
steering their votes tactically, thereby ensuring that, on this occasion,
much of the 'bias' in the SMP system was at the expense of the
Conservatives (Johnston *et al.* 1999; Rossiter *et al.* 1999b).

A third point to be noted about the figures in Table 2.3 is that the
system can also produce unusual election results in terms of who
'wins' office. In 1951 the Conservative Party won more seats than
Labour despite having fewer votes. In February 1974 it was Labour's
turn to benefit, winning more seats than the Conservatives despite
having fewer votes. As for the point about strong government, the
only example of a 'hung' parliament (where no single party had an
overall majority) was in February 1974. We have to go back to before
the Second World War to find other examples (1929, 1923, twice in
1910). However, there have been a number of governments with very
small majorities, where the practice of 'strong' government has been
somewhat curtailed. The most prominent example was as a result of
the October 1974 election when Labour had only a majority of three.
By April 1976, due to resignations and by-election losses, the government had lost majority status and for the remainder of its term
it relied on the support of smaller parties, especially the Liberals.
(This was the period of the 'Lib–Lab pact'.) Other close election
results were in 1950 (when Labour had a majority of five seats) and
1964 (when Labour's majority was four). The Conservative government elected in 1992 had a majority of just 21 seats. Due to a process
of attrition (primarily death and subsequent loss of by-elections, and
in some cases desertion to other parties) the government's majority
was gradually whittled away, leaving it vulnerable to backbench
revolts.

On the basis of the UK experience, to what extent does SMP meet
the requirements of simplicity, stability and constituency representation which were introduced at the start of the chapter? It cannot
be disputed that it is simple, both to use and to understand, and this
fact will be ever more evident as we examine the other main electoral
systems in use. But is simplicity really the issue? It is all very well
being able to understand what is going on, but what do I actually
gain from this if my preferred candidate (and my preferred party) is

resoundingly defeated election after election, perhaps because I happen to live in a non-marginal constituency? In other words, the benefit of simplicity can be (and is often) at the cost of fairness – fairness to smaller parties and to the supporters of smaller parties, fairness to those voters 'trapped' in seats which are safely held by parties they do not support.

Why should the question of simplicity be any more important for British voters than for any other voters? It clearly has not been seen as a relevant factor by those countries which have recently adopted proportional systems: in Mediterranean, Central and Eastern Europe, Japan or New Zealand – the latter replacing SMP with a mixed system. Indeed, it is hard to find any evidence of higher levels of voter confusion in other countries. For instance, there are no perceptible differences in the numbers of spoiled or invalid votes (see below, pp. 202–3). For that matter, when Northern Ireland voters moved towards the more complex single transferable vote system (which we deal with in Chapter 6) for local elections in the 1970s, 'the system [did not] prove complicated for voters': the numbers of invalid votes did not rise (Bogdanor 1981: 147).

There are a number of issues to consider under the rubric of government 'stability', and we will be returning to this, in far more detail, in Chapter 9. For the moment, let us deal with one aspect which is prominent in the British debate, namely the argument that the plurality system has an in-built mechanism to produce single-party parliamentary majorities and hence 'strong' government. For some time this used to be formalized as a 'cube rule' (Butler 1963; Kendall and Stuart 1950), which can be summarized as follows: if the ratio of votes that two parties receive is $A:B$, then this will result in the following ratio of seats, $A^3:B^3$. In other words, the plurality system is said to exaggerate the winning party's lead, making it easier to win a clear majority of the seats, and hence promoting greater parliamentary stability. With the onset of electoral volatility from the 1970s, and the declining hold of the two larger parties (particularly as a result of the electoral rise of the Liberals/Liberal Democrats), it has been far less easy to predict the relationship between votes and seats, leading Vernon Bogdanor (1981: 180; also Butler 1983; Curtice and Steed 1982; though see Norris and Crewe 1994) to conclude that 'the cube law has ceased to hold in Britain'. This is confirmed by analysis of recent elections which shows no perceptible evidence of vote–seat distortion (Curtice 1992). Needless to say, if the electoral system can no longer guarantee a parliamentary majority for the party winning the most votes (as evidenced by the 1974 results), then this raises doubts about the utility of the argument that it promotes stable government.

Despite the evident demise of the cube rule, of course it can be argued that the record of postwar British electoral politics speaks for itself. British governments have tended to be long-lasting and stable, in contrast to the record of other European countries. Here attention is paid to the instability of coalitions and the dangers that can hold for political system stability (Pinto-Duschinsky 1999). The common examples cited are Fourth Republic France (1946–58), Weimar Germany (1919–33) and postwar Italy. More recently, there have been references to the frequency of elections in Ireland since the early 1980s, especially the three elections held over an eighteen-month period in 1981–2. Here 'stability' is taken to mean 'longevity': that is, the length of time governments remain in office. While it is easy to refer to unstable cases like Italy – which has tended to change government virtually every year – it is also quite easy to find examples of countries, like Luxembourg or Sweden, where coalition governments are the norm and yet where governments enjoy long lives. We will return to this issue in Chapter 9, when dealing with international comparisons and with other meanings of the word 'stability'.

The third requirement of an electoral system, which is particularly prominent in the British debate, is that it should incorporate constituency representation. Just like the legend of the 'bobby on the beat', there tends to be a certain nostalgic imagery attached to the idea of the constituency politician, to the idea that voters throughout the land have constituency representatives promoting their special interests and needs.

But how significant a factor is constituency representation? For instance, to what extent can one argue that Sir Russell Johnston had a proper mandate to represent his constituency, when only 19 per cent of the electorate actually voted for him? Similar questions can be raised about those 47 per cent of MPs elected in 1997 without an overall majority of support in their constituency. Furthermore, what significance has constituency representation in a parliamentary party system which discourages independent action; where MPs are whipped into the voting lobbies? There is not exactly great scope for individual constituency representation in the legislature when MPs are expected to toe the party line. This is not to deny the fact that constituent contact with MPs is significant and increasing and that MPs are making ever increasing use of parliamentary question time to promote constituency concerns (Cain *et al.* 1987; Franklin and Norton 1993), and that such activities clearly affect the personal vote of MPs (Norton and Wood 1990). But parliamentary questions represent only a part of the work of the Commons; it is in the area of legislation – in the legislative role of MPs – that questions could perhaps be raised. A politician who pays attention to constituency concerns may not have quite so much time to devote to legislative details (Bowler and Farrell 1993; Cain *et al.* 1987).

There are other questions worth raising over the issue of constituency representation. For instance, there is a question mark over the representation of those voters who backed a losing candidate: for example, to what extent are the interests of a Conservative supporter being served by a sitting Labour MP? Finally, there is the issue of whether, in fact, constituency representation is compatible with stable government. Almost by definition a good constituency MP (particularly if from the governing party) is not necessarily a good team player in parliament. For instance, in cases in which specific constituency interests conflict with party policy, such an MP may be unwilling or unable to toe the party line. Given the right circumstances, this could threaten government stability (Whiteley and Seyd 1999).

2.2 Britain's Long Road to Electoral Reform

The question of electoral reform has gained a certain prominence in Britain, particularly since the election of a new Labour government in 1997 which has placed electoral reform high on its agenda. As an examination of late nineteenth- and early twentieth-century British history reveals, however, this is not the first time electoral reform has had such prominence (Bogdanor 1981; Butler 1963; Hart 1992). Indeed, on one occasion – in 1918 – the single transferable vote was very nearly adopted as the method of election for a third of parliamentary constituencies. Furthermore it is interesting to note how the main themes of the debate have not changed a great deal over time.

Because the issue of electoral reform in Britain has been so closely bound up with the process of democratization, much time has been spent on areas of electoral law which are unrelated to voting rules. In particular, attention has focused on the process of enfranchisement – on the gradual extension of voting rights to men and later to women – and on constituency boundaries and their revision (Butler 1963). These issues are not dealt with here, as we are more concerned with the electoral system itself: that is, the voting rules used in British elections.

The first main period of debate was from the mid-nineteenth century through to the early 1930s. A series of attempts – in 1867, 1884, 1910, 1917 and 1931 – were made to change the voting rules for election to the House of Commons. This coincided with the development of democracy, mass enfranchisement and the origins of the existing party system. Three electoral systems featured in these debates: the limited vote, the alternative vote and the single transferable vote (STV). It was the latter of these which attracted the most attention, particularly among those pushing for change. STV originated in the writings of Thomas Hare from the 1850s onwards. His work – particularly his *Treatise on the Election of Representatives, Parliamentary and Municipal* (1859) – greatly affected people like the philosopher John Stuart Mill, who at the time was a Member of Parliament (Hart 1992). Mill sought unsuccessfully to have Hare's single transferable vote system ('hare-brained', as it was dubbed by critics) introduced in the 1860s. Later, in the 1880s, the Proportional Representation Society was formed with the principal aim of lobbying for STV.

Looked at from the perspective of the beginning of the twenty-first century, there is something quite familiar about a number of the aspects of these early debates. First, there is a close similarity in the nature of the people calling for electoral reform. In the 1880s and early 1900s the Proportional Representation Society featured prominently, working in coalition with minority groupings in the major parties. Similar coalitions between groups within the main parties and organizations such as the Electoral Reform Society (the successor to the PR Society) are prominent in the current debate. Second – and seemingly in stark contrast to the 'founding fathers' of the USA (McLean 1992) – there is not a lot of evidence that British politicians took much trouble to study electoral systems and to understand them. Jennifer Hart's (1992) review of the earlier debates shows how little critics of electoral reform seemed to know about the workings of electoral systems. Similar observations are not uncommon in the contemporary debate.

Finally, there are evident similarities in the themes which featured in both debates. In both cases the principal theme has been strong government. However, in the earlier debates, whereas there was a concern to protect minority interests, this was not in the sense we would understand this today, where PR is often proposed to facilitate the representation of ethnic minorities, but rather in the sense that the position of the minority elite was seen as endangered by the process of mass enfranchisement. The elite faced the prospect of losing power to the masses, and in this sense 'strong government' was under threat. In addition – and for much the same reasons – there was a desire to limit the power of parties, to control the dangers to democracy of factions and caucuses (particularly as, it was felt, these have a tendency to encourage extremes).

These questions were behind one significant change in the electoral system (in the 1860s) and several more ambitious proposals for change which were all defeated in the Commons. The change in 1867 was the adoption of the limited vote for thirteen three-seat constituencies and one four-seat constituency introduced by the Reform Act of that year. Prior to the Reform Act, most of the parliamentary constituencies elected two members, which tended to exaggerate the bias in favour of larger parties inherent in SMP. Under the limited vote system, electors were given three votes in a four-seat constituency and two votes in a three-seat constituency. As Bogdanor (1981: 101) observes, its intention was to 'allow [a] minority to be represented on as little as one-third of the vote'. While there is some evidence that the system did help to protect minority interests, it did not do so consistently (Lakeman 1974: 83–4). Furthermore, it 'encouraged the development of a party machine whose purpose it was to ensure that only majorities were represented' via elaborate vote management strategies (Bogdanor 1981: 104).

The Third Reform Act of 1884–5 abolished the limited vote and with it went most of Britain's multi-seat constituencies: the single-seat constituencies date from this period. One main consequence of the experiment with the limited vote was that it weakened the case for further attempts at electoral reform. There was little appetite for another experiment. This reluctance was clear in each of the subsequent pushes for electoral reform: in 1910, 1916–17 and 1931. Each of these episodes is dealt with in detail in the available histories

(Bogdanor 1981; Butler 1963; Hart 1992). It is worthwhile spending a moment on the 1916–17 Speaker's Conference proposals, however, particularly as this was the one occasion when the electoral reformers came enticingly close to getting their way. In 1916 a Speaker's Conference was established to come up with proposals relating to franchise extension and its consequences. Its 1917 report proposed STV for borough constituencies – about a third of the constituencies – and the alternative vote (used in Australia, and discussed in Chapter 3) for the remaining (predominantly rural) constituencies. It was the STV proposal which attracted the bulk of attention. Here was a clear attempt to protect the minority elite from the dangers of mass enfranchisement, particularly in urban areas where the Labour Party stood to make great gains. The proposal attracted widespread support in the subsequent parliamentary debate, particularly among those members not affected by it. Ultimately, it was rejected, but only after a series of votes in the Commons and the Lords in which the proposal was repeatedly rejected and reintroduced. Indeed, its initial rejection, in the first Commons vote, was by only a narrow margin. Just eight votes prevented the adoption of STV for one-third of constituencies. The result could hardly have been closer. With the rejection of the proposal, and 'as a rather picturesque anomaly' (Bogdanor 1981: 129), STV was only introduced in four of the seven university seats (representing university graduates; see Blackburn 1995: 70–1). Otherwise the electoral system remained unchanged.

With the exception of one more push for electoral reform in 1931 – when the alternative vote was the system being promoted – nothing much was heard on the question until the early 1970s, when Britain entered into its second main period of debate over electoral reform. A number of factors coincided to drive electoral reform back on to the agenda. The most significant of these was the growing instability of the British voter as revealed by the 1974 election results (Farrell *et al.* 1994). As was discussed above when examining Table 2.3, the patently unfair result for the Liberal Party in that year, whose large votes in both elections were not translated into large numbers of seats, and the disproportionate benefit in seats for Labour in February 1974 (when the party received more seats than the Conservatives despite having fewer votes), once again raised questions about the electoral system. By the mid-1970s, the advocates of electoral reform were no longer being dismissed as 'harmless and rather amusing cranks, like nudists or the eaters of nut-cutlets' (Lord Avebury cited in Hart 1992: 279). Indeed, they received a further fillip from three more developments in the 1970s: the outbreak of the 'troubles' in Northern Ireland, Britain's accession to the European Community, and the debate over regional devolution.

First, with the collapse of the devolved political system in Northern Ireland in the early 1970s, and in an effort to reduce communal tensions in the province, the British government reintroduced the single transferable vote for all elections other than Westminster elections (STV had been used there in the 1920s before being abolished by the Unionist-dominated government). Subsequently in 1979 STV was further extended to European Parliament elections in Northern Ireland. Second, Britain's accession to membership of the European Community in 1973 coincided with the move towards the first Community-wide election of the European Parliament (in 1979), and the question over whether there should be a uniform electoral system across the Community. In a House of Commons vote in 1977 on whether a PR list system (see Chapter 4) should be adopted, Labour (in a free vote) divided and the Conservatives voted against, thereby leaving Britain (that is, excluding Northern Ireland) as the only part of the European Community to elect its MEPs under SMP (Bowler and Farrell 1993). Third, the mid-1970s debates over Scottish and Welsh devolution included questions over what system to use for the new regional assemblies to be elected if devolution were successful. Despite pressures from smaller parties, however, the Labour government came out against the use of a PR system, and the devolution proposals were ultimately defeated, albeit by a technicality, in a referendum.

The coincidence of electoral instability, and the regional and EC debates, meant that electoral reform was high on the political agenda. In 1975 the Hansard Society established a Commission on Electoral Reform, chaired by the historian and Conservative peer, Lord Blake. Its report in the following year proposed a mixed electoral system (that is, a version of the system used in Germany; see Chapter 5), with three-quarters of the Commons elected in single-seat constituencies and the remainder elected on regional lists. Coinciding with this report, an all-party National Committee for Electoral Reform was established, chaired by Lord Harlech. This was designed to coordinate the various organizations calling for reform, and it too attracted a great deal of attention. After several years of appearing neutral as to which PR system to promote, it eventually came down firmly in favour of STV.

Largely as a result of the activities of the National Committee and its influential backers, electoral reform remained on the agenda of British politics into the 1980s. However, the fact remained that, for the most part, electoral reform was the concern of smaller parties and small minorities within the larger parties. Neither the Conservative nor Labour hierarchies were prepared to embrace electoral reform, fearing that this would endanger their chances of forming single-party majority governments. By the end of the 1980s, however – and after having lost three elections in succession – the Labour Party began to show signs of a new emphasis. The view was being expressed more frequently within party ranks that it could no longer hope to defeat the Conservatives by itself, that some form of coalition was inevitable. Given the long-held view of the Liberals (now Liberal Democrats) in favour of PR, this meant that any future coalition arrangement with them would be likely to have to include an agreement on electoral reform.

The Labour Party's Damascas-like conversion to favouring electoral reform involved a number of key stages, starting with the work of an internal working party (the Plant Commission) in 1991–3, followed soon after by high-level negotiations with the Liberal Democrats, and culminating, in 1997, in election manifesto promises to introduce PR for European Parliament elections, and for elections to assemblies which would be established under a new round of regional devolution proposals. Most significantly, the 1997 Labour manifesto also included a promise to hold a referendum on electoral reform for the House of Commons.

And if the doubters might have expected the party to quietly drop these proposals (especially the latter) in the euphoria of dramatic electoral victory in 1997, any such doubts would very quickly have been dispelled. With lightening speed, the new Labour government rushed through its devolution proposals, including the adoption of mixed electoral systems for the new assemblies in Scotland, Wales (both elected in 1999) and London (elected in 2000); introduced a PR list system for European Parliament elections (first used in 1999); and in December 1997 established an Independent Commission on Electoral Reform, chaired by Lord (Roy) Jenkins, which was given the brief of recommending an electoral system to be offered to voters, in a referendum, as an alternative to SMP (Farrell 2000). The

Jenkins Commission produced its report in October 1998, proposing a complicated new system known as 'Alternative Vote Plus' – in essence a mixed electoral system (see Chapter 5, especially p. 114; Farrell 2000; Margetts and Dunleavy 1999). At the time of writing (January 2000), the Jenkins proposals are still being debated over, and the current belief is that, if there is a referendum, it will not be until after the next general election.

2.3 The Electoral Reform Debate in Other SMP Countries

To broaden the treatment somewhat, it is worthwhile reviewing the debates over electoral reform in a series of other SMP countries, namely Canada, India, New Zealand and the USA. Of the four countries selected for inclusion here, just one (New Zealand) has actually abandoned SMP, but not all of the others have been entirely immune from debate over change.

Clearly, in recent years, the most dramatic case has been New Zealand, whose electors voted in 1993 to replace SMP with a mixed system (Denemark 2000; see also Chapter 5 below). This vote was the product of a long process of national debate which dates from the end of the 1970s when the parliament established a Select Committee on Electoral Law whose main purpose was to assess the operation of the existing electoral system. The committee's scope also included the right to assess the question of electoral reform. Its report in 1980 did not favour replacing SMP with PR, but significantly this conclusion was not supported by the Labour minority on the Committee, who called for the establishment of a wide-ranging Royal Commission on Electoral Reform. When next in government, in 1985, the Labour Party went ahead and established such a Commission, and in its report in December 1986, the Commission recommended the replacement of SMP with what it called a 'mixed member proportional' system.

Not much else happened on this issue until 1990 when, in a highly disproportionate election result, Labour was flung out of office and the new National government (with 48 per cent of the vote, but 69 per cent of the seats), elected on a manifesto of reform and change, had little choice but to take on the question of electoral reform (Vowles 1995). In 1992 an 'indicative', or non-binding, referendum was held. This consisted of two parts. In part A, voters were asked whether the current SMP system should be retained, or replaced by another electoral system. If they rejected SMP, in part B, they were offered a choice of four other electoral systems to choose between: a 'supplementary member system' (somewhat akin to the British Hansard's proposals of the mid-1970s); STV; the mixed system; and the alternative vote system as used in Australia.

Given the general levels of disquiet about the political system (as revealed in the opinion polls) and the close attention which had been paid to the mixed system (not least by the 1986 Royal Commission report), the results of the 1992 referendum were not that surprising in the sense that voters showed a clear desire to change towards the mixed system. What was surprising was the size of the vote for change. Just short of 85 per cent of voters rejected SMP, and two-thirds of voters (65 per cent) were in favour of the mixed system (Harris 1992).

This result was non-binding. It triggered another referendum campaign, with the voters being offered a clear choice between the existing SMP system and the favoured alternative of the mixed system. This time the result would be binding. After a long, informative and somewhat heated debate, the referendum in November 1993 produced a result, which, while not exactly overwhelming, was certainly conclusive enough to ensure that the system would be changed. On a turnout of 83 per cent, 53.9 per cent voted for the mixed system and 46.1 per cent voted for SMP (Harris 1993; Vowles 1995). The first election under the new mixed system was held three years later, in October 1996 (Vowles *et al.* 1998b).

Electoral reformers (and scholars) in other SMP countries have followed the New Zealand developments with keen interest, and nowhere more closely than in Canada. Much like we saw above in the case of Britain, over the years the question of electoral reform has arisen from time to time in Canadian debate. For instance, in the 1920s there was a failed attempt to adopt the alternative vote. Prior to the 1960s there was some experimentation with the single transferable vote at provincial level. In 1979 a Task Force on Canadian Unity recommended the adoption of a mixed system to replace SMP at national level, but its proposals were rejected by the Trudeau government. Similarly, proposals by the leader of the New Democratic Party and other scholarly suggestions around that time (for example, Irvine 1979) were also ignored.

The problem was that for a long time the political elite tended not to pay much attention to the issue. This is most dramatically shown by the case of the Royal Commission on Electoral Reform and Party Financing (the Lortie Commission), set up in 1989 to carry out a root-and-branch survey of the Canadian electoral process and how it might be reformed. Despite its supposed remit of 'electoral reform', the Commission was specifically excluded from examining the electoral system. Its 1991 report, consisting of four volumes, incorporating 23 commissioned academic studies and totalling thousands of pages, covered just about every subject area imaginable under the rubric of electoral reform and party finance, with the singular exception of the Canadian electoral system. According to Donley Studlar, this 'represents a historic missed opportunity to analyze the potential of alternative electoral systems' (1998: 55).

In the early 1990s, as part of the negotiations over constitutional and regional reform in Canada, there were indications that the political elite might finally be considering the question of electoral reform at least for elections to the upper chamber. However, with the failure of the Senate reform proposals in 1992, electoral reform was left on the back burner, where it has remained ever since despite the protestations of some pressure groups, smaller parties and much of the Canadian political science community (see Flanagan 1998; Milner 1998; Studlar 1998; Weaver 1998), and despite the fact that the two elections which have occurred since 1992 have been probably among the most disproportional in Canadian history (Milner 1998: 42–3).

Table 2.4 provides some evidence of the degree of disproportionality in recent Canadian elections, revealing the same kind of double-digit 'difference' proportions as we saw in the British case (Table 2.3). Much attention has been given to the 'electoral earthquake' of 1993 (Erickson 1995) which saw the governing Progressive Conservative Party's number of parliamentary seats plummet from 169 (and an overall majority) to just two. Having enjoyed a 14.3 per cent advantage in seats over votes in 1988, the Progressive Conservatives' meltdown was not helped by a highly disproportional deficit of 15.2 per cent in its seat proportion relative to its vote. And this vote–seat deficit was not greatly improved in the subsequent 1997 election.

Another SMP case which, so far at any rate, has resisted any moves towards electoral reform is India, the world's largest democracy with some 600 million voters. In its first thirty years of independence

Table 2.4 Disproportionality in recent Canadian elections

	Bloc Québécois[a]			Liberal Party			New Democrat Party			Progressive Conservatives			Reform		
	Vote (%)	*Seat (%)*	*Diff. (%)*	*Vote (%)*	*Seat (%)*	*Diff. (%)*	*Vote (%)*	*Seat (%)*	*Diff. (%)*	*Vote (%)*	*Seat (%)*	*Diff. (%)*	*Vote (%)*	*Seat (%)*	*Diff. (%)*
1988		–n.a.–		31.9	28.1	–3.8	20.4	14.6	–5.8	43.0	57.3	+14.3	2.1	0.0	–2.1
1993	13.5	18.3	+4.8	41.3	60.0	+18.7	6.9	3.1	–3.8	16.0	0.8	–15.2	18.7	17.6	–1.1
1997	10.7	14.6	+3.9	38.4	51.5	+13.1	11.0	7.0	–4.0	18.9	6.7	–12.2	19.3	19.9	+0.6

Notes: Percentages to not add up to 100 because of the exclusion of independents. In the 'Diff.' columns a positive sign implies that the party gained a greater share of seats than its share of the vote, a negative sign implies it received a lesser share of seats.
[a] The party was first established in 1990.
Source: Election results.

India followed an impeccable SMP tradition in the sense that the Congress Party secured safe parliamentary majorities, on the basis of consistent pluralities (but never majorities) of the vote. Throughout this period the party faced a divided opposition. Things changed dramatically in 1977 when the opposition parties formed a common front against Indira Gandhi's state of emergency (her government had set aside constitutional rights in 1975–7). Congress's vote fell by more than one-third to 35 per cent, and this was magnified by the SMP electoral system to the extent that its seat proportions fell by more than half (56 per cent) to a then all-time low of 28 per cent (Rangarajan and Patidar 1997). (This low point was beaten in 1996 when Congress's seat proportion dropped to just under 26 per cent.) Congress won power again in 1980 and held it through much of the 1980s, but the spell of Congress supremacy had been broken. Congress's hold of power has been interrupted by periods of coalition government in 1977 and 1989, and an unstable government in 1996 which lasted barely two years.

The cases of Canada and India share a few traits in common, not least the tendency for some dramatic turn-arounds in electoral fortunes for prominent parties (the Progressive Conservatives and Congress) and the consistently disproportional results for small parties. On the face of it, there does not appear to be much to distinguish these cases from New Zealand or Britain whose politicians have, since the early 1990s, revealed themselves to be more amenable to discussing (and in New Zealand's case implementing) electoral reform. No simple explanations can be provided for these differences, apart from the obvious sort of points, such as the fact that a large proportion of India's population remain illiterate, which might be seen as a reason for ruling out more complex electoral systems (though this same fact did not prevent post-apartheid South Africa adopting PR list), or the ability of the federalized nature of both systems to provide a 'safety-valve' of regional assemblies where smaller parties can win some influence. One point which certainly does seem significant in at least partially explaining why there is a reluctance to attempt electoral reform in Canada and India relates to what might be called a delicate institutional balance which some fear might be endangered by too much tinkering with the system. In the Canadian case this relates to the perceived dangers of regional parties and the separatist debate, to 'a general sense of institutional vulnerability as far as the federal distribution of power is concerned

– an unarticulated fear that tampering with electoral institutions would only exacerbate the situation' (Milner 1998: 50). According to Rangarajan and Patidar (1997: 35), SMP has retained support in India 'due in part to the practice of reserving seats for socially under-privileged groups' (scheduled castes and tribes, and in the future possibly also women).

When compared with the recent process of electoral reform in New Zealand and the steady-state positions of Canada and India, the USA can be seen as representing something of an in-between case, in the sense that there are signs, particularly since the 1990s, of a willingness to embrace electoral reform, but only at local or at most state level. At federal level the USA remains steadfastly resistant to change, nor for that matter is there much if any mainstream discussion about the possibility of change. And this is not just in terms of public debate; the academic community has also remained largely immune from discussions of electoral reform. Indeed, it is ironic that while much of the academic literature on electoral systems focuses on the US case, very little of this actually deals with the voting system used in the United States. For the most part the attention is on issues of redistricting and voting rights (as we saw in Chapter 1). As Douglas Amy has observed: 'the American voting system is the aberration. Ours is one of the few developed countries that continues to cling to a plurality system, and among those few, ours is the only one in which no public debate over the desirability of this system is occurring' (Amy 1993: 4; also Dunleavy and Margetts 1995). As Amy's comprehensive study points out, in those instances where electoral reform at federal level is raised there are the standard battery of objections ready to shoot it down. Other systems are said to be too complex, promoting the dangers of unstable government, fringe parties and the loss of constituency representation, and giving too much power to the party elites. But the most significant reason why electoral reform does not appear on the American national agenda seems to be a basic lack of interest on the part of the voters (and presumably by implication, the elite). In other words, while people may think there are problems with the system – as shown most particularly by the low levels of esteem for politicians generally and, perhaps, by very low turnout – there is no great groundswell of opinion in favour of electoral reform as one possible means of changing things. Another factor which undoubtedly contributes to the lack of concern about the electoral system is the fact that the US government tends to be 'divided', in the sense that it is common for one party to control the presidency while another controls Congress. This is quite different from the British case where one party can control all of government for extended periods, and where it is recognized that a major reason for this is the distorting effects of the electoral system. Finally, the nature of the US party system is an important factor in explaining the lack of concern about electoral reform in the USA. This is revealed both by the weakness of US parties (Wattenberg 1998), which ensures little attention to national vote trends, and also by the fact that the USA 'now stands alone in the world as the homeland of a system that is almost perfectly two-party . . . [and] if only two parties run candidates than even a plurality rule system may operate quite proportionally' (Dunleavy and Margetts 1995: 24).

But the USA has not been entirely devoid of any attention to other electoral systems, and this is where it parts company with Canada and India. For instance, in the earlier part of the twentieth century there were notable efforts to adopt STV at local government level, with some success. As Leon Weaver (1986: 140) notes: 'PR systems have been used in approximately two dozen cities (for city councils and school boards). These cases might conceivably be counted as five dozen if one wishes to count the school communities in Massachusetts PR cities and in the New York City community school boards as separate cases.' Lest we take this to mean that STV was on a dramatic growth curve in this period, it is well to note Weaver's important qualifier that 'PR systems have constituted a very small sample – a fraction of 1 per cent – when compared with the total number of electoral systems in this country'. Moving into the second half of the twentieth century the use of STV in American local government was on a steep decline. At the time of writing, STV is used only in Cambridge, Massachusetts (for city council and school committee elections) and in New York City (for community school board elections). The USA also makes relatively widespread use of the two-round system (such as used in France; see Chapter 3). In some southern states (notably Louisiana) the two-round system is even used in congressional elections.

In the light of recent Supreme Court decisions which have raised doubts over the long-term viability of 'majority–minority' constituencies (discussed on p. 16 above), alternative means will have to be found to help protect and promote the interests of ethnic minorities, particularly in the southern states. According to a review of recent trends by Richard Engstrom (1998), prominent among these alternative means has been a growing interest in new electoral systems. At least 40 local governments in five states have adopted limited voting in recent years, while close to 60 local governments in five states have adopted some element of cumulative voting. (These systems are dealt with in the next section.)

As we shall see below, cumulative and limited voting are members of the plurality family of electoral systems. Across the USA there is also some evidence of a growing interest in proportional electoral systems, particularly among smaller parties, single-issue candidates and significant lobbying organizations. 'A decade ago', according to two proponents of electoral reform, proportional representation 'sounded foreign and probably unconstitutional to many Americans . . . Today, hundreds of publications (including our largest-circulation newspapers and magazines) regularly discuss voting system reform' (Ritchie and Hill 1998: 101).[3] In the 1990s both Cincinnati and San Francisco held referendums on proportional systems (offering the single transferable vote, also known as 'choice voting', as the alternative), which in each case garnered the support of four in ten voters. There has been some discussion in Congress about the possibility that states might once again be able to use PR to elect their Congressmen (Cynthia McKinney's Voter's Choice Act). New Mexico and Vermont have recently held debates over the introduction of the alternative vote (also known as 'instant runoff'). 'Overall, PR activism in the United States is greater than at any time since before World War II' (Ritchie and Hill 1998: 102).

2.4   Other Plurality Systems

As with many of the electoral systems explored in this book, SMP offers scope for variation, in this case around the common theme of 'plurality'. One of the most obvious alternatives is the use of plurality systems in multi-member constituencies, with voters being given as many votes as there are seats to be filled (generally free to vote across party if desired). As with SMP, in these 'block vote' systems the victors are those candidates winning the plurality of the votes in the constituency. According to Reynolds and Reilly's recent review of comparative trends (1997), block systems are currently used for the following elections: the Palestinian Authority, Bermuda, Fiji, Laos, the US Virgin Islands, Thailand, the Maldives, Kuwait, the Philippines and Mauritius. It is also used for some local government constituencies in the United Kingdom.

Jordan and Mongolia abandoned block voting in the early 1990s because of unease over the disproportionality of the result. And this is the basic point that needs to be stressed about this system. For while it may apparently give a greater say to voters (greater personal choice) in deciding which candidates of their preferred party they may wish to vote for, the fact is, however, that most voters vote the straight party ticket. In consequence the system greatly exaggerates the disproportionality of the plurality system. In other words, the maxim which will be stressed throughout this book, that the larger the district magnitude the greater the proportionality of the system, is reversed in the case of block systems: the more seats to be filled per constituency in a block system the greater the disproportionality.

Two further variants of the plurality family get around the disproportional tendencies of the block system while retaining the multi-member constituencies, one by reducing the number of votes that a voter can cast, the other by allowing voters the right to express more than one vote against a candidate. These systems, known respectively as the limited vote and the cumulative vote, are generally categorized as 'semi-proportional' due to the fact that they make life a bit easier for small parties.

The limited vote first came to prominence in debates over electoral reform in mid-nineteenth-century Britain, where, as we have seen, it was used between 1867 and 1885. For a time it was also used in Gibraltar. It is still in use for the election of the Spanish Senate, and for local government elections in five US states. The objective behind the limited vote is simple: allowing the voter fewer votes than the number of seats to be filled reduces the chance for a large party to have its full slate of candidates elected (which, as we have seen, is the danger with the block vote system); there is more chance for a candidate of a smaller party to be elected.

The cumulative vote emerged at around the same time as the limited vote as another means of trying to reduce the disproportional tendencies of the block voting system. Under this system the voter retains the same number of votes as seats to be filled, only in this case they can give two or more votes to one candidate: that is, the votes can be 'cumulated'. The obvious advantage of this system is that it allows a voter to express a very strong preference for an individual candidate while at the same time being able to vote for other candidates.

The cumulative vote was first used in the Cape Colony in the 1850s, where it remained as the system for electing the Legislative Council until the early twentieth century. It was also used towards the end of the nineteenth century for the election of schools boards in the UK (Bowler *et al.* 2000). But its widest use, particularly of late, has been in the USA. It has had a long history in Illinois where it was used for elections to the state House of Representatives from 1870 to 1980. As we saw above, cumulative voting has become more popular in recent years as a means of furthering the representation of minorities: it has so far been adopted in five US states for the election of all or part of their governing boards.

Under these systems there is some scope to increase the 'proportionality' of the result. In contrast to the block vote system, under the cumulative and the limited systems as district magnitude increases so does overall proportionality (Lijphart *et al.* 1986). Engstrom (1998: 233) shows this by way of example (for limited voting taking the case of where a voter has just one vote): when there are two seats to be filled a candidate requires 33.3 per cent of the vote; in a three-seat constituency the proportion falls to 25 per cent; in a four-seat constituency it falls to 20 per cent, and so on.

An additional means of increasing proportionality is available in the limited vote system, whereby as the vote becomes more 'limited' the vote proportion required to win a seat decreases (Lakeman 1974; Lijphart *et al.* 1986). For instance, as Engstrom shows (1998: 232–3), in a four-seat constituency if a voter has three votes, a candidate needs 42.9 per cent of the vote to be elected; if a voter has two votes, the proportion drops to 33.3 per cent; and if the voter has just one vote, it drops to just 20 per cent. This last case, where a voter has just one vote in a multi-seat constituency, was the system used by Japan from 1948 to 1994, where it was given the title of single non-transferable vote (SNTV). In 1994 Japan switched to a mixed system (as discussed below in Chapter 5). Currently SNTV is used in Jordan (after it abandoned the block vote), Vanuatu, and for 125 out of 161 seats in the Taiwanese parliament (Reynolds and Reilly 1997).

The fact is, of course, that the limited (SNTV) and cumulative vote systems are at best semi-proportional; while they can be used to make life a bit easier for smaller parties, life will never become that easy. The experience of their use in a range of contexts demonstrates how smaller parties are far from guaranteed greater representation: a major calculation has to be made in determining the correct number of candidates to run in order to win seats without danger of diluting the vote too much. Among the reasons Japan switched from SNTV to a mixed system in the mid-1990s was because the system was credited with having encouraged candidate rivalry, and having discouraged the parties from appealing to a broader spectrum of voters. Overall, then, while these systems may represent some improvement on SMP in terms of helping smaller parties win seats, PR proponents will always argue that they do not go far enough.

2.5 Conclusion

SMP (and its plurality cousins) remains one of the most commonly used systems in the world, certainly in terms of per head of population (although India alone accounts for a large proportion of that total). While some countries are showing signs of a possible willingness to change to an alternative electoral system (and, in one case, New Zealand, has actually changed), equally there are prominent cases where electoral reform remains firmly off the agenda.

It should become steadily more apparent as we progress through this book that there is no such thing as the perfect electoral system, even if some systems have certain advantages over others. This chapter has shown some of the obvious disadvantages of SMP: it produces disproportional results; smaller parties are underrepresented; supporters of smaller parties waste their votes. But, as we have seen, SMP does also have a number of apparent advantages, particularly in terms of its promotion of single-party, stable government; the central role of constituency representation; and its much trumpeted simplicity. In attempting to weigh up the pros and cons of this (or, indeed, any) system we can only go so far when we treat the system in isolation. A full analysis can only be made on the basis of comparisons with other systems. We start in the next chapter with consideration of SMP's close neighbour, the majoritarian systems.

3

Majoritarian Electoral Systems: Two-Round Systems and the Alternative Vote

As we saw in the previous chapter, Sir Russell Johnston (Liberal Democrat) won the seat of Inverness, Nairn and Lochaber in the 1992 British general election with just 26 per cent of the vote. It is results like this that give the single member plurality (SMP) system a bad name. One view often expressed in political circles is that if it were possible to clear up these sorts of anomalies – but without 'destroying' the 'essential' character of SMP – then the system would not receive such a bad press. The ideal compromise is said to be one where the electoral system is still easy for the average voter to understand; where it produces strong and stable government; where there still is a single MP representing a single constituency; and, in addition, where that MP enjoys the support of the majority of his or her constituents. The critical new ingredient, therefore, is that each MP is elected with an overall majority, as opposed to the situation which prevailed in the 1997 British election when only 53 per cent of MPs were elected with an overall majority of all the votes in the constituency, a not uncommon result (Punnett 1991).

In terms of the three main features of electoral systems introduced in Chapter 1, the main point of distinction between the majoritarian systems and SMP is over the 'electoral formula'; there are also some differences over 'ballot structure'. The electoral formula distinction may appear quite simple, but it is seen as crucial by the proponents of majoritarian systems. Instead of requiring only a *plurality* of votes (that is, more votes than any of the other candidates but not necessarily an overall majority) in order to win the seat, a candidate must get an overall *majority* (that is, at least 50 per cent plus one), hence the title 'majoritarian' systems.

The ballot structure distinction really only relates to the Australian majoritarian system, known as the alternative vote. As we shall see, under the alternative vote, voters rank-order all the candidates on the ballot paper: in other words the ballot structure is 'ordinal'. Things are not quite so straightforward under the two-round system (such as used in France) which, as we see in section 3.1, consists essentially of two 'categoric' ballots on different polling days either a week or a fortnight apart. Both majoritarian systems share in common with SMP a 'district magnitude' of one: the country is divided into a series of one-seat constituencies (though multi-seat constituencies have been used). Once again, in other words, we are dealing with non-proportional electoral systems: proportionality on a seat-by-seat basis can only occur when there are multi-seat constituencies and a proportional electoral formula.

Majoritarian electoral systems are seen as a compromise by those people who wish to see improvements to the SMP system, but who are not in favour of the adoption of proportional representation. Whether, in fact, it is correct to view majoritarian systems as a compromise is dealt with later. But first we need to examine the two main types of majoritarian systems in use. We start, in section 3.1, with a discussion of the two-round system, with particular emphasis on France. Section 3.2 outlines the alternative vote system which is most closely associated with Australia where it is used for lower house elections. The chapter concludes, in section 3.3, with an assessment of the majoritarian electoral systems.

3.1   The Two-Round System

As ever, this system has several possible names: run-off, two-ballot, second ballot. In this book, the term 'two-round system' will be applied to those systems which require voters to vote on two separate occasions. As we shall see, of course, there are variants of this system. Two-round systems are common in many of those countries with directly elected presidents (Blais and Massicotte 1996; Jones

1995, 1997). Counted among these are Austria, Bulgaria, Chile, Colombia, Ecuador, France, Finland, Madagascar, Mali, Mozambique, Poland, Portugal, Russia and Ukraine. This system is far less common in the case of legislative elections. It is most closely associated with France where it was used for elections to the Chamber of Deputies from 1928 to 1945; it was readopted by the French Fifth Republic in 1958, and has also been used for presidential elections (Cole and Campbell 1989). From time to time it has been replaced, most recently in 1986–8 by proportional representation (also France has opted for a PR system for its European Parliament elections).

In the first part of the twentieth century many European countries passed through a two-round stage for parliamentary elections, *en route* from plurality to proportional electoral systems, among them Austria, Belgium, Germany, Italy, the Netherlands, Norway, Spain and Switzerland (in some of these cases using multi-member constituencies). Two-round systems have gained a certain popularity in a number of the post-Soviet bloc states, among them Belarus, Kyrgystan, Macedonia, Moldova, Tajikistan and Uzbekistan. Ukraine used a two-round system in 1994 before abandoning it for a mixed electoral system in 1998 (Birch 1997). Albania, Hungary and Lithuania have incorporated two-round systems as part of their mixed systems (see Chapter 5 below). According to Reynolds and Reilly's survey of comparative trends, two-round systems are used for legislative elections in over thirty countries. Apart from the countries already mentioned, most of the remainder share in common the fact that they are 'territorial dependencies of the French Republic, or have been historically influenced in some way by the French' (1997: 43). Two-round systems have also been used quite widely in the USA for lower-level elections, and in some southern states even for Congressional elections.

The remainder of this section focuses on the French case, whose presidential and legislative electoral systems rather neatly encapsulate the two forms of two-round systems. As we have seen, the central feature of this system is two rounds of voting taking place on two different polling days. The principal objective is to ensure (or at least increase the likelihood) that the candidate elected will have an overall majority of support in the constituency, more than 50 per cent of the votes cast (in single-seat constituencies). France uses a *majority–plurality* version of two-round voting for its legislative elections and a *majority–run-off* version for its presidential elections.

In both cases the first stage is deceptively like an SMP election: the French voters simply select their preferred candidate. If a candidate receives an overall majority of the votes – such as happened in 22 per cent of cases in the 1988 French legislative elections and 12 per cent of cases in 1993 (Cole and Campbell 1989: 191; Goldey 1993) – then they are deemed elected and there is no need for a second ballot. Where no candidate receives an overall majority, then a second round of voting takes place, one week later for legislative elections, two weeks later for presidential elections. It is at this point that the two French systems vary.

In the case of legislative elections, using the majority–plurality version of the two-round system, only those candidates who receive a minimum percentage of votes are allowed to proceed to the second ballot. This minimum is set at 12.5 per cent, not of those who voted, but of the registered voters.[1] In other words, in the 1997 legislative election when 68.5 per cent of the electorate turned out to vote in the first round, on average candidates needed more than 18 per cent of the total vote in order to qualify for the second round. This minimum figure is designed to reduce the number of candidates in the second ballot and therefore to increase the likelihood that the MP finally elected has an overall majority of votes. Note that it does not *guarantee* a majoritarian result. This is because there is always the possibility that more than two candidates receive 12.5 per cent of the vote in the first round – in theory anything up to seven or eight candidates could receive 12.5 per cent of the vote – and once there are more than two candidates, then there is no guarantee of a majoritarian result; indeed, in this round all a candidate requires to get elected is a plurality of the vote. Only with two candidates can a majoritarian result be guaranteed. Of course, often candidates who manage to receive the minimum percentage of votes in the first round pull out of the race anyway so as to increase the chances for a particular candidate from another party (such as when there is a coalition bargain). (Indeed, it used to be possible for candidates to enter the race for the first time in the second round. Since 1958 all candidates must have been on the first ballot to qualify.) According to Cole and Campbell (1989: 168), in the 1988 legislative elections there were nine 'triangular contests' in the second ballot. In 1993 there were fifteen triangular contests, representing 3 per cent of all constituencies (Goldey 1993).

An unusual feature of the French electoral process is that the ballot papers are produced by the parties themselves, not by the state. There are a set of regulations which govern the style and content of the ballot paper: it should measure approximately 10 cm × 15 cm; it should have the candidate's name (and that of the replacement, thus avoiding the need for a by-election) and party affiliation; it can contain further information as desired, such as a party's slogan or symbol, or background on the candidate (Holliday 1994). Each party provides its own ballot paper. To vote, the elector chooses the appropriate ballot paper of the party they support, places it in the envelope provided, and pops it into the ballot box. An example of a ballot paper for one of the French Green parties is provided in Figure 3.1.

The electoral rules for presidential elections are simpler. In this majority–run-off version of the two-round system, only the candi-

ÉLECTIONS LÉGISLATIVES - SCRUTINS DE MARS 93
Département du NORD - 13ᵉ Circonscription

ENTENTE DES ÉCOLOGISTES
GÉNÉRATION ÉCOLOGIE - LES VERTS
Mᵐᵉ DOMINIQUE MARTIN-FERRARI
Journaliste
Suppléant : RENAUD JOUGLET
Conseiller Municipal de Téteghem

Figure 3.1   A French majority–plurality two-round ballot paper

Table 3.1   The 1995 French presidential election

	First round (24 April) (%)	Second round (7 May) (%)
Lionel Jospin (Socialist Party)	23.3	47.4
Jacques Chirac (Rally for the Republic)	20.8	52.6
Edouard Balladur (Rally for the Republic)	18.6	
Jean-Marie Le Pen (National Front)	15.0	
Robert Hue (Communist Party)	8.6	
Arlette Laguiller (Workers' Struggle)	5.3	
Philippe de Villiers (Another Europe)	4.7	
Dominique Voynet (Greens)	3.3	
Jacques Cheminade (Federation for a New Solidarity)	0.3	
Turnout	78.4	79.7
Invalid votes	2.2	4.7
Valid votes	76.2	82.0

Source: Mackie and Rose (1997).

dates with the highest and second highest number of votes are allowed to run in the second round; all other candidates are excluded. There being only two candidates left in the race, the final result is majoritarian. Technically speaking, of course, the final result often does not actually represent a majority of the electorate because only a certain percentage actually turn out to vote and therefore it is only a majority of the voters which determines the result. This point is even more significant in the cases where the turnout is lower in the second round of voting, as happened in 1965 and 1969. For instance in 1969 turnout dropped from 77.6 per cent in the first round to 65.5 per cent in the second. As a result General de Gaulle's 'majority' over François Mitterrand of 52.2 per cent represented in reality just 45.3 per cent of the French electorate.

The 1995 French presidential election result is given in Table 3.1. This provides a good example of the strategic nature of the system. On the face of it, this election was a battle between the Left and the Right, with the Socialist candidate, Lionel Jospin, taking up the mantle from the extremely unpopular François Mitterrand, who was retiring from politics. Underlying this battle was an even more bitter strategic struggle between the two main candidates of the Right, the former prime minister and long-standing mayor of Paris, Jacques Chirac, and the then prime minister, Edouard Balladur, who had entered the race as hot favourite.

At the start of the campaign there were predictions that Jospin would be defeated in the first round, leaving the second round to be fought over by the two candidates of the Right. This was seen as a potentially dangerous scenario, and one of the weaknesses of the two-round system. If it had actually occurred, then the supporters of left-of-centre parties would have been denied the right to vote for any candidate of their persuasion in the second round. In the event, and despite the fact that his campaign started late, Jospin managed to produce a dramatic recovery in the Socialist vote, and topped the poll in the first round with 23.3 per cent of the vote. Meanwhile, Chirac, who fought a blistering campaign, pushed Balladur into third place and out of the race.

In the second round, a fortnight later, Chirac emerged the victor with 52.6 per cent of the vote. But it should be noted that this second-round election saw an unprecedented 5 per cent of voters who spoiled their votes. As a result, Chirac received the active support of less than half the total French electorate.

3.2 The Alternative Vote System

The alternative vote electoral system was devised in the 1870s by W. R. Ware, a professor at the Massachusetts Institute of Technology. As Jack Wright (1980: 54) points out, in the debates of the late nineteenth century about Australian independence and the setting up of the federation, considerable interest had been shown in the merits of preferential voting. This interest continued into the early years of the new federation. The basic argument was that SMP – the system first adopted – risked a situation where parties would suffer unfairly from vote-splitting. This point was illustrated by a by-election in Western Australia, when a Labor candidate was elected with 35 per cent of the vote, reflecting the fact that the support of the non-Labor side was split between three other candidates. Soon after that, in 1918, what was known as preferential voting, or majority preferential voting, was introduced for elections to the Australian House of Representatives. (In fact, the first use of a version of the alternative vote system in Australia was in the state of Queensland in 1892.)

Most Australian states also use the alternative vote for state lower house elections.

According to Reynolds and Reilly (1997: 37), the alternative vote offers 'a good example of the regional diffusion of electoral systems . . . the past, present and likely future use of [the alternative vote] has all occurred within the Oceania region'. Other countries in the region which have used or are considering the alternative vote include Nauru, Papua New Guinea (1964–75; see Reilly 1997a) and Fiji (recommended as the next electoral system by the 1996 Constitution Review; see Lal and Larmour 1997). The alternative vote is not exclusive to the Oceania region, however. Ireland uses it for presidential and parliamentary by-elections; it was used in parts of Canada from the 1920s to the 1950s (Alberta, Manitoba, and for a brief period in British Columbia; see Flanagan 1998); Sri Lanka has used a version of it for presidential elections since 1978; the US state of Alabama used what it called a 'second-choice' system between 1915 and 1931, before reverting back to a two-round system (Reilly 1997b); in Britain the new London mayor was elected in 2000 by a system called the 'supplementary vote'.

In short, then, the alternative vote has been applied in quite a range of different electoral arenas; however, inevitably most attention has been devoted to its use in Australia. Although outside Australia this electoral system is usually referred to as the alternative vote, preferential voting is a more appropriate title.[2] 'Alternative' implies an either/or system – such as the two-round system, for instance – whereas, in reality, the voters are being asked to rank-order a number of candidates 1, 2, 3 and so on. Indeed, in Australia, voters have to rank-order *all* the candidates on the ballot paper; otherwise, their vote is declared invalid. An example of an Australian ballot paper is provided in Figure 3.2 for the electoral division (that is, constituency) of Moore. In essence very similar to an SMP ballot paper, the big difference is that voters vote in order of preference for all the candidates, in this case all five candidates. (Note the non-alphabetical ordering of candidates' names; in Australia the parties determine the order of the candidates.)

Table 3.2 provides an illustration of how the alternative vote system can produce a result quite different from one obtained under SMP. In the Hinkler division of Queensland, in the 1998 Australian federal elections, there were six candidates running for one seat, and there were 72,356 valid votes. The first count consisted of the sorting

BALLOT PAPER
HOUSE OF REPRESENTATIVES
WESTERN AUSTRALIA

ELECTORAL DIVISION OF
MOORE

Number the boxes from 1 to 5 in the order of your choice.

☐ LLOYD, Alan R
AUSTRALIAN DEMOCRATS

☐ WATSON, Mark
GREY POWER

☐ FILING, Paul
LIBERAL

☐ STEELS, Brian
THE GREENS (W.A.)

☐ BLANCHARD, Allen
AUSTRALIAN LABOR PARTY (ALP)

Remember...number _every_ box to make your vote count.

Australian Electoral Commission. /AEC

Figure 3.2   An Australian alternative vote ballot paper

Table 3.2 An alternative vote election result: division of Hinkler (Queensland) in the 1998 Australian federal elections

	Count one	Next count	Count two	Next count	Count three	Next count	Count four	Next count	Count five	
Paul Neville (National)	26,471	+45	26,516	+223	26,739	+807	27,546	+8,877	36,423	Elected
Cheryl Dorron (Labor)	29,021	+39	29,060	+353	29,413	+987	30,400	+5,533	35,933	
Ray Pearce (Green)	1,139	+48	1,187	Excluded						
Marcus Ringuet (Hanson's One Nation)	13,739	+61	13,800	+169	13,969	+441	14,410	Excluded		
Lance Hall (Australian Democrats)	1,677	+116	1,793	+442	2,235	Excluded				
Cindy Rolls (Citizens Electoral Council)	309	Excluded								

Source: Australian Electoral Commission.

of the ballot papers in order of the first-preference votes. Under SMP, Cheryl Dorron (Labor Party) would have been elected as the candidate with the most votes (a respectable 40 per cent of the valid vote, as compared to 37 per cent for her nearest rival, Paul Neville of the National Party). However, under the alternative vote system, a candidate must receive more than 50 per cent of the vote (that is, at least 36,179 votes in this case). Therefore, it was necessary to 'exclude' the candidate with the fewest votes, Cindy Rolls (Citizens Electoral Council), and re-sort her 309 ballot papers according to the second preferences of the voters.

Rolls's votes transferred pretty evenly to the other candidates, with a bit over a third going to Lance Hall of the Australian Democrats, and the rest divided between the remaining candidates. Unsurprisingly, given the small amount of votes being transferred, the result of this second count was inconclusive: still none of the candidates had an overall majority. The third count, therefore, consisted of the exclusion of the next weakest candidate – this time Ray Pearce (Green – 1,187 votes). Again more than a third of the preferences transferred to the Australian Democrats, just under a third went to the Labor candidate, and the other two candidates shared the remainder. The margin separating the top two candidates remained largely unchanged, and still no candidate had more than 50 per cent of the vote, so a fourth count was required, involving the exclusion of Lance Hall and the transfer of his 2,235 votes. The bulk of these were shared evenly by the top two candidates, and yet again no single candidate emerged with an overall majority, although Labor's Cheryl Dorron (42 per cent) still held a healthy lead over Paul Neville of the National Party (38 per cent).

The fifth and final count, therefore, consisted of the exclusion of Marcus Ringuet, the candidate representing the far-right One Nation party of Pauline Hanson. Since only two candidates were left in the race this meant that one of them had to be elected in this round; one of them had to get an overall majority. Despite the fact that Dorron had been leading from the outset, the final victory went to Neville, who received 62 per cent of Ringuet's transfers – understandable given that National is positioned closer on the political spectrum to Hanson's One Nation than is Labor – giving him a final vote tally of 36,423 (50.3 per cent) as against 35,933 votes (49.7 per cent) for Dorron.

Another good example from 1998 of where the alternative vote produced a very different result to SMP was provided by the Blair division in Queensland, where Pauline Hanson was the candidate expected to win – a cause of some trepidation to the mainstream parties which balked at her extremist policies. If this had been an SMP election, Hanson would have been the clear winner, with 36 per cent of the first-preference vote, beating her nearest rival, Cameron Thompson of Labor, who had just 22 per cent. In the event, however, it was Thompson who would emerge as the winner, after eight counts, with a final vote of 53 per cent, against Hanson's 47 per cent.

It should not be assumed that the Hinkler and Blair cases – where the transfer of preferences can produce results different to what would be obtained under SMP – are typical. In his review of trends since the 1970s, Clive Bean (1997) observes that, on average, this happens in only about 5–10 per cent of constituencies, and therefore rarely has any significant effect on the national election result. Indeed, Bean's research suggests just two occasions, 1961 and 1969, when the national election result would have been very different had SMP been the electoral system instead of the alternative vote (Bean 1986).

3.3   Assessing Majoritarian Electoral Systems

An assessment of the majoritarian electoral systems needs to consider two main aspects: their systemic consequences, particularly in terms of the parties' shares of votes and seats; and their strategic consequences, in terms of how the parties and the voters make use of the systems. Let us consider each in turn.

Tables 3.3 and 3.4 present percentages of votes, seats and vote–seat differences in France and Australia in postwar elections (only since 1962 in France, the first election held under the Fifth Republic). These tables provide easy comparisons with the trends in British elections which we saw in the previous chapter (Table 2.3). Overall, when drawing comparisons between SMP and the two majoritarian systems, the trends are strikingly similar. Table 3.3 reveals a systematic bias in the French system against the parties on the two extremes, reflecting the tendency – in the two-round system – for voters to gravitate towards the centre as the candidates of the extreme parties (more usually the Communists or the National Front) are excluded. The 1997 election was particularly interesting in this regard. For

Table 3.3   French legislative elections, 1962–97: vote and seat percentages

	Socialist Party[a]			Communist Party			Gaullists		
	Vote (%)	Seat (%)	Diff. (%)	Vote (%)	Seat (%)	Diff. (%)	Vote (%)	Seat (%)	Diff. (%)
1962	19.8	22.5	+2.7	21.9	8.8	−13.1	33.7	49.5	+15.8
1967	18.9	25.1	+6.2	22.5	15.3	−7.2	33.0	40.6	+7.6
1968	16.5	12.1	−4.4	20.0	7.0	−13.0	38.0	60.0	+22.0
1973	19.1	18.8	−0.3	21.4	15.4	−6.0	26.0	37.6	+11.6
1978	22.8	21.5	−1.3	20.6	18.1	−2.5	22.8	30.0	+7.2
1981	36.6	56.5	+19.9	16.1	9.2	−6.9	21.2	16.9	−4.3
1986[b]	31.3	35.6	+4.3	9.7	5.8	−3.9	26.8	26.3	−0.5
1988	36.6	46.8	+10.2	11.2	4.3	−6.9	19.1	22.2	+3.1
1993	19.0	10.0	−9.0	11.2	4.0	−7.2	19.7	45.0	+25.3
1997	23.5	41.8	+18.3	9.9	6.6	−3.3	15.7	23.2	+7.5

	Union for French Democracy			National Front		
	Vote (%)	Seat (%)	Diff. (%)	Vote (%)	Seat (%)	Diff. (%)
1978	22.0	26.2	+4.2	0.3	0.0	−0.3
1981	18.9	12.4	−6.5	0.2	0.0	−0.2
1986[b]	15.8	23.0	+7.2	9.8	6.3	−3.5
1988	19.0	23.4	+4.4	9.8	0.2	−9.6
1993	19.6	37.7	+18.1	12.7	0.0	−12.7
1997	14.7	18.7	+4.5	14.9	0.2	−14.7

Notes: Percentages do not add up to 100 because not all parties have been included.
[a] Including Radical Socialist Party from 1962 to 1968.
[b] PR election in 1986.
Sources: Mackie and Rose (1991, 1997); electoral returns.

instance, despite having its highest ever vote, the National Front (with 14.9 per cent of the vote) ended up with just one seat. The three mainstream parties all benefited from high vote–seat distortions in their favour, particularly the Socialists whose seat percentage was 18 points higher than their share of the vote. The single exception to this centrifugal trend was in 1986 when a PR electoral system was used. Note how in this case the percentage variations between votes and seats were much smaller across the board. Note also how the

Table 3.4   Australian House of Representatives elections, 1949–98: vote and seat percentages

	Labor Party			Liberals			Country/National		
	Vote (%)	Seat (%)	Diff. (%)	Vote (%)	Seat (%)	Diff. (%)	Vote (%)	Seat (%)	Diff. (%)
1949	46.0	38.8	−7.2	39.4	45.5	+6.1	10.9	15.7	+4.8
1951	47.6	43.0	−4.6	40.6	43.0	+2.4	9.7	14.0	+4.3
1954	50.0	47.1	−2.9	38.6	38.8	+0.2	8.5	14.1	+5.6
1955	44.6	38.5	−6.1	39.7	46.7	+7.0	7.9	14.8	+6.9
1958	42.8	36.9	−5.9	37.2	47.5	+10.3	9.3	15.6	+6.3
1961	47.9	49.2	+1.3	33.6	36.9	+3.3	8.5	13.9	+5.4
1963	45.5	41.0	−4.5	37.1	42.6	+5.5	8.9	16.4	+7.5
1966	40.0	33.3	−6.7	40.2	49.6	+9.4	9.7	16.3	+6.6
1969	47.0	47.2	+0.2	34.8	36.8	+2.0	8.6	16.0	+7.4
1972	49.6	53.6	+4.0	32.1	30.4	−1.7	9.4	16.0	+6.6
1974	49.3	52.0	+2.7	34.9	31.5	−3.4	10.8	16.5	+5.7
1975	42.8	28.4	−14.4	41.8	53.5	+11.7	11.3	18.1	+6.8
1977	39.6	30.7	−8.9	38.1	54.0	+15.9	10.0	15.3	+5.3
1980	45.1	40.8	−4.3	37.4	43.2	+5.8	8.9	16.0	+7.1
1983	49.5	60.0	+10.5	34.4	26.4	−8.0	9.2	13.6	+4.4
1984	47.5	55.4	+7.9	34.4	30.4	−4.0	10.6	14.2	+3.6
1987	45.8	58.1	+12.3	34.6	29.1	−5.5	11.5	12.8	+1.3
1990	39.4	52.7	+13.3	35.0	37.2	+2.2	8.4	9.5	+1.1
1993	44.9	54.4	+9.5	37.1	33.3	−3.8	7.2	10.9	+3.7
1996	39.2	32.4	−6.8	39.0	52.0	+13.0	8.2	12.2	+4.0
1998	40.0	44.6	+4.6	34.1	43.2	+9.1	5.3	10.8	+5.5

	Democratic Labor Party				Australian Democrats		
	Vote (%)	Seat (%)	Diff. (%)		Vote (%)	Seat (%)	Diff. (%)
1955	5.2	0.0	−5.2	1977	9.4	0.0	−9.4
1958	9.4	0.0	−9.4	1980	6.6	0.0	−6.6
1961	8.7	0.0	−8.7	1983	5.0	0.0	−5.0
1963	7.4	0.0	−7.4	1984	5.4	0.0	−5.4
1966	7.3	0.0	−7.3	1987	6.0	0.0	−6.0
1969	6.0	0.0	−6.0	1990	11.3	0.0	−11.3
1972	5.2	0.0	−5.2	1993	3.8	0.0	−3.8
1974	1.4	0.0	−1.4	1996	6.7	0.0	−6.7
1975	1.3	0.0	−1.3	1998	5.1	0.0	−5.1
1977	1.4	0.0	−1.4				
1980	0.3	0.0	−0.3				

Note: Percentages do not add up to 100 because not all parties are included.
Sources: Mackerras (1996); election results.

smaller parties tended to fare much better, particularly the extremist National Front.

In Australia, smaller parties (the Democratic Labor Party and the Democrats) have never managed to win a seat (Table 3.4), even though in some cases they have more votes than the British Liberal Democratic Party which *does* win seats under SMP. This indicates how majoritarian systems can, and do, produce results which are even more inequitable than SMP (Dunleavy *et al.* 1998). The interesting case to note here is the National Party which consistently benefits from more seats than its relatively small vote warrants. This reflects the fact that, as a farmers' party, its vote is geographically focused in agricultural areas (McAllister 1992). Just as with SMP (as shown, for instance, by the Nationalist parties in Britain), a party benefits greatly from a good geographical concentration in its vote.

Apart from the unfair treatment of smaller parties, the majoritarian systems can also produce anomalous majorities, similar to those we saw with SMP in the previous chapter. For instance, in seven of the 21 Australian elections in Table 3.4 (that is, in 1949, 1955, 1958, 1963, 1975, 1977, 1980), the Liberal Party was awarded more seats than the Labor Party despite having won fewer votes. Then, for a period, from 1983 to 1993, there was a systematic bias in the seats-to-votes ratio for the governing Labor Party – a trend which bears a marked resemblance to that enjoyed for some time by the British Conservatives under SMP (see Table 2.3). This helped to explain the dominance of the Labor Party in Australian politics throughout the 1980s and early 1990s, a dominance which was shattered in 1996 (and when, for the first time in a decade, the party was awarded a lower share of seats than its vote warranted). In 1996 and 1998 the electoral system seems to have worked to the benefit of the Liberal Party.

In conclusion, the evidence from both majoritarian systems suggests electoral trends which are strikingly similar to those for SMP. Smaller parties are disadvantaged by the highly disproportional results; larger parties are advantaged; parties with a good geographical concentration in support tend to do better. In Australia, governments with a majority of seats are the norm; in France, while there have been very few instances of large single-party majorities in the National Assembly (the Gaullists in 1968; the Socialists in 1981), to a large degree this has been dissipated by the fact that generally stable coalitions (centre-right or centre-left) have been pretty easily formed.

When dealing with the strategic consequences of majoritarian electoral systems, it is useful to take each system in turn: as we have seen there are some quite significant differences between the two majoritarian systems, and this is particularly notable with regard to ballot structure. Let us start with the two-round system, dealing simply with the French case. The fact that polling takes place on two separate occasions has a number of consequences for the political system, some positive, some negative, some over which observers are divided. Among the obvious benefits is the fact that the system maintains the simplicity of SMP, requiring voters to do no more than simply tick a box or pick a ballot paper (of obvious advantage in highly illiterate societies). More significantly, the two-round system has been credited with an important role in encouraging a politics of 'centrism' in France – requiring parties to cooperate and form alliances in order to reap full benefit from its disproportional tendencies (Elgie 1997; Taagepera and Shugart 1989) – and in helping maintain coherent party organizations (Schlesinger and Schlesinger 1990, 1995). Of the two versions of the two-round system, Sartori (1997: 65–7) expresses a strong preference for the majority–plurality version, on the grounds that it encourages more serious bargaining between the parties, anxious to strike deals over which candidates will go through to the second round; by contrast, under the majority–run-off version, there is no incentive for the parties to engage in serious bargaining: smaller parties have nothing to lose from fielding candidates and seeking to outbid the established parties. In short, according to Sartori, majority–plurality systems are more effective than majority–run-off systems in encouraging a politics of centrism.

But, of course, the fact that voters have to return and vote on a second occasion (except where a candidate has actually achieved more than 50 per cent of the vote in the first round) does also suggest some negative consequences. At an extreme, for instance, close, knife-edge election results in the first round may only feed a mood of 'electoral uncertainty', which in the wrong circumstances could have detrimental effects on system stability. More generally, the simple fact that voters have to vote twice places additional burdens (and costs) on electoral administrators (at least one reason why some two-round systems have switched to the alternative vote), on parties and politicians, and on voters. In the latter case, this can manifest itself in lower turnout in the second round, reflecting not only voter exhaustion, but also perhaps a degree of disquiet over the reduced choice available: for instance, arguably the very high number of invalid votes in the second round of the 1995 election (Table 3.1) could, in part, reflect voters' dissatisfaction with the choices available. Domenico Fisichella (1984: 185) has coined the phrase 'orphaned electorate' to refer to those voters whose first choice of candidates are excluded in the second round. As we saw above, the 1995 presidential election very nearly offered an extreme example of this: if the Socialist candidate, Lionel Jospin, had been excluded after the first round, this would have resulted in centre-left voters being forced to choose in the second round between two candidates both of the centre-right. Sartori profoundly disagrees with the sort of interpretation provided by Fisichella: he is in no doubt that the two-round system, which he refers to as the 'double ballot' system, has clear advantages over any other electoral system: 'All other electoral systems are one-shot; the double ballot, and the double ballot only, is a two-shot system. With one shot the voter shoots very much in the dark; with two shots he or she shoots, the second time, in full daylight' (Sartori 1997: 63).

At first glance, the alternative vote system seems fairer than any of the other systems considered so far, for a range of reasons. First, unlike SMP (and on occasions under the majority–plurality version of two-round voting), the candidate elected has more votes than all the other candidates combined; he or she enjoys majority support in the constituency, giving a greater sense of legitimacy to the electoral result. Second, this system also allows the voters more say over who they want to represent them: if it is not to be their first choice, then they can choose a second. Third, because voting takes place on one day, there is no possibility for the parties to adopt manipulative strategies to try and maximize their gains; there is no second round of voting a week or fortnight later. Fourth, and more fundamentally, some have argued that the alternative vote can play a useful role, particularly in emerging democracies, in helping to foster closer cooperation between parties, encouraging them to engage in 'preference swapping' and a politics of centralism (Horowitz 1997; Reilly 1997c). If true, this argument provides a powerful alternative to the more common position in the academic literature which holds that proportional representation systems are best suited to promoting a politics of accommodation (for example, Lijphart 1999a; see Chapter 9 below).

On the other hand, there are reasons for suggesting that the alternative vote is not always fairer than the other electoral systems so far considered. For instance, under the Australian electoral rules, a voter must vote for all the candidates on the ballot paper. Such a requirement is peculiar to Australia, and it is one major reason for the higher number of invalid votes in Australia than elsewhere (McAllister and Makkai 1993). Whether the requirement to complete all the preferences produces a 'more democratic' result is debatable. It adds considerable burden to the vote process; and it has opened the way for the party machines to make use of 'how to vote' cards to direct voters on how to complete preferences. Arguably it diminishes the whole point of preferential voting if the order of preferences is pretty much determined in advance by party strategists (Wright 1986).

Not all countries using the alternative vote system have this requirement that all preferences must be completed, although this in turn opens up the possibility of large numbers of non-transferable votes, in some cases resulting in the candidate finally elected not actually having the support of the majority of voters. In any event, there is still a large number of wasted votes under the Australian system: as we have seen 49.7 per cent of those who voted in the Hinkler division in 1998 did not support the winning candidate. In common with the two-round and SMP systems, therefore, a large proportion of voters remain unrepresented.

In some cases, steps have been taken to 'simplify' the alternative vote so as to help reduce the burden on voters (and also play a role in reducing the dangers of too many fringe candidates picking up stray preferences). This was certainly behind the decision to have the new London mayor elected by a system called the 'supplementary vote', in which the voter has just two preferences. If no candidate achieves an overall majority on the first count, all but the top two candidates are eliminated and their ballot papers are redistributed on the basis of second-preference votes – in effect, a majority–run-off election held on the same day. Credited as a 'British invention' (for example, Norris 1995a), in fact, as Ben Reilly (1997b) observes, this variant has a much longer and wider pedigree, versions of it having been used in Alabama in the first part of the twentieth century, and as long ago as 1892 in the Australian state of Queensland.

3.4 Conclusion

Majoritarian electoral systems have clear selling points, certainly so far as opponents of proportional representation systems are concerned. Like SMP, these systems maintain the tradition of constituency representation, with single seats. The two countries best known for using these systems, Australia and France (Fifth Republic), have good records of stable government, incorporating strong single-party, or at least cohesive coalition, majorities. There is little scope for voter confusion: both the two-round and the alternative vote systems are easy to use and easy to understand. While the Australian practice of requiring that voters turn out and complete all vote preferences may add to the burden of voting, there is no reason why such a practice needs to be followed elsewhere.

If the majoritarian electoral systems share the positive features of SMP, they also share most of the negative features. Smaller parties are disadvantaged, certainly small parties which lack geographic concentrations in their support bases. For the same reasons as apply under SMP, it is questionable how 'fair' such systems are to smaller parties, and to the supporters of smaller parties. These issues can only be resolved by a move towards some form of proportional representation. However, as we shall see in the following chapters, the introduction of PR cannot be achieved without some costs of its own.

4

The List Systems of Proportional Representation

The electoral systems which we have looked at so far (together with the STV system discussed in Chapter 6) share a number of features in common. First, they are constituency-based: that is, the country is divided into a series of geographically defined constituencies, each represented by one MP (or, in the case of STV, several MPs). Second, and related, voting is candidate-based, not party-based: that is, voters choose between the candidates put forward by the parties. In other words, these systems can be characterized as consisting of the 'direct' election of MPs rather than their 'indirect' election via party lists. A third factor which many of the systems share in common is that they have been traditionally associated with Anglo-American countries.

In this chapter we deal with one of the most commonly used family of electoral systems, the list systems of proportional representation. In Table 1.2 we saw how just under half (29) of our sample of 59 'democracies' use a list system for their national elections. It has long been used by most West European countries, the exceptions being the UK, Ireland (which uses STV), Germany (which partially uses it in its 'mixed' system), and generally, though not always, France. List systems are also dominant across Latin America and in many of the newer African democracies as well.

One point must be stressed at the outset. There is no single list system – there are considerable variations in the different types of list systems. And, of course, the most significant difference relates to those cases where list is 'mixed' with another system such as single member plurality. For this reason, mixed electoral systems are dealt with separately in the next chapter.

The basic principle behind the list systems is simple enough. Each party draws up a list of candidates in each constituency. The size of the lists is based on the number of seats to be filled. In its most basic form, voters vote for parties instead of candidates (though see section 4.4). The proportion of votes each party receives determines the number of seats it can fill. For example in the 1997 British general election, the three main parties won the following proportions of votes:

Labour	43.2%
Conservatives	30.7%
Liberal Democrats	16.8%

If we imagine for a moment that the electoral system being used was a pure form of list PR – with the whole of the UK being treated as one vast constituency and with minimal distortion to proportionality – this would have resulted in the following distribution of seats:

Labour	285 seats (43.2%)
Conservatives	202 seats (30.7%)
Liberal Democrats	111 seats (16.8%)

This is strikingly different from the actual seat distribution of:

Labour	418 seats (63.4%)
Conservatives	165 seats (25.0%)
Liberal Democrats	46 seats (7.0%)

As no party would have an overall majority, the result would have been the formation of a coalition government. Obviously, this is a hypothetical example, and, in fact – as we shall see – in no case is such a degree of complete proportionality ever actually achieved. The list systems of PR incorporate their own distortions to proportionality. As we shall see below, this is primarily due to the fact that list systems tend to use subnational constituencies, or regions, and because of the inevitable distorting effects of all electoral formulas.

The chapter starts, in section 4.1, with a brief discussion of the origins of the various list systems. This is followed by three sections which examine the mechanics of these systems according to electoral formula (4.2), district magnitude (4.3) and ballot structure (4.4). Finally, in section 4.5, we assess the operation of list systems and their consequences.

4.1 The Origins of PR List Systems

The origins of PR list systems are associated with four people in particular: Thomas Hare (England), Victor d'Hondt (Belgium), Eduard Hagenbach-Bischoff (Switzerland), and A. Sainte-Laguë (France). As we shall see, a number of the features of the contemporary list systems are named after these individuals. But it would be a mistake to give them all the credit. The origins of list systems coincided with the development of representative democracy, and particularly with suffrage extension and the development of mass parties.

As we have seen in previous chapters, from the first steps in the development of electoral systems, Britain differed from its continental European neighbours, many of whom at an early stage had adopted majoritarian electoral systems, involving run-off elections. For the most part, this was in single-seat constituencies, though in Belgium, Luxembourg and Switzerland the constituencies were multi-seat. Only Denmark, Finland and Sweden did not pass through this interim phase of using majoritarian electoral systems. The move towards majoritarian electoral systems represented a clear attempt to avoid a situation where MPs could be elected without an overall majority of support in their constituencies. However, it soon became evident that this was not sufficient to prevent disproportional results at the national level. The earliest pressures for electoral reform in favour of proportional representation were felt in Belgium and Switzerland in the late nineteenth century. In both cases, as 'divided societies' (with ethnic and religious divisions), there was a desire to adopt an electoral system which could equalize the representation of the different communities involved.

Societies pressuring for electoral reform were formed: in Switzerland (the Association Réformiste de Genève) in 1865, and in Belgium (the Association Réformiste pour l'Adoption de la Représentation Proportionnelle) in 1881 (Victor d'Hondt was one of the founders). The efforts of these groups culminated in a conference at Antwerp in 1885 at which the relative merits of electoral systems recently devised by Thomas Hare (single transferable vote) and Victor d'Hondt (list PR) were discussed. D'Hondt's proposal for a list system of election was chosen as the most appropriate method. Given the absence from the conference of any representative of the British Proportional Representation Society, such a conclusion was probably inevitable. Subsequently, in 1899, Belgium became the first country to adopt a list system of proportional representation. This was the d'Hondt system, designed appropriately by a Belgian national. Finland became the next country to adopt PR in 1906, followed by Sweden in 1907. By 1920 most continental European countries had switched to a list system. As we see next, however, from there on the story becomes more complex.

4.2   Electoral Formulas: Largest Remainders and Highest Averages

There are considerable variations between the different types of list systems in use. It is beyond the scope of this book to attempt a comprehensive overview of all the different systems (see Carstairs 1980; Hand *et al.* 1979; Lijphart 1994a). The basic point of distinction is between one set of systems which determine seat allocation by *subtraction*, and another set which do so by *division*. The former is technically referred to as the 'largest remainder' systems, which operate with the use of an electoral quota. Different types of quotas are possible. The most common are the Hare and Droop quotas. List systems which operate with divisors are referred to technically as the 'highest average' systems. There are two types of highest average system in use: the d'Hondt method which is by far the most common (in the USA this is referred to as the Jefferson method), and the modified Sainte-Laguë method which is associated most with Scandinavian countries. The best way to grasp the variations between the two sets of list systems is to make use of hypothetical examples.

  The *largest remainder system* is used in Austria, Belgium, Denmark (for upper-tier allocations), Greece and Iceland; Italy formerly used it for lower house elections. Among the newer democracies which use largest remainder systems are South Africa, Colombia, Cost Rica and the Czech Republic. The central feature of this system (referred to in the USA as the Hamilton method) is an electoral quota. In its most basic form (though it can get more

Table 4.1   A hypothetical example of the operation of the largest remainder system

Total valid vote = 1000
Number of seats = 5
Hare quota (1000/5) = 200

	First round votes	Hare quota	Seats	Second round remainder	Seats	Total seats
Blue	360	200	1	160	1	2
Red	310	200	1	110	0	1
Orange	150	–	0	150	1	1
Green	120	–	0	120	1	1
Psychedelic	60	–	0	60	0	0

complex), the counting process occurs in two rounds. In the first round, parties with votes exceeding the quota are awarded seats, and the quota is subtracted from their total vote. In the second round, those parties left with the greatest number of votes (or the 'largest remainder') are awarded the remaining seats in order of vote size. This counting process is shown by the example in Table 4.1. Here we have five parties running for five seats. The total valid vote is 1,000 votes. In this example we make use of the Hare quota, which is the most commonly used. This is often referred to as the 'simple quota' and it is used in Colombia, Costa Rica and Madagascar, in Austria and Belgium at the constituency level, and in Denmark (and formerly Italy) for higher-tier seat allocation (see below, pp. 80–1). The Hare quota is calculated as follows: total valid vote divided by the number of seats, or 1000 ÷ 5 = 200.

The first stage of the counting process consists of sorting the votes into different piles for each of the parties. Here we see that the votes received by both the Blue Party (360 votes) and the Red Party (310 votes) exceed the quota (200 votes) and therefore each is awarded one seat in the first round. Next, the quota is subtracted from the Blue and Red totals, resulting in the following distribution of remaining votes: Blue, 160; Orange, 150; Green, 120; Red, 110; Psychedelic, 60. Since three more seats remain to be filled, these are awarded to the parties with the largest remaining votes: Blue, Orange and Green. The final result, therefore, is two seats for the Blues, and one each for Red, Orange and Green.

As the example suggests, the largest remainder system produces proportional results: smaller parties have an easier task in winning seats than they would in the systems discussed in the previous chapters. In this case the Green Party won the same number of seats as the Red Party despite having barely a third of the vote. The largest remainder system, therefore, tends to favour the smaller parties, especially when using the Hare quota. The relative importance of remainders in the allocation of seats can be reduced by using a lower quota, thereby making it more difficult for smaller parties to win seats. Two alternative quotas are used in some cases, the Droop quota (often referred to as the Hagenbach-Bischoff quota), and the Imperiali quota. The Droop quota, which is used, for instance, in Greece, South Africa and the Czech Republic, and which also plays a central role in the single transferable vote system, will be discussed in detail in Chapter 6. It is calculated by dividing the total valid vote by the number of seats plus one, adding one to the result and ignoring fractions. The Imperiali quota (which was used in Italy until 1993) is calculated by dividing the total valid vote by the number of seats plus two. As the following example shows – using the figures from Table 4.1 – these different formulas produce progressively smaller quotas:

Hare	votes ÷ seats	$1,000 ÷ 5$	$=200$
Droop	[votes ÷ (seats + 1)] + 1	$[1,000 ÷ (5 + 1)] + 1$	$=167$
Imperiali	votes ÷ seats + 2	$1,000 ÷ (5 + 2)$	$=143$

Lower quotas result in more seats being allocated to parties receiving a full quota and fewer being allocated by remainders, and therefore somewhat less proportional results. If the example in Table 4.1 is recalculated using the Imperiali quota instead of the Hare quota, this produces quite a different result. Since the Blues and Reds now qualify for two quota seats each, and the Orange Party for one quota seat, this means that all five seats are filled in the first round, without any need to take account of remainders. The final tally is two seats each for the Blue and Red parties, and one seat for Orange. The Green Party does not win a seat.

The *highest average system* is far more common than the largest remainder system. Instead of using a quota, it operates according to a divisor method. The system derives its name from the method by which seats are allocated to the parties. Each party's votes are divided by a series of divisors to produce an average vote. The party with the 'highest average' vote after each stage of the process wins a seat, and its vote is then divided by the next divisor. The process is continued until all the seats have been filled. Two main types of divisors are in operation: the d'Hondt system (with the divisors 1, 2, 3, 4 and so on, used in Argentina, Brazil, Bulgaria, Finland, Israel, Luxembourg, Mozambique, the Netherlands, Portugal, Spain, Switzerland, Turkey and Uruguay) and the modified Sainte-Laguë system (with the divisors 1.4, 3, 5, 7 and so on, used in Denmark, Norway and Sweden).[1]

Table 4.2 presents the election results for the same hypothetical example as above, this time using the d'Hondt highest average system. (In order to provide a 'real world' example of a list system in action, the Box 4.1 summarizes a recent count in Finland, which uses the d'Hondt highest average system.) The counting process is quite simple. First, the votes are sorted into piles for each of the parties. These totals are then divided by the d'Hondt divisors 1, 2, 3, and so on until all the seats have been allocated. The seats are awarded to those parties with the highest averages. Because in this example it is a five-seat constituency, literally this means that we are looking for the five highest numbers in the table. In this example, the italics indicate the sequence in which the seats have been filled. The seats are allocated in the following sequence:

Table 4.2　A hypothetical example of the operation of the d'Hondt highest average system

Total valid vote = 1000
Number of seats = 5

	Votes	*Votes divided by 1*		*Votes divided by 2*		*Votes divided by 3*	*Total seats*
Blue	360	360	*1st seat*	180	*3rd seat*	120	2
Red	310	310	*2nd seat*	155	*4th seat*	103	2
Orange	150	150	*5th seat*	75			1
Green	120	120					0
Psychedelic	60	60					0

Box 4.1   The d'Hondt Electoral System in Finland[2]

The Finnish parliament (which is unicameral) comprises 200 MPs, elected in fixed four-year cycles. With the exception of the autonomous province of Åland, which elects one MP, Finnish district magnitude ranges from seven to thirty seats. As we shall see below, voting is candidate-based: that is, the lists are open and the ranking of the parties' candidates is based entirely on their personal votes.

Table 4.3 provides a summary of how seats were allocated in the region of North Karelia in 1991. As we would expect with a d'Hondt system and a relatively small district magnitude, the larger parties won all seven seats. This was particularly notable in the case of the Electoral Alliance of Centre, Liberal and Christian parties whose vote proportion of 40.1 per cent was translated into a seat tally of 57.1 per cent (that is, 17 per cent more seats than their share of the vote should have allowed them). In general, however, the result was pretty proportional: none of the other parties had a difference between the proportion of votes and the proportion of seats that was greater than 7 per cent.

First seat	360 votes	Blue
Second seat	310 votes	Red
Third seat	180 votes	Blue
Fourth seat	155 votes	Red
Fifth Seat	150 votes	Orange

While this result is more proportional than under single member plurality or majoritarian systems – in the sense that smaller parties like the Orange Party have a chance of winning seats – it should be noted that this is a less proportional result than was achieved in the largest remainder example in Table 4.1: the Green Party does not win a seat. This result is consistent with the argument that d'Hondt is one of the least proportional of the list electoral formulas (Lijphart 1994a). This point will be explored in Chapter 7 when we deal with the question of proportionality of electoral systems.

A much more proportional result can be achieved by replacing the

Table 4.3   The d'Hondt highest average system in practice: the Finnish region of North Karelia in 1991

Total valid vote = 92,257
Number of seats = 7

	Votes	Votes divided by 1	Votes divided by 2	Votes divided by 3	Votes divided by 4	Total seats
Electoral Alliance of Centre, Liberal and Christian parties	37,028	37,028 (1)	18,514 (3)	12,343 (6)	9,257 (7)	4
Social Democratic Party	27,721	27,721 (2)	13,861 (4)	9,240		2
National Coalition Party	12,438	12,438 (5)	6,219			1
Electoral Alliance (Finnish Rural Party and 3 minor parties)	6,443	6,443				0
Left Wing Alliance	4,783	4,783				0
Greens	3,702	3,702				0
Communist Workers' Party	104	104				0
Humanity Party	38	38				0

	Votes (%)	Seats (%)	Diff. (%)
Electoral Alliance of Centre, Liberal and Christian parties	40.1	57.1	+17.0
Social Democratic Party	30.0	28.6	−1.4
National Coalition Party	13.5	13.5	–
Electoral Alliance (Finnish Rural Party and 3 minor parties)	7.0	0.0	−7.0
Left Wing Alliance	5.2	0.0	−5.2
Greens	4.0	0.0	−4.0
Communist Workers' Party	0.1	0.0	−0.1
Humanity Party	0.0	0.0	–

Note: The bracketed numbers in italics indicate the order in which seats were allocated.
Source: Kuusela (1995).

Table 4.4   A hypothetical example of the operation of the modified
Sainte-Laguë highest average system
Total valid vote = 1000
Number of seats = 5

	Votes	Votes divided by 1.4		Votes divided by 3		Votes divided by 5	Total seats
Blue	360	257	*1st seat*	120	*3rd seat*	72	2
Red	310	221	*2nd seat*	103	*5th seat*	62	2
Orange	150	107	*4th seat*	50			1
Green	120	85					0
Psychedelic	60	42					0

d'Hondt divisors of 1, 2, 3, 4 and so on with the odd-integer divisor
series, 1, 3, 5, 7 and so on. This is known as the pure Sainte-Laguë
system (in the USA it is known as the Webster method), and according to Lijphart (1994a: 23) it 'approximates proportionality very
closely and treats large and small parties in a perfectly even-handed
way'. This system, which is generally seen as 'too proportional', is
very rare. It was recently adopted in New Zealand as part of its new
mixed system (see Chapter 5). The practice over time has been to
modify the first integer, replacing 1 with 1.4. This reduces the overall
proportionality because it is that bit harder for small parties to win
seats. According to Lijphart, as a result, modified Sainte-Laguë lies
on a scale of proportionality somewhere between d'Hondt and pure
Sainte-Laguë.

Table 4.4 shows an election count with modified Sainte-Laguë
using the same hypothetical case as before. The presentation is the
same as for Table 4.2, only this time the divisors are 1.4, 3, 5 and so
on. The result is the same, but the sequence in which the seats are
allocated varies. The result is as follows:

First seat	257 votes	Blue
Second seat	221 votes	Red
Third seat	120 votes	Blue
Fourth seat	107 votes	Orange
Fifth seat	103 votes	Red

If the election had been fought using pure Sainte-Laguë divisors (1, 3, 5 and so on), the result would have been far more proportional, namely:

First seat	360 votes	Blue
Second seat	310 votes	Red
Third seat	150 votes	Orange
Fourth seat	120 votes	Green
Fifth seat	120 votes	Blue

In summary, this section has assessed the three main electoral formulas in use in PR list systems. According to Arend Lijphart's research, separate from the effects of district magnitude, the electoral formula which produces the most proportional result is the largest remainder system with the Hare quota; modified Sainte-Laguë highest average forms an intermediate category; and the least proportional systems are d'Hondt highest average and largest remainder with the Imperiali quota (Lijphart 1986a, 1994a; the ranking of electoral systems in terms of proportionality is dealt with in Chapter 7). The fact is, however, that all these systems incorporate some element of disproportionality. This can be minimized by having a large district magnitude or by 'two-tier' seat allocations, as we see in the next section.

Disproportionality can also be reduced by the process of *apparentement*. As we have seen, in the list systems, smaller parties can have many 'wasted' votes: that is, situations in which they do not have enough votes to fill seats. It can happen that a series of small parties miss winning any seats by relatively small margins. *Apparentement* refers to a situation in which parties formally agree to link their lists – where two or more parties declare that they are contesting the election as an alliance (Valen 1994). The ballot papers are not affected; the parties still appear as separate lists. However, in the counting process all their spare votes are pooled, increasing the prospect that one of the smaller parties will succeed in having an extra candidate elected. *Apparentement* is used most commonly in d'Hondt systems (notably the Netherlands, Israel and Switzerland) to compensate for disproportionality. In the past it was also used in Scandinavian countries (Denmark, Norway and Sweden), but for the most part they stopped using it with the move towards Sainte-Laguë, and later modified Sainte-Laguë (Carstairs 1980: 216–18; Lijphart 1994a: 134–7).

4.3 District Magnitude: Constituency Size and Two-Tier Districting

At the start of the chapter it was pointed out that the best way to maximize proportionality is to have the entire country as one vast constituency. Once we start to carve up a country into smaller constituencies an element of disproportionality is introduced. The basic relationship for all proportional systems is: the larger the constituency size (and, hence, the larger the district magnitude) the more proportional the result. This relationship is examined in detail in Chapter 7 below. But the basic idea should make sense. If a country is divided up into small constituencies, there is a far greater number of voters whose votes are wasted in the counting process. For instance, depending on the different electoral formulas used in the examples in the previous section, the supporters of the Psychedelic Party and sometimes also of the Green Party did not see their votes translated into seats. If that experience is repeated across the country, then there is the prospect of a lot of voters just missing the chance of having their preferred party elected in their constituency. In the aggregate, therefore, the result is disproportional.

As the size of constituencies increases, so also do the prospects for a proportional result. The ideal situation – as far as proportionality is concerned – is one where the entire nation is one constituency. This is the practice in Israel and the Netherlands. In Israel all 120 members of the Knesset are elected on a national level. In theory that should mean that in order to be elected a candidate needs only 1/120th, or 0.83 per cent, of the total national vote. However, this 'pure' proportionality is reduced somewhat, both by the electoral formula which is used (d'Hondt – the least proportional of the list formulas) and by the requirement that a party must win at least 1.5 per cent of the national vote to qualify for seats (legal thresholds are discussed below). The Netherlands comes closer to a purely proportional result. All 150 members of the Tweede Kamer (Second Chamber) are elected on the basis of the national distribution of party votes. A candidate needs just 1/150th, or 0.67 per cent, of the total national vote to be elected. This means that, depending on the turnout, a party can be represented in parliament with fewer than 60,000 votes. In fact it is possible for candidates to be elected with even smaller proportions. To prevent this possibility there is a minimum threshold of 0.67 per cent of the vote which a party must win in order to qualify for any seats (in 1998 this amounted to 57,361 votes).

The problem with national-level representation is that it reduces the contact between representatives and voters. In effect there is no such thing as a constituency politician. There is a danger that the geographical location of MPs (either by birth or residence) may be concentrated in the urban, more populated areas, leaving whole swathes of the population 'unrepresented'. One solution to this – which is the Dutch practice – is to have the party lists drawn up at the regional level. This means that even if the question of who wins seats is determined by the national vote, at least those candidates elected will be more evenly spread across the country.

The more common practice is to divide the country up into regions or constituencies. However, these are not constituencies in the sense in which one understands them in a single member plurality system. In all cases the constituencies are larger than under SMP, and in some cases quite substantially so. According to Lijphart's (1994a) detailed overview, the smallest average constituencies are in Greece (with about five seats), while the largest are in Portugal (with about 24 seats). Therefore, it is not possible to call the MPs elected under these systems 'constituency politicians' in the sense used, say, in the UK. This point is reinforced by the fact that voters are voting for parties and not candidates and therefore constituency representation does not feature so highly in the voting process (Katz 1980; see also the discussion on ballot structure below).

It is possible to build into the system a means of increasing the proportionality of the result without having overly large constituencies. Technically this is referred to as 'two-tier districting', where a certain number of seat allocations are determined in a 'higher tier' such as the wider region, or even across the nation as a whole. This two-tier method irons out any discrepancies at the constituency level and produces a result which is more proportional. The basic idea is that any votes which have been 'wasted' at the first tier – that is, all remaining votes which have not been used to fill seats – are pooled and the distribution of the remaining seats is determined in the second tier. This practice is followed by all the countries using the largest remainder system or the modified Sainte-Laguë highest average system. Consistent with the fact that the d'Hondt system is the least proportional of the list formulas in use, none of the countries using it bother with a second tier.

Two different procedures are followed: 'remainder transfer' in the largest remainder cases and 'adjustment-seats' in the modified Sainte-Laguë highest average cases (Lijphart 1994a: 32). The 'adjustment-seats' system entails a certain fixed proportion of seats which are set aside and 'awarded to the parties in the appropriate numbers to compensate them for any shortfall in the seats they won in the constituencies' (Gallagher *et al*. 2000: 311). In Denmark and Iceland the proportion is about 20 per cent; in Sweden, 11 per cent; and in Norway, 5 per cent. In the 'remainder transfer' system the proportions of higher-tier seats are not fixed in advance, but the outcome is the same. This practice is followed in Austria, Belgium and Greece (and formerly Italy).

For all the effects on proportionality of electoral formula and district magnitude, the list systems often contain features which give an in-built advantage to larger parties. It is common for the electoral law to include a legal threshold below which parties are not awarded any seats. In other words, this is a cut-off point which is designed to reduce the number of tiny, splinter parties in the system. The best-known example of such a legal threshold is in Germany where a party must win at least 5 per cent of the list vote (or – even more difficult – win three constituency seats) before it can be awarded any seats. In 1987, for instance, the German Green Party won 8.3 per cent of the vote which translated into 42 (or 8.5 per cent) seats. In the 1990 first all-German election, the party won only 4.8 per cent of the vote in the western part of Germany and so lost all its seats.[3]

Legal thresholds can vary greatly in size and method of operation. As we have seen, the lowest one is used in the Netherlands where a party must get at least 0.67 per cent of the vote. In Denmark the threshold is set at 2 per cent; in Sweden it is 4 per cent; in Poland it is 7 per cent. Some thresholds apply to the upper-tier allocation only. In these cases they are used to top up the gains of the larger parties. In Austria a party needs only to win one constituency seat to qualify for upper-tier seats, which is not too onerous given that the average constituency has twenty seats (Gallagher *et al*. 2000). The most controversial example of topping-up was in Greece in 1981 and 1985 with a system which was euphemistically referred to as 'reinforced

PR'. A party had to win at least 17 per cent of the national vote to qualify for upper-tier allocation. This caused some marked distortions in the results, and in 1989 the restriction was dropped. Probably the most elaborate threshold rule is in the Czech Republic where a party must obtain 5 per cent of the national vote. However, if it is in coalition then this threshold is made less onerous, so that a coalition of two parties requires 7 per cent of the vote, a coalition of three requires 9 per cent, a coalition of four requires 11 per cent, and so on.

4.4   Ballot Structure: Closed and Open Lists

Ballot structure is particularly important in the case of list systems. Since the basis of the system is a vote for party, rather than for candidate, there has to be a means of determining the allocation of seats between the party candidates. In other words, once we have used the electoral formula to work out how many seats each party is to be allocated, we next need some mechanism for working out which seats are to go to which candidates. In theory this should be a very simple exercise. Each party draws up a list of candidates for the given region and the seats are allocated according to the rank order used in the list. For instance, imagine a hypothetical situation where the Blue party in a particular region (say a seven-seat region) has selected its seven candidates and listed them in the following order, where we can guess the reasons (in parentheses) for the rank order:

> Candidate 1 (long standing activist; party fund-raiser)
> Candidate 2 (woman)
> Candidate 3 (leading industrialist)
> Candidate 4 (woman)
> Candidate 5 (party headquarters functionary)
> Candidate 6 (teacher)
> Candidate 7 (son of local business owner)

If in the subsequent election the party wins three seats then the first three names on the list are awarded the seats. If the party wins two seats then only Candidates 1 and 2 are elected. This is referred to as a 'closed' list, or a non-preferential system. For the most part it is used in 'newer democracies', such as Argentina, Columbia, Costa

Rica, Israel, Portugal, Spain, Turkey and Uruguay. It is also used in Germany for the list seats. It was also briefly used by France in the 1986 legislative elections. Figure 4.1 provides an example of a Spanish ballot paper. This is the ballot for the Convergència I Unió Party, where the candidate names are listed in the rank order set by the party. The act of voting for this party consists basically of picking up this ballot paper and dropping it into the ballot box.

It is easy to see the advantages for the party elite of such a system. They can draw up their lists in such a way so as to maximize the chances for their preferred candidates to be elected. There are clear advantages to this system wherever a party wants to increase its proportion of female MPs (for example, by 'zipping', with every second candidate being a woman), or, perhaps, guarantee a minimum proportion of seats to ethnic minorities. A good example of this is provided by the first democratic election of post-apartheid South Africa in April 1994. The SMP electoral system of the old regime had been replaced by list PR. As Figure 4.2 shows, the ballot paper contained party names and logos, and colour photographs of the party leaders. This was a closed list system; the voter was instructed as follows: 'make your mark next to the party you choose'. As Andrew Reynolds (1994: 58) observed, these 'national, and unalterable, candidate lists allowed parties to present ethnically heterogeneous groups of candidates which, it was hoped, would have cross-cutting appeal'.

But there are also clear disadvantages to such a system. The individual voters have absolutely no say over *who* represents them. The list is drawn up by the parties and all the voter can do is select one list for one party. The voter has no say over the rank order, apart, that is, from joining the party and trying to get involved in the internal candidate selection process. (Of course, precisely the same criticism can be levelled at the SMP system; see Chapter 2.)

Most of the list systems operate a more flexible, or 'open' ballot structure, and are, to varying degrees, preferential systems (Katz 1986; Marsh 1985). The least open of these are in Austria, Belgium, the Netherlands, Norway and Sweden. Figure 4.3 provides an example of the Belgian case, where voters have two choices. They may either cast a vote for one party (by ticking the relevant box under the party name) or a vote for one candidate (by ticking the relevant box next to the candidate). In theory, expressing a personal vote for one of the candidates has the effect of moving that candidate higher up the rank ordering. In practice, however, a candidate

ELECCIONES A CORTES GENERALES 1989
ELECCIONS A CORTS GENERALS 1989

DIPUTADOS
DIPUTATS

BARCELONA

Doy mi voto a la candidatura presentada por:
Dono el meu vot a la candidatura presentada per:

CONVERGENCIA I UNIO
(C. i U.)

MIQUEL ROCA i JUNYENT *(C.D.C.)*
JOSEP M.ª CULLELL i NADAL *(C.D.C.)*
JOSEP M.ª TRIAS DE BES i SERRA *(C.D.C.)*
LLIBERT CUATRECASAS i MEMBRADO *(U.D.C.)*
RAFAEL HINOJOSA i LUCENA *(C.D.C.)*
MARIA EUGÈNIA CUENCA i VALERO *(C.D.C.)*
FRANCESC HOMS i FERRET *(C.D.C.)*
JORDI CASAS i BEDOS *(U.D.C.)*
LLUIS MIQUEL RECODER i MIRALLES *(C.D.C.)*
PERE BALTÀ i LLÓPART *(C.D.C.)*
ANTONI CASANOVAS i BRUGAL *(C.D.C.)*
SANTIAGO MARTINEZ i SAURI *(U.D.C.)*
JOSEP NICOLÀS DE SALAS i MORENO *(C.D.C.)*
SARA BLASI i GUTIERREZ *(C.D.C.)*
MARCEL RIERA i BOU *(C.D.C.)*
IGNASI JOANIQUET i SIRVENT *(U.D.C.)*
LLUIS ARBOIX i PASTOR *(C.D.C.)*
JOAN GRAU i TARRUELL *(C.D.C.)*
JOSEP M.ª OLLER i BERENGUER *(C.D.C.)*
RAMON TOMÀS i RIBA *(U.D.C.)*
YOLANDA PIEDRA i MAÑES *(C.D.C.)*
JOAN USART i BARREDA *(C.D.C.)*
LLUIS BERTRAN i BERTRAN *(C.D.C.)*
OLGA CAMPMANY i CASAS *(U.D.C.)*
MIQUEL SÀNCHEZ i LOPEZ *(C.D.C.)*
ANA M.ª PAREDES i RODRIGUEZ *(C.D.C.)*
JOAN MASAFRET i CADEVALL *(C.D.C.)*
MARTA VIGAS i GINESTA *(U.D.C.)*
ALFONS CASAS i GASSÓ *(C.D.C.)*
JOSEP MASSÓ i PADRÓ *(C.D.C.)*
FRANCESC XAVIER MIRET i VOISIN *(C.D.C.)*
VICTOR PEIRÓ i RIUS *(U.D.C.)*

Suplentes – *Suplents*

ANA M.ª DEL VALLE i RODRIGUEZ *(C.D.C.)*
ALBERT TUBAU i GARCIA *(C.D.C.)*
MIQUEL COLL i ALENTORN *(U.D.C.)*

Figure 4.1   A Spanish PR list ballot paper

BALLOT PAPER

PAN AFRICANIST CONGRESS OF AZANIA		PAC	
SPORTS ORGANISATION FOR COLLECTIVE CONTRIBUTIONS AND EQUAL RIGHTS		SOCCER	
THE KEEP IT STRAIGHT AND SIMPLE PARTY		KISS	
VRYHEIDSFRONT - FREEDOM FRONT		VF-FF	
WOMEN'S RIGHTS PEACE PARTY		WRPP	
WORKERS' LIST PARTY		WLP	
XIMOKO PROGRESSIVE PARTY		XPP	
AFRICA MUSLIM PARTY		AMP	
AFRICAN CHRISTIAN DEMOCRATIC PARTY		ACDP	
AFRICAN DEMOCRATIC MOVEMENT		ADM	
AFRICAN MODERATES CONGRESS PARTY		AMCP	
AFRICAN NATIONAL CONGRESS		ANC	
DEMOCRATIC PARTY - DEMOKRATIESE PARTY		DP	
DIKWANKWETLA PARTY OF SOUTH AFRICA		DPSA	
FEDERAL PARTY		FP	
LUSO - SOUTH AFRICAN PARTY		LUSAP	
MINORITY FRONT		MF	
NATIONAL PARTY - NASIONALE PARTY		NP	
INKATHA FREEDOM PARTY - IQEMBU LENKATHA YENKULULEKO		IFP	

Presented by the Voter Education Programme of the Independent Electoral Commission.

Figure 4.2   A South African PR list ballot paper

86

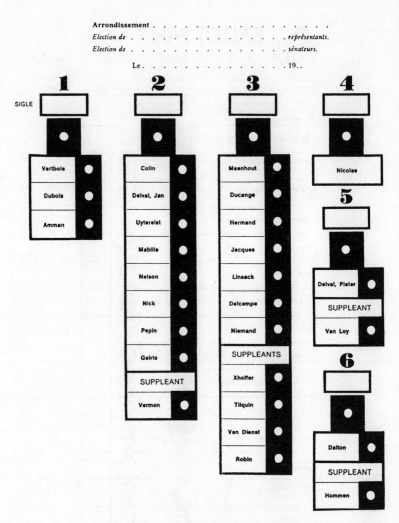

Arrondissement . . . .
Election de . . . . *représentants.*
Election de . . . . *sénateurs.*

Le . . . . 19 . .

Figure 4.3   A Belgian PR list ballot paper

placed low in the rank order requires a very large personal vote in order to 'leap-frog' into a winning position. This is because the 'party' votes are used to top up the personal votes of the candidates placed high on the party list, giving them a huge advantage over the candidates lower in the rank order (Berghe 1979). The usual pattern is that the supply of available party votes is generally exhausted before they can be of any use to candidates closer to the bottom of the party list, so that only a tiny proportion of seat allocations are affected by unusually large personal votes for individual candidates (De Winter 1988).

An intermediate category of openness is presented by cases like Finland or Italy (before reforms in the 1990s) where personal votes have a real influence on candidate rank order.[4] In Italy it used to be the case that voters could either simply vote for their preferred party, or else they could also write down the names or numbers of up to three or four (depending on constituency size) preferred candidates under the party name. Unlike the Belgian case where party votes have a strong influence on retaining the original candidate rank order, in Italy the seats were allocated to those candidates with the most personal votes, so personal votes could make a difference. However, for the most part only about 30 per cent of Italian voters made use of preferential voting (Marsh 1985: 368), though the percentage tended to be significantly greater in southern Italy, reflecting higher degrees of 'clientelism'. There were prominent occasions when personal voting made a real difference, for instance in the 1983 election when the porno star 'La Ciciollina' received a huge personal vote and was swept into parliament. The Italian ballot structure tended to encourage the clientelistic and factional tendencies in the political system, and in the early 1990s the electoral law was changed so that only one personal vote could be declared. In 1993 – in the furore over political scandals – the electoral system was replaced altogether (see below, and Chapter 5).

Luxembourg and Switzerland operate the most flexible ballot structures of all. An example of the Luxembourg ballot paper is provided in Figure 4.4. Here voters have as many votes as there are seats to be filled. They have three choices: (1) cast a 'list vote' for the party, thereby giving one vote to each of the party's candidates; (2) cumulate two personal votes on one candidate (as indicated by the two boxes next to each candidate's name in Figure 4.4; this option is referred to as 'cumulation'); or (3) give personal votes to candidates

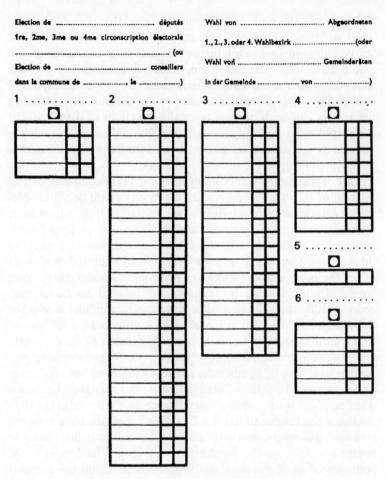

Figure 4.4   A Luxembourg PR list ballot paper

on more than one party list. This latter option is known as *panachage* and, according to Marsh (1985: 369), on average it has been used by about 8 per cent of Swiss voters and 18 per cent of Luxembourg voters.

4.5 The Operation of Two List Systems

As we have seen, there are a large number of countries using list PR and many variants of the system. In this section we will focus on two prominent examples, the Netherlands and Italy, the former an example of a highly proportional system with a large number of parties represented in parliament, the latter also a case of a highly fragmented party system, where, in part, due to disquiet over the operation of PR, the electoral system was first amended and then, in 1993, replaced by a new one. Let us start with a bit of context on each of them.

As we shall see in Chapter 7, the Netherlands has one of the most proportional electoral systems in the world. It uses highest average d'Hondt with a very large district magnitude. In effect, the entire country is one constituency, so that, according to Rudy Andeweg and Galen Irwin (1993: 89), 'The proportional distribution of seats is as close as possible to the proportion of votes that the parties have achieved.'

The operation of PR in the Netherlands has been seen as a major factor in the long-standing tradition of successful political 'accommodation' in Dutch politics. But this has not stopped the emergence of a debate about electoral reform, which rose to some prominence in the 1980s. Two main issues have driven this debate. First, there is some attention to the lack of MP–voter links, inevitable given the absence of parliamentary constituencies. Ken Gladdish refers to academic surveys in the early 1970s which found that Dutch citizens considered their MPs as largely irrelevant to their local concerns. In the case of one of these surveys it was found that 'At national level, members of the Royal Family turned out to be the object of slightly more frequent contacts than individual MPs' (Gladdish 1991: 101). This attitude of indifference is reciprocated by the Dutch MPs. A cross-national survey of parliamentarians in the early 1980s found that, in 'the task of mediation between groups and individuals', British and German MPs 'scored highly'; by contrast, this activity 'was virtually ignored by the Dutch' (Gladdish 1991: 102).

A second issue which has driven the debate about electoral reform in the Netherlands is the stability of government. This issue was brought to a head in the 1960s by the new Democrats 66 (D66) Party which laid great stress on the inconclusiveness of Dutch elections, the length of time it took to form a government after an election, and the complexity of governments which were formed. This relates to the point often raised about whether PR can really guarantee proper democratic accountability if the governments are formed more on the basis of post-election negotiations, rather than as a result of clear electoral mandates (see Chapter 9 below). In the Netherlands this issue was compounded by the fact that the three confessional parties were always in government: new parties like D66 could not get a look in.

In 1967 a parliamentary committee, known as the Cals–Donner committee, was established to examine constitutional reform, looking into such matters as whether the Dutch should adopt a presidential system of government. Among the proposals in its 1971 report, the Cals–Donner committee called for the replacement of nationwide PR with a system of twelve regional lists. At first this proposal seemed to carry some weight, particularly as it was endorsed by the Labour Party. However, after a long debate, the committee's proposals were finally rejected in early 1975, and for some time after that, little attention was given to the issue of electoral reform in the Netherlands.

Debate since the early 1990s over the accountability of Dutch politicians to their voters has once again led to speculation about possible electoral reform, in which the Netherlands might move towards some form of mixed system, such as used in Germany (see Chapter 5). One of the prime movers of recent proposals along such lines was the D66 Party, which was now in government as part of the 'Purple Coalition' elected in 1994. The issue was dropped, however, after strong resistance in the parliament. But D66 continues pushing an electoral reform agenda, and just prior to the change of government in 1998, the party proposed a move to an electoral system which would increase the degree of contact between MPs and their voters. Given that D66 joined the new government elected in 1998, it is likely that this issue will continue to receive attention.

Italy has shared a lot in common with the Netherlands, notably the high degree of proportionality of its electoral system, and the large number of parties competing for seats and ultimately winning representation in parliament. One significant difference between the two countries is that the Italians have not just talked about electoral reform; as we shall see in the next chapter, they have gone ahead and radically changed their electoral system.

As one of the few political systems with a powerful second chamber, Italy used two versions of list PR. For the lower house, the Chamber of Deputies, the system was largest remainder Imperiali (with personal voting) in 32 electoral districts, with a distribution of remainders through a national pool (with quota rules applying). For the Senate, the system was highest average d'Hondt (without personal voting).

The Chamber of Deputies' ballot structure was 'open', with voters being permitted to express between three and four personal votes (depending on the size of the region) on the ballot paper. To use the personal vote option the voters needed to know either the names or numbers of the candidates (and the party they were running for); the names were not even provided in the polling booth. As we have seen, the personal vote option was only used by about 30 per cent of voters on average. However, in parts of Italy the percentage was far higher, particularly in the south and the islands of Sardinia and Sicily, where candidates and parties made great efforts to try to influence the personal vote. In some cases personal voting was greater than 50 per cent. There were accusations that organized lobbies, and even, in some cases, organized crime, played a role in trying to influence votes in favour of their particular candidates. In 1991 a constitutional referendum was held to reduce the number of personal votes allowed to just one.

The major reform of the Italian electoral system was in 1993 when, in the wake of a major scandal over the proprieties of the established parties and politicians, the Italians voted in a referendum to abolish list PR for the Senate. Subsequently this prompted the politicians to also change the electoral system for the Chamber of Deputies. The details of the referendum debate and the nature of the electoral reforms are long, complex and convoluted (see Donovan 1995; Katz 1996). The basic result is that the two houses of the legislature have ended up with electoral systems which share common features, but which are quite distinct in some important respects. The basic point of similarity is that, in each case, three-quarters of MPs are elected to represent individual constituencies, while one-quarter are elected on PR lists, and in this sense both systems can be categorized as mixed electoral systems, which are considered in Chapter 5. However, in the case of the Senate the allocation of the list seats is based on the overall (single) vote for each party. By contrast, in the

Chamber of Deputies' electoral system the voters have two separate votes, one for constituency politicians and one for party lists.

What have been the implications of PR for these two systems? Both have been characterized by a large number of parliamentary parties – with up to as many as 14 parties represented in the parliament – and, in consequence, coalition governments are the norm. In the Netherlands there have been more than seventeen changes of government since the war, while Italy has had more than twice that figure (see Chapter 9 for further discussion). In Tables 4.5 and 4.6 we follow the practice of the previous chapters and examine the electoral systems in terms of percentage vote–seat differences. Given the large number of parties in each system, it has been decided to present only the 'difference' figures so as to save space. The percentages of votes and seats are not presented; instead, the parties have been grouped under one of three categories: large (votes greater than 9 per cent), medium (votes between 2 and 9 per cent), and small (votes less than 2 per cent). Furthermore, not all parties are included: many of the smaller parties are transitory, and, particularly in the case of Italy, are regionally based.

Both tables reveal very low levels of disproportionality: the difference figures are the lowest of all the electoral systems dealt with so far (and lower than the trends discussed in Chapters 5 and 6 below). Nevertheless, there are some areas of similarity with the trends in other electoral systems. In particular the largest parties still benefit most from higher proportions of seats relative to share of votes. This is most notable in the case of the Italian Christian Democrats, demonstrating the benefits to that party of a strong geographical concentration in its support base (in the south), and explaining why it should be most resistant to change. It is also worth noting how it is only with the Christian Democrats that we see high levels of disproportionality. By contrast, there is no sign of any particular gains being made by smaller parties in the system (quite the contrary). This raises questions about just how significant a role the electoral system played in producing political instability in Italy; other factors seem also to have had a role.

The smaller the party the less beneficial the distorting effects of the electoral system. In the Netherlands we see that the record of disproportionality in the case of medium-sized parties is quite mixed; the smaller parties generally do least well (though, by contrast with single member plurality, the picture for these small parties

Table 4.5 Differences between vote and seat percentages in the Netherlands, 1959–98

	1959	1963	1967	1971	1972	1977	1981	1982	1986	1989	1994	1998
Large parties (average vote >9%)												
Catholic People's Party	+1.1	+1.4	+1.5	+1.5	+0.3							
Christian Democratic Appeal						+0.8	+1.2	+0.6	+1.4	+0.7	+0.5	+0.9
Labour Party	+1.6	+0.7	+1.1	+1.4	+1.4	+1.5	+1.0	+0.9	+1.4	+0.8	+0.7	+1.0
Liberal Party	+0.5	+0.4	−0.4	+0.4	+0.3	+0.8	—	+0.9	+0.6	+0.1	+0.8	+0.6
Medium-sized parties (average vote between 2 and 9%)												
Anti-Revolutionary Party	−0.1	—	+0.1	+0.1	+0.5							
Christian Historical Union	−0.1	+0.1	−0.1	+0.4	−0.1							
Communist Party	−0.4	−0.1	−0.3	+0.1	+0.2	−0.4	−0.1	+0.2	−0.6			
D66			+0.2	+0.5	−0.2	−0.1	+0.2	−0.3	−0.1	+0.1	+0.5	+0.3
Democratic Socialists'70				—	−0.1	—	−0.6					
Political Reformed Party	—	−0.3	—	−0.3	—	−0.1	—	+0.1	+0.3	+0.1	−0.4	+0.2
Radical Political Party				−0.5	−0.1	+0.3	—	−0.4	—			
Small parties (average vote <2%)												
Centre Party							−0.1	−0.1	−0.4			
Evangelical People's Party							−0.5	—	−0.2			
Farmers' Party	−0.7	−0.1	−0.1	−0.4	+0.1	−0.1	−0.2	−0.3				
Middle Class Party				−0.2	−0.4							
Pacifist Socialist Party	−0.5	−0.3	−0.2	−0.1	−0.2	−0.2	−0.1	−0.3	−0.5	−0.3	+0.2	
Reformed Political Federation						−0.6	+0.1	−0.2	−0.2	−0.3	+0.2	—
Reformed Political Union	−0.7	—	−0.2	−0.3	−0.5	−0.3	−0.1	−0.1	−0.3	+0.1	—	—

Notes: The difference percentage is calculated by subtracting the percentage of seats each party was awarded from the percentage of votes it won. A positive sign indicates that the party was awarded a greater share of seats proportionate to its vote, a negative sign indicates it received a lesser share of seats, a dash indicates perfect proportionality. Not all parties are included. Blank spaces indicate that the party is no longer in existence.
Sources: Mackie and Rose (1991); election results.

Table 4.6 Differences between vote and seat percentages in Italy, 1953–92

	1953	1958	1963	1968	1972	1976	1979	1983	1987	1992
Large parties (average vote >9%)										
Christian Democrats	+4.5	+3.4	+3.1	+3.2	+4.0	+3.0	+3.1	+2.8	+2.8	+3.0
Communist Party/Democratic Left	+1.6	−0.8	+1.0	+1.2	+1.2	+1.6	+1.5	+0.6	+1.5	+0.9
Socialist Party	–	−0.1	–	–	+0.1	−0.6	–	+0.1	+0.6	+0.1
Medium-sized parties (average vote between 2 and 9%)										
Liberal Party	−0.8	−0.6	−0.7	−0.9	−0.6	−0.5	−0.4	−0.4	−0.4	−0.1
Radical Party						−1.1	−0.6	−0.5	−0.5	−0.1
Republican Party	−0.8	−0.4	−0.4	−0.6	−0.7	−0.9	−0.6	−0.5	−0.4	−0.1
Social Democrats	−1.3	−0.9	−1.0	–	−0.5	−1.0	−0.5	−0.4	−0.3	−0.2
Social Movement MSI	−0.9	−0.8	−0.8	−0.6	+0.2	−0.5	−0.4	−0.1	−0.3	–
Small parties (average vote <2%)										
Proletarian Democracy							−0.8	−0.4	−0.4	–
South Tyrol People's Party	–		+0.1							
Val d'Aosta Union		+0.1	+0.1	−0.1	−0.1	−0.1	+0.1	+0.1	+0.1	+0.1

Notes: The difference percentage is calculated by subtracting the percentage of seats each party was awarded from the percentage of votes it won. A positive sign indicates that the party was awarded a greater share of seats proportionate to its vote, a negative sign indicates it received a lesser share of seats, a dash indicates perfect proportionality. Not all parties are included. Blank spaces indicate that the party is no longer in existence.

Sources: Mackie and Rose (1991, 1997).

is quite rosy). In Italy, the picture looks quite different. Here we see the smallest parties apparently having a better time of things than the medium-sized parties. There are two reasons for this. First, the Italian electoral system was less proportional and the effects of this were felt most by the medium-sized parties. Second, many of the smallest Italian parties are regionally based and therefore benefit from a higher geographic concentration in their vote. This is particularly noticeable in the case of the South Tyrol People's Party which managed to achieve virtually perfect proportionality at each election.

4.6 Conclusion

In their various forms, the list systems of PR have proved to be the most popular with the electoral engineers, and for good reason. These systems undoubtedly give the greatest amount of control to the party headquarters, particularly in the case of closed lists where the voters have no say over which politicians are elected, but also in the case of those systems with larger district magnitudes where the average voter has little chance of knowing much about the individual candidates. List systems are also popular with many political reformers because of their greater proportionality, and also because, at least in theory, they allow greater scope for implementing policies to increase the representation of women and minority ethnic groupings (for further discussion, see Chapter 7).

Given the prominence of the list systems generally, the fact that so many recently democratizing countries have chosen to adopt a version, the fact that (with the exception of Ireland) it has become the basis for the common electoral system for the European Parliament, and the fact that with very few exceptions (Italy in 1994, France in 1988) there is little sign of countries dropping this system once adopted, there has always been good reason for arguing that in time we should see all countries eventually adopting a version of list PR as their electoral system. History seemed to bear this out. As we have seen, in a large number of cases (the STV countries appear to be the main exceptions), countries have moved from SMP, through some form of majoritarian system and on to list PR.

However, trends in electoral reform since the 1990s suggest an entirely new pattern. In particular, the tendency now increasingly is to experiment with more nuanced forms of electoral systems, mixing the proportional benefits of list PR with the direct-contact benefits of single member plurality. Suddenly the mixed systems have become very much in vogue, as we shall see next.

5

Mixed Electoral Systems

For all the positive features of the different list systems of proportional representation reviewed in the previous chapter, the one negative point which they are all seen to share in common, so far as many supporters of SMP and majoritarian systems are concerned, is the lack of constituency representation. The alternative of regional politicians elected on regional lists, or even (as in Israel) national politicians elected on national lists, is not viewed by some with much enthusiasm. The electoral systems examined in this chapter are seen as providing an ideal solution because of their hybrid nature in offering both SMP and PR elections in the one system.

There has been much debate over the correct title for the set of systems being looked at in this chapter, and this in large part reflects differences over how to define them. Of course, it used to be much simpler because for a long time this category of electoral system was associated with just one country – (West) Germany. But even then there were a range of different titles on offer, among them: 'additional member', 'compensatory PR', 'mixed member proportional', 'personalized PR', 'two-vote' (for example, Jesse 1988).

Now Germany is no longer alone. The 1990s witnessed what can best be described as an explosion in the use of electoral systems which have by now been given the generic title 'mixed electoral systems'. According to one authoritative source as many as 29 different countries currently use a form of mixed system for some aspect of their national election: this represents about one-fifth of the world's population (Massicotte and Blais 1999).

Trying to settle on an acceptable definition of a mixed electoral system is not helped by the fact that the scholars themselves appear to be in some disagreement: depending on which of the highly useful overviews one reads, it is possible to arrive at a range of different definitions (for example, Massicotte and Blais 1999; *Representation* 1996; Shugart and Wattenberg 2000a). Massicotte and Blais (1999: 345), for instance, define mixed systems as involving 'the combination of different electoral formulas (plurality or PR; majority or PR) for an election to a single body'. According to Shugart and Wattenberg (2000a), however, such a definition is too broad, since it allows for the inclusion of those cases where, for instance, PR is used in some parts of the country while a plurality or majoritarian formula is simultaneously being used in other areas. Their preference is for a narrower definition in which mixed systems are seen as a variant of the two-tier systems outlined in the previous chapter (see p. 80 above). The distinguishing feature for Shugart and Wattenberg is that one tier must allocate seats 'nominally' (that is, where 'votes are cast for candidates by name and seats are allocated to individual candidates on the basis of the votes they receive') and the other tier must allocate seats by lists (as in the case of the systems reviewed in the previous chapter) (Shugart and Wattenberg 2000a).

Given the fact that Germany has by far the longest record in using this electoral system, the bulk of this chapter focuses on the German case. Then, in section 5.3, we explore the variations between the different mixed systems currently in use across the world, revealing some significant distinctions from the German model. At one extreme, as we shall see, the alteration is so great as to make the system 'majoritarian', rather than the proportional system used in Germany.

5.1   The Operation of Germany's Mixed Electoral System

In the years immediately following the Second World War, when Germany was divided into zones under the control of occupying powers, there was concern that any new German state which would emerge should avoid the mistakes of the Weimar period. It was the British in particular who were anxious to introduce an electoral system which would both avoid the dangers of too many parties entering the system and destabilizing it, and at the same time incorporate the British tradition of constituency representation. Ultimately it was the German political parties who designed the system, but the form it took was greatly influenced by British experiments in

Land (or state-level) elections in their zone (Carstairs 1980; Roberts 1975). It is worth noting that even though this system is largely a postwar invention, in certain respects it does have an 'ancient lineage' (Pulzer 1983: 104). According to Peter Pulzer, mixed constituency and list systems were proposed as early as 1914, and 'The nearest presentiment to the present-day system was proposed by C. H. Bornemann in 1931'. In fact, the earliest known case of a mixed electoral system in Germany was in the kingdom of Württemberg from 1906 to 1918. Indeed, this is the earliest known example of a mixed electoral system anywhere (Massicotte and Blais 1999), and in this sense the mixed electoral system could certainly be seen as a progeny of Germany.

In 1949 the electoral law for the new Federal Republic proposed that 60 per cent of MPs would be elected by SMP in single-seat constituencies, and 40 per cent elected by PR list. The lists, which were closed (that is, the rank ordering of candidates was determined by the parties), were drawn up on a *Land* basis. From the beginning there was a minimum threshold: a party had to win at least one constituency seat or 5 per cent of the vote in any one *Land* to qualify for list seats. In its early form, this was not a 'two-vote' system: the elector cast just one vote and this served both as the vote for the constituency candidate and for the party list of the party to which the candidate belonged.

Electoral law changes in 1953 produced the electoral system which, with only slight amendment, has been used by the German Federal Republic ever since. There were three changes in 1953. First, a 'two-vote' element was introduced: a 'primary vote' (*Erststimme*) for constituency MPs; and a 'secondary vote' (*Zweitstimme*) for the list MPs. Second, the proportion of list MPs was increased to 50 per cent. Third, the legal minimum threshold was increased, so that to qualify for list seats a party had to win at least 5 per cent of the vote in the whole federation (though there were some exemptions). There was a further change to the threshold rule in 1956 whereby parties now had to win either 5 per cent nationally or three constituency seats.

There was another temporary change to the threshold rule before the 1990 election. Given the exceptional nature of that election – occurring so soon after unification of the country – the federal court ruled that for this election the 5 per cent clause should apply separately in the two parts of the country: that is, the western part which had formed the original Federal Republic, and the recently merged eastern part, which used to be the 'German Democratic Republic'. The reason for this amendment was to ensure that smaller parties – lacking suitable partners in the other part of the state – would not be disadvantaged. In the event, it was the faction-ridden Green party which was to fall foul of this clause. The west and east Green parties did not merge before the election and therefore their respective vote totals were counted separately. The eastern Greens (*Grüne/Bündnis'90*) won 6 per cent of the vote in the eastern part of Germany, passing the 5 per cent threshold; but the western Greens won only 4.8 per cent of the vote in the western part and therefore were not eligible for any seats. As Boll and Poguntke (1992) make clear, if the two parties had merged before the election, their combined vote would have been exactly 5 per cent and they would have received considerably more seats (probably in excess of thirty) than the eight which were allotted to them on the basis of the eastern vote. Contrast this with the result for the former East German Communist Party (PDS). Its national vote was only 2.4 per cent which ordinarily would have guaranteed it no seats. However, it won 11.1 per cent of the vote in the east (just 0.3 per cent in the west) and therefore was eligible for 17 seats under the amended rules.

In terms of the three elements of electoral systems which we have been examining throughout this book the major difference between the mixed electoral system and the other list systems dealt with in the previous chapter is in the area of ballot structure. As we shall see, because the list vote is so crucial to how the system operates (at least in Germany), this ensures that the larger district magnitude of the list vote, together with its proportionate electoral formula, translates into highly proportional results. Indeed, whatever distortion there is in the election result is largely caused by the operation of the 5 per cent threshold. The basic point, therefore, is that in terms of average district magnitude there is nothing very unusual about the electoral system used in Germany. Nor for that matter is there anything unusual about the electoral formulas. The constituency seats are determined on the basis of SMP, and the list seats are determined by the largest remainder system using the Hare quota (see Chapter 4, section 4.2).[1] It is in the areas of ballot structure and counting rules that the mixed electoral system reveals its special qualities.

The German voter has two votes for the two types of MPs. In the most recent 1998 election, for instance, the voters were electing a

Bundestag of 656 MPs: 328 (50 per cent) of these were elected to represent individual constituencies, and 328 (50 per cent) were elected from the regional lists (allocated at the *Land* level). It is important to note that the allocation of the list seats is computed on the basis of the full Bundestag membership (that is, as if the PR list election were the whole election). In the polling station, each voter receives a ballot paper much like the one shown in Figure 5.1, and is asked to tick two boxes: first, on the left-hand side of the ballot paper for a constituency candidate, and second, on the right-hand side for a regional list. The first vote is for a candidate, while the second vote is for a party.

Three points need stressing at this stage. First, the location of the different votes on the ballot paper is deliberate. The constituency vote is called the 'primary vote' (*Erststimme*); it is supposed to be more important than the list vote. However, as Taagepera and Shugart (1989: 130) point out, this is really a 'psychologically important nuance', intended to create the impression that the constituency vote is more significant. As we shall see in a moment, when considering the counting rules, 'the real impact is rather the reverse'. Second, the party list vote used in Germany is a closed list: German voters have no influence over the rank ordering of the candidates on the party lists (short of joining a party and trying to influence the process of candidate selection). Third, (since 1953) there is no requirement for the elector to cast both votes for the same party. In the ballot paper in Figure 5.1, it is quite acceptable for a voter to, say, mark an 'X' next to Bernhard Jagoda of the CDU, and another 'X' next to the FDP. This would also be quite a rational voting strategy (Schoen 1999). As we shall see below, this practice of 'ticket-splitting' has become increasingly significant in German electoral behaviour.

The election count proceeds in three stages. First, there are counts in each constituency to determine which candidate is elected and to work out the total number of constituency seats for each of the parties in each of the federal *Länder*. Since these are SMP contests, the candidates with most votes in each constituency are elected, regardless of whether or not they have an overall majority of the votes in the constituency. As we see in Table 5.1 (the 'first vote') this produces a highly disproportional result, with most of the smaller parties picking up no seats. Indeed, it is usually the case that only the two larger groupings, the Christian Democrats (CDU and CSU)

Sie haben 2 Stimmen

hier 1 Stimme
für die Wahl
eines Wahlkreisabgeordneten
(Erststimme)

hier 1 Stimme
für die Wahl
einer Landesliste (Partei)
(Zweitstimme)

| 1 | **Dr. Kreutzmann, Heinz**
Parl. Staatssekretär
Borken (Hessen) **SPD**
Kellerwaldstraße 7 | Sozialdemo-
kratische Partei
Deutschlands | ○ |

| 2 | **Jagoda, Bernhard**
Obersekretär a.D.
Schwalmstadt-Treysa **CDU**
Am Weißen Stein 31 | Christlich Demo-
kratische Union
Deutschlands | ○ |

| 3 | **Wilke, Otto**
Elektromeister
Diemelsee-Adorf **F.D.P.**
Bredelarer Straße 1 | Freie
Demokratische
Partei | ○ |

| 4 | **Funk, Peter**
Werkzeugmacher
Baunatal 6 **DKP**
Triftweg 6 | Deutsche
Kommunistische
Partei | ○ |

| 5 | **Keller, Gerhard**
Zivildienstleistender
Frielendorf 2 **GRÜNE**
Friedhofsweg 30 | DIE GRÜNEN | ○ |

| ○ | **SPD** | Sozialdemokratische
Partei Deutschlands
Leber, Matthöfer, Jahn,
Frau Dr. Timm, Zander | 1 |

| ○ | **CDU** | Christlich Demokratische
Union Deutschlands
Dr. Dregger, Zink, Dr. Schwarz-
Schilling, Frau Geier, Haase | 2 |

| ○ | **F.D.P.** | Freie Demokratische
Partei
Mischnick, von Schoeler,
Hoffie, Wurbs, Dr. Prinz zu
Solms-Hohensolms-Lich | 3 |

| ○ | **DKP** | Deutsche Kommunistische
Partei
Mayer, Knopf, Frau Dr. Weber,
Funk, Frau Schuster | 4 |

| ○ | **GRÜNE** | DIE GRÜNEN
Frau Ibbeken, Hecker, Horacek,
Kerschgens, Kuhnert | 5 |

| ○ | **EAP** | Europäische
Arbeiterpartei
Frau Liebig, Haßmann, Stalleicher,
Frau Kaestner, Stalla | 6 |

| ○ | **KBW** | Kommunistischer Bund
Westdeutschland
Schmierer, Frau Monich,
Frau Eckardt, Dresler, Lang | 7 |

| ○ | **NPD** | Nationaldemokratische
Partei Deutschlands
Philipp, Brandl, Sturtz,
Lauck, Bauer | 8 |

| ○ | **V** | VOLKSFRONT
Gotz, Taufertshofer, Konig,
Riebe, Frau Weißert | 9 |

Figure 5.1   A German MMP ballot paper

Table 5.1　The 1998 German federal election

	First (constituency) vote			*Second (list) vote*		*Final result*	
	Vote (%)	*Seats No.*	*Seats (%)*	*Vote (%)*	*Additional seats No.*	*Total seats No.*	*Total seats (%)*
SPD	43.8	212	64.6	40.9	86	298	44.5
CDU	32.2	74	22.6	28.4	124	198	29.6
CSU	7.3	38	11.6	6.7	9	47	7.0
FDP	3.0	0	0	6.2	43	43	6.4
GP	5.0	0	0	6.7	47	47	7.0
PDS	4.9	4	1.2	5.1	32	36	5.4
DR	2.3	0	0	1.8	0	0	0
DV	0.0	0	0	1.2	0	0	0
Others	1.5	0	0	3.0	0	0	0

Note: SPD (Social Democrats), CDU (Christian Democratic Union), CSU (Christian Social Union), FDP (Free Democrats), GP (Greens), PDS (Party of Democratic Socialism), DR (The Republicans), DV (Deutsche Volksunion).
Source:　Electoral returns.

and the Social Democrats, stand any chance of winning constituency seats. Indeed, this was the case from 1957 to 1987 (Pulzer 1983: 100). The 1990 election was unusual in that two small parties (the FDP and the former Communists, PDS) each managed to win one constituency seat, in large part as a consequence of the disruption caused by German unification. In 1994, the PDS won four constituency seats, and thereby succeeded in passing the electoral threshold (of at least three constituency seats). In the light of this result, some consideration was given to tightening up the rules so as to make it more difficult for a party like the PDS to enter the Bundestag through this route; however, this 'looked too much like blatant political manipulation to receive much support' (Scarrow 2000).

In 1998 the PDS once again won four constituency seats, all in East Berlin constituencies, which was consistent with its campaign strategy of geographically targeting its vote. However, on this occasion – and possibly against its own expectations – the party also succeeded in winning 5.1 per cent of the list vote, thereby passing the 5 per cent threshold for the first time. As Jeffery and Hough observe, in the light of this result, the PDS will in future elections 'face the fascinating dilemma of which route to follow: targeting a small number of constituencies on the first vote, and/or building on 1998's success and bringing out a nationwide hurdle-clearing vote' (1999: 82).

The crucial extra ingredient, separating mixed electoral systems from SMP, is the second vote where smaller parties have a much greater chance of winning seats. Table 5.1 shows the distribution of second votes (that is, list votes) for all the parties. It is interesting to note how the percentage of second votes of most of the smaller parties was higher than that of their first votes (the exception was the Republican Party which, like most far-right parties, went for a personal vote). To an extent this reflects the fact that supporters of smaller parties are conscious of how their votes matter more under PR elections (we return to this issue in Chapter 7 below); but in the specific circumstances of the German case, the main factor driving this is undoubtedly the 5 per cent threshold rule.

Once the votes of parties failing to win 5 per cent of the list vote (or three constituency seats) had been excluded – the Republicans (DR), Deutsche Volksunion (DV) and a spate of tiny parties – the Hare quota is applied to determine the total number of seats to which each of the remaining parties is entitled (for discussion on largest remainder Hare, see pp. 71–3 above). The results of this calculation are shown in the final two columns of Table 5.1. Since this part of the election is using a PR system, the proportion of seats (that is, the column headed 'total seats (%)') reflects very closely the proportion of list votes (the column headed 'second vote (%)').

The first two stages in the counting process (that is, the counting of first and second votes) are common to most mixed systems. It is in the third and final stage that a very important distinction arises. The nature of this distinction is elaborated in section 5.3 below, for now we will examine how it works in the German case. The basic point of the German system is that it should produce a proportional result. In order to achieve this, it is important that the larger parties should not be overly advantaged by the greater ease with which they win constituency seats. Therefore the operating principle of this third stage in the German count is that the total number of constituency seats won by the parties should be *subtracted* from the total number of list seats they have been allocated (and remember that the list seats are allocated at the *Land* level). This is why the German electoral system is generally referred to as an 'additional member' system, because the result of this subtraction determines the number of additional members to which each party is entitled.

Before discussing the final stage in the counting process, we need to take account of an anomaly which can result from the fact that constituency seats are subtracted from list seats. It is quite possible for a party to gain more constituency seats in any one *Land* than the total to which its share of the vote would entitle it. Whenever this happens the party is allowed to retain its extra seats (*Überhangmandate*, overhang or surplus seats), and the size of the Bundestag is enlarged temporarily until the next election.[2] In the past, this was not a regular occurrence: up until 1990, the number of surplus seats in any one election had never exceeded five (all for the CDU in 1961). In the 1990 election, however, there were six surplus seats, all won by the CDU and as a result the final tally of seats for the CDU increased from 262 to 268, and the membership of the 1990 Bundestag was increased from 656 to 662 MPs.

Surplus seats proved to be decisive in the 1994 Bundestag election. In total there were 16 surplus seats: four won by the SPD (in Bremen and Brandenburg), and 12 won by the CDU (in Baden-Württemberg, Mecklenburg-Vorpommern, Sachsen-Anhalt, Thuringia and Saxony). This meant that what otherwise would have been a very slim Christian Democrat–Free Democrat Bundestag majority of just two seats became in fact a relatively comfortable majority of ten seats. As Philip Cole (1995: 10) observes, this result had 'enormous political repercussions', particularly for the FDP, because 'If Chancellor Kohl's majority had really been only two, the smart money would have been on him ditching the FDP in a favour of a Grand Coalition with the SPD'.

In 1998 it was the turn of the Social Democrats to benefit from winning surplus seats, 13 in total, all but one in eastern Germany. As a result, the total size of the Bundestag was increased from 656 to 669. The Social Democrats ended up with a total of 298 parliamentary seats. Strictly speaking, the truly proportional result should have been 285 seats (that is, 298 seats minus 13 surplus seats). Most of the Social Democrats' seat tally comprised constituency seats (212 seats); they were awarded an additional 86 list seats. None of the other parties benefited from surplus seats on this occasion. The Christian Democratic Union's seat total of 198 seats was made up of 74 constituency seats and 124 list seats. The respective figures for the remaining parties were as follows: Christian Social Union 47 seats, of which 38 were constituency seats and nine were list; the Free Democrats 43 seats, of which all were list seats; the Greens 47 seats, of which all were list seats; the Party of Democratic Socialism 36 seats, of which four were constituency seats and 32 were list seats.

5.2   Proportionality, Parties and Politics in Germany

The combination of the surplus seats together with the operation of the 5 per cent electoral threshold has reduced the overall level of proportionality of the German electoral system in recent elections. As Table 5.2 shows, not since the 1950s has Germany experienced such high levels of disproportionality. This reflects the great significance of German unification in 1989. Just as in the late 1940s and 1950s, Germany is passing through a period of electoral instability and change (Jeffery 1999), and this exposes the distortions in the German version of the mixed electoral system.

There is another interesting trend worth noting in Table 5.2, relating to the 'difference' columns for each of the parties. With few exceptions, the ratio is positive: that is, the disproportionality of the system usually favours *all* the parties, large and small; the only exceptions are the Free Democrats in 1972 and 1983, and the Greens in 1980, 1983 and 1990. What we are seeing here is the effect of the 5 per cent rule. In other words, the system is excluding tiny parties from any representation and all the remaining parties are benefiting from a small surplus in their proportions of seats. But the overall message from this table is that, despite the distortions of the 5 per cent threshold and the surplus seats, the overall level of disproportionality in German elections is low. For instance, as we shall see, the difference between vote per cent and seat per cent is consistently lower than that produced by the single transferable vote in Ireland (see Table 6.3 below).

It is quite common in debates about electoral reform to draw simple conclusions from the experiences of countries using particular systems. Certainly, some pretty straightforward conclusions would seem to suggest themselves from the German experience. For instance, despite being a PR system, it has not resulted in a proliferation of minor parties (Jeffery 1999). Another feature which has tended to attract considerable attention is the role of the Free Democrats as the 'pivotal' party. As Table 5.3 shows, the Free

Table 5.2   German federal elections, 1949–98: percentage of votes and seats

	Christian Democratic Union			Christian Social Union			Social Democrats		
	Vote (%)	*Seat (%)*	*Diff. (%)*	*Vote (%)*	*Seat (%)*	*Diff. (%)*	*Vote (%)*	*Seat (%)*	*Diff. (%)*
1949	25.2	28.6	+3.4	5.8	6.0	+0.2	29.2	32.6	+3.4
1953	36.4	39.2	+2.8	8.8	10.7	+1.9	28.8	31.0	+2.2
1957	39.7	43.7	+4.0	10.5	10.7	+0.2	31.8	34.0	+2.2
1961	35.8	38.5	+2.7	9.6	10.0	+0.4	36.2	38.1	+1.9
1965	38.0	39.5	+1.5	9.6	9.9	+0.3	39.3	40.7	+1.4
1969	36.6	38.9	+2.3	9.5	9.9	+0.4	42.7	45.2	+2.5
1972	35.2	35.7	+0.5	9.7	9.7	–	45.8	46.4	+0.6
1976	38.0	38.3	+0.3	10.6	10.7	+0.1	42.6	43.1	+0.5
1980	34.2	35.0	+0.8	10.3	10.5	+0.2	42.9	43.9	+1.0
1983	38.2	38.4	+0.2	10.6	10.6	–	38.2	38.8	+0.6
1987	34.5	35.0	+0.5	9.8	9.9	+0.1	37.0	37.4	+0.4
1990	36.7	40.5	+3.8	7.1	7.7	+0.6	33.5	36.1	+2.6
1994	34.2	36.3	+2.1	7.3	7.4	+0.1	36.4	37.5	+1.1
1998	28.4	29.6	+1.2	6.7	7.0	+0.3	40.9	44.5	+3.6

	Free Democrats			Green Party		
	Vote (%)	*Seat (%)*	*Diff. (%)*	*Vote (%)*	*Seat (%)*	*Diff. (%)*
1949	11.9	12.9	+1.0			
1953	9.5	9.9	+0.4			
1957	7.7	8.2	+0.5			
1961	12.8	13.4	+0.6			
1965	9.5	9.9	+0.4			
1969	5.8	6.0	+0.2			
1972	8.4	8.3	–0.1			
1976	7.9	7.9	–			
1980	10.6	10.7	+0.1	1.5	0.0	–1.5
1983	7.0	6.8	–0.2	5.6	5.4	–0.2
1987	9.1	9.3	+0.2	8.3	8.5	+0.2
1990	11.0	11.9	+0.9	5.0	1.2	–3.8
1994	6.9	7.0	+0.1	7.3	7.3	–
1998	6.2	6.4	+0.2	6.7	7.0	+0.3

Note: The vote per cent is the number of 'second' (i.e. list) votes. Percentages do not add up to 100 because smaller parties and 'Others' have been excluded.
Sources: Mackie and Rose (1991); official returns.

Table 5.3   German federal governments, 1949–98

Election	Coalition parties	Chancellor
1949	CDU/CSU, FDP, DP	Konrad Adenauer (CDU)
1953	CDU/CSU, FDP (until 1956), DP, GB/BHE (until 1955), FVP (from 1956)	Konrad Adenauer (CDU)
1957	CDU/CSU, DP (until 1960)	Konrad Adenauer (CDU)
1961	CDU/CSU, FDP	Konrad Adenauer (CDU) (until 1963) Ludwig Erhard (CDU)
1965	CDU/CSU, FDP (until 1966) CDU/CSU, SPD	Ludwig Erhard (CDU) Kurt-Georg Kiesinger (CDU)
1969	SPD, FDP	Willy Brandt (SPD)
1972	SPD, FDP	Willy Brandt (SPD) (until 1974) Helmut Schmidt (SPD)
1976	SPD, FDP	Helmut Schmidt (SPD)
1980	SPD, FDP (until 1982) CDU/CSU, FDP	Helmut Schmidt (SPD) Helmut Kohl (CDU)
1983	CDU/CSU, FDP	Helmut Kohl (CDU)
1990	CDU/CSU, FDP	Helmut Kohl (CDU)
1994	CDU/CSU, FDP	Helmut Kohl (CDU)
1998	SPD, GP	Gerhard Schröder (SPD)

Note: CDU (Christian Democratic Union), CSU (Christian Social Union), SPD (Social Democrats), FDP (Free Democrats), GP (Greens), DP (German Party), GB/BHE (Refugees Party).
Source: Updated from Jeffery (1999).

Democrats have been in almost every postwar German government. The exceptions are: in 1957–61, when the Christian Democrats had a sufficiently large number of seats not to need them; in 1966–9, when the Christian Democrats and Social Democrats formed a 'grand coalition'; and, most recently, as a result of the 1998 election, when the Social Democrats and Greens formed a 'red–green' coalition.

Throughout postwar (West) German history, the practice has tended to be that goverment changed hands, not as a result of an election, but rather because a party switched sides in the Bundestag.

For the most part, of course, attention has focused on one party, the Free Democrats. A prominent example was in 1982 when the Free Democrats switched allegiance from the Social Democrats under Helmut Schmidt to the Christian Democrats under Helmut Kohl. To some people it is galling to think that a party whose vote share rarely rises to double figures could have such a hold on the reins of power. In 1998, however, 'the German electorate cast their ballots with unaccustomed gusto to produce the first ever voter-led change in power in postwar Germany' (Jeffery and Hough 1999: 78).

The mixed electoral system is frequently extolled as offering a panacea to the 'problems' of disproportionality resulting from SMP, or the 'problems' of a lack of constituency representation in list systems. Here, we are told, is a system which incorporates constituency representation while, at the same time, producing proportional election results. This argument presupposes two things: first, that German constituency MPs operate in a similar fashion to, say, British constituency MPs, and, second, that the constituency MPs are *seen* as significant within the system. The principal piece of evidence in support of the latter is the fact that the constituency vote is seen as *primary*, as superior to the list vote, indicating that the political system attaches more importance to the constituency part of the election.

However, this is a pretence. As we saw above, what matters in determining the overall allocation of seats is the list vote, not the constituency vote. Furthermore, there are no by-elections. A retired or deceased politician is replaced by the next highest name on the party list in that region. This applies to both constituency and list replacements, and for one very good reason. If, for example, list replacements were determined by the next highest name on the list while constituency replacements resulted from by-elections, this might be seen as devaluing constituency seats. A party would not be able to guarantee that it would win the by-election. Therefore, the rational strategy for parties under such a scheme would be to maximize the number of list seats they seek to win in elections and minimize their constituency seats.

As far as the parties in Germany are concerned, therefore, there are no significant differences between the two classes of MPs. This point is reinforced by the parties' campaign strategies, where it is usual for constituency candidates to also have their names on party lists: if they lose the constituency election (as, indeed, happened to Helmut Kohl in 1998) they will almost certainly secure a place as a result of the list election (providing the party wants to ensure their return and has placed them high enough on the list).

The party leaderships may not see the two sets of MPs as different, but evidence from a survey of the members of the Bundestag in the mid-1980s suggests that the constituency MPs do see their role as different from that of list MPs, paying closer attention to constituency concerns. The bulk of the MPs asked (70 per cent) felt that 'representatives from single-member districts are more accountable' to the voters (Lancaster and Paterson 1990: 466). This finding may need some qualification, however, especially when we try to get a true impression of what German MPs mean by constituency service. For instance, it has been stressed by Geoffrey Roberts (1975: 221) that German MPs do not have 'a sensitivity toward the constituency relationship; it did not exist before 1949, and has not been highly developed since then'. Furthermore, German voters do not seem too interested in the distinction between the two types of MPs: indeed, 'Most voters are completely unaware of the names of their constituency candidates' (Jesse 1988: 113). Finally, there is the fact that because Germany is a federation, voters have multiple levels of representatives (for example, *Land* politicians, local councillors) to choose from when raising constituency problems so 'constituency members necessarily play a smaller role in dealing with grievances than in Britain, a unitary and highly centralized country' (Bogdanor 1984: 57).

There is one important respect in which the two types of seats are quite clearly different, and that is the fact that one system disproportionately favours the larger parties. With the recent exception of the PDS (see above), there is little point in smaller parties concentrating their resources on trying to win constituency seats, because, as we have seen, the SMP electoral system virtually guarantees that they will be unsuccessful. This fact introduces an element of 'strategic voting' into the mixed electoral system, something which appears to have been exploited with remarkable success by the Free Democrats.

Ticket-splitting is a feature of many electoral systems where voters are either voting in different levels of elections at the same time (for example, the USA or Australia) or where there is a preferential voting system which allows voters to vote across party lines (as in

Ireland). Germany represents an important example of the latter, because its electoral system, since 1953, allows voters to vote for one party with their first vote and, if they want, for a different party with their second. Because smaller parties stand a far better chance in the second-vote list election, they tend to concentrate their resources on that campaign and, for the most part, treat the first-vote SMP election, as a lost cause. The Free Democrats have utilized ticket-splitting to their advantage, encouraging their supporters to vote, in a 'coalition fashion', for whichever party they currently share office with. The idea is that Free Democrat supporters should use their constituency votes to support the coalition partner; in return, the coalition partner's supporters are encouraged to give their list vote to the Free Democrats, to help it over the 5 per cent hurdle.

Ticket-splitting has been on the increase: in 1961 just 4.4 per cent of votes were split; by 1987 this figure had increased to 13.7 per cent; in the 1990 reunification election it reached a level of 16.2 per cent (Jesse 1988; Roberts 1988; Schoen 1999). Table 5.4. gives an indication of the relationship between ticket-splitting and party coalition arrangements (though see Schoen 1999). Between 1969 and 1982 the Free Democrats were in coalition with the Social Democrats. As the table shows, in all the elections during this period (and particularly in 1972), a large proportion of FDP voters gave their constituency vote to Social Democrat candidates. By contrast, in the 1983 and 1987 elections, when the Free Democrats were in coalition with the Christian Democrats, the ticket-splitting of the Free Democrats was now predominantly in favour of the Christian Democrats.

Table 5.4   Constituency votes of FDP list voters, 1961–87 (%)

Constituency vote to	1961	1965	1969	1972	1976	1980	1983	1987
CDU/CSU	8.1	20.9	10.6	7.9	8.0	13.3	58.3	43.2
SPD	3.1	6.7	24.8	52.9	29.9	35.5	10.1	13.1
FDP	86.5	70.3	62.0	38.2	60.7	48.5	29.1	38.7

Source: Roberts (1988).

5.3   Other Mixed Electoral Systems

As indicated at the start of this chapter, Germany is no longer alone in using a mixed electoral system. It has been joined by three other established democracies, Italy in 1993, Japan in 1994, and New Zealand in 1993. More dramatically, with the process of democratization, spreading right across the world, but focused most particularly on developments in the former Soviet Union and East and Central Europe, a host of other countries have rushed to adopt mixed systems. Massicotte and Blais's review (1999) finds 29 countries making use of mixed systems for national-level elections, representing one-fifth of the world's population. Operating with a more exclusive definition of a mixed electoral system, Shugart and Wattenberg (2000a) produce a list of 17 countries, all of which have adopted these systems in the 1990s.

From our sample of 59 countries, introduced in Chapter 1 (Table 1.2), mixed systems are currently being used in 16: namely, Bolivia, Ecuador, Germany, Hungary, Italy, Japan, Lithuania, Mexico, New Zealand, Panama, the Philippines, Russia, South Korea, Taiwan, Ukraine and Venezuela. This is using quite a loose definition of mixed systems. Once we use the more restrictive definition (discussed on p. 98 above) – namely, that one tier allocates seats nominally and the other tier allocates them by lists – this removes Ecuador and Panama from the sample (Shugart and Wattenberg 2000a). The Philippines are also excluded given the quirky nature of their system in preventing any party from winning more than three list seats (Bolongaita 1999).[3]

By definition, there is quite a range of different mixed systems in operation, and 'Therefore, generalizing about them is risky' (Massicotte and Blais 1999: 362). Scholars like Massicotte and Blais (1999) and Shugart and Wattenberg (2000a) have made great strides towards producing suitable typologies of mixed systems. To simplify matters somewhat, let us focus, in ascending order of importance, on four areas of variation between the various forms of mixed system currently on offer.

We can start with the simplest variation, in which the voter is given just one vote. As we saw above, such a system was initially used in the Federal Republic of Germany between 1949 and 1953, when voters voted just once and their vote was used twice: (1) to elect the constituency candidate, and (2) to add to the party total in the regional list. As was pointed out in the previous chapter (pp. 91–2), a single-vote mixed system was adopted for the Italian Senate as a result of the 1993 referendum. In the mid-1970s, a report of the Hansard Society proposed a single-vote mixed system for Britain (Roberts 1977), though nothing ever came of this. One reason given for such an adaptation is that it simplifies the act of voting, and thus reduces the potential for voter confusion (though it could be argued that the process of counting might appear more opaque in consequence). In addition, it removes any possibility of ticket-splitting. There are very few countries which use this single-vote version of the mixed system. As Table 5.5 shows, only Taiwan makes use of it for lower house elections.

Table 5.5   Variations in mixed systems for national (lower house) elections

	Constituency electoral system	List electoral system	Proportion of list seats (%)	Type of system[a]
Bolivia	SMP	d'Hondt	48	MMP
Germany	SMP	LR Hare	50	MMP
Hungary	Maj–plurality	Droop[b]	54	MMM[c]
Italy	SMP	LR Hare	25	MMM[d]
Japan	SMP	d'Hondt	40	MMM
Lithuania	Maj	LR Hare	50	MMM
Mexico	SMP	LR Hare	40	MMM[e]
New Zealand	SMP	Ste-Laguë	46	MMP
Russia	SMP	LR Hare	50	MMM
South Korea	SMP	LR Hare	15	MMM
Taiwan	SNTV[f]	LR Hare	30	MMM
Ukraine	SMP	LR Hare	50	MMM
Venezuela	SMP	d'Hondt	50	MMP

Notes: Based on the cases of mixed systems from our sample range of countries (see Table 1.2). Except for Taiwan, all cases use a two-vote mixed system.
[a] MMP = mixed member proportional; MMM = mixed member majoritarian.
[b] Two tiers of seat allocation. Upper tier uses d'Hondt.
[c] The upper tier in the list election provides some correction. In addition, the upper-tier allocation takes account of votes received by parties whose candidates were defeated at the constituency level.
[d] There is some correction caused by the fact that the list votes for each party are reduced on the basis of the number of votes required to win a constituency seat by each of its successful candidates at the constituency level.
[e] Some proportionality is maintained by the provision that no party may receive more than 8% over-representation.
[f] SNTV = single non-transferable vote (see p. 46 above).
Sources: Massicotte and Blais (1999); Shugart and Wattenberg (2000a).

A second distinction between different types of mixed systems relates to the electoral formulas used for each part of the election. In the case of the list election, this is no great surprise: just as with list systems generally, there is plenty of scope to choose between a number of different electoral formulas, and, as Table 5.5 reveals, there is quite a range of different electoral formulas, with a slight tendency to favour largest remainder Hare. More interesting are those cases where the electoral formula for the constituency election makes use of a majoritarian system, rather than the usual SMP formula. For instance, in Hungary the constituency seats are determined by a two-round system (the majority–plurality version used to elect the French Assembly; see pp. 52–3 above) rather than by SMP. In Taiwan, the 'semi-proportional' single non-transferable vote system is used (see p. 46 above). The system proposed for Britain by the recent report of the Jenkins Commission (see pp. 36–7 above) would use the Australian alternative vote to elect the constituency MPs. In principle, however, using a majoritarian system rather than a plurality system to elect constituency MPs is hardly of much significance, since the eventual result should still be the same, namely a proportional result determined by the list vote (though see below).

Third, it is possible to alter the proportions of list and constituency seats. For instance, in Japan 300 (40 per cent) of the 500 parliamentary seats are constituency seats and the remaining 200 seats – distributed across 11 regions – are elected by PR list (for details, see Shiratori 1995). In other words, this is a 60:40 split, in comparison to the German 50:50 split. The Italians have adopted an even more extreme ratio of constituency to list seats: 75 per cent constituency seats and 25 per cent list seats. In South Korea the list seats comprise a mere 15 per cent of the total. If the Jenkins proposals are adopted in Britain, this would result in a similarly low ratio of constituency to list seats: Jenkins proposes that list seats should constitute between 15 and 20 per cent of the total (Farrell 2000). This raises the question of at what stage the divide becomes so large that the system ceases being proportional, because the ratio of list seats is too small to compensate for the disproportional results of the constituency election. It has been argued that 'at least one-quarter of seats should be adjustment seats, if full reintroduction of PR is desired' (Taagepera and Shugart 1989: 131). This would imply that South Korea (15 per cent), Italy (25 per cent) and possibly also

Taiwan (30 per cent) are not fully proportional. However, in all these cases the issue is largely superfluous, because, as we shall see next, all (with the slight exception of Italy) operate a non-correctional version of the mixed system. This is where we get to the fourth, and most significant, distinction between types of mixed electoral systems.

As was pointed out earlier, a core feature of the German electoral system is the notion that list seats should be 'additional' to the constituency seats. To this end, the final seat tally is calculated by subtracting the number of constituency seats each party wins from the total number of list seats to which it is entitled. As Eckhard Jesse (1988: 110) points out, in the mid-1950s there was a debate in Germany about possibly reforming the electoral system. It was proposed that constituency seats should not be *subtracted* from the list seats; rather the two sets of seats should be *added* together. This apparently small technical change (dubbed the 'gap' system, or *Grabenwahlsystem*) in the calculation rules of the mixed system would have dramatic repercussions for its overall proportionality, a point recognized by the Free Democrats who managed to block it.

The significance of this alteration to the mixed system is immense. Its effect is to drastically reduce the proportionality of the election result, in effect turning a mixed member *proportional* (MMP) system, into a mixed member *majoritarian* (MMM) system. This can be illustrated by observing the Russian case, which uses this majoritarian form of a mixed system (or MMM).

The December 1993 Russian election – the first under the new electoral system – produced a multi-party system, with a wide range of parties elected to the parliament, representing a wide set of different interests (McAllister and White 1995). Headline news in all the media focused on the dramatic electoral victory of the ultra-nationalist Liberal Democratic Party of Russia (LDPR) led by the outspoken Vladimir Zhirinovsky. With almost a quarter (23 per cent) of the total vote, the LDPR won more votes than any other party. As a result Zhirinovsky and his party were propelled into the limelight as representing a clear threat to the leadership of President Boris Yeltsin, whose preferred party, the reformist Russia's Choice, had been beaten into second place (15 per cent).

What escaped the attention of many of the journalistic observers at the time was the fact that even though the LDPR won by far the most votes in the system, it did not win the most seats. It ended up with 70 seats (16 per cent) as compared with 96 seats (22 per cent) for Russia's Choice. As Table 5.6 shows, the discrepancy was due to the large number of constituency seats won by Russia's Choice (56 seats, as against just 11 seats for the LDPR). Had the Russians been using the German (MMP) version of the mixed system, the election result would have been very different. Instead of adding the list and constituency totals together, the result would be based on subtracting one from the other. The final result for the LDPR would have probably been of the order of 100 seats, while Russia's Choice would have ended up with fewer than 70 seats. It is in the discrepancy between votes won and seats awarded for the two biggest parties that we see the highest scores in the difference column of Table 5.6: Russia's Choice benefited by 6.2 per cent in its proportion of seats,

Table 5.6   The 1993 Russian election: State Duma

	List vote (%)	List seats	Const. seats	Total seats	Total seats (%)	Difference between list votes and total seats (%)
Russia's Choice	15.4	40	56	96	21.6	+6.2
LDPR	22.8	59	11	70	15.8	−7.0
Communist Party	12.4	32	33	65	14.6	+2.2
Agrarian Party	7.9	21	26	47	10.6	+2.7
Women of Russia	8.1	21	4	25	5.6	−2.5
Yabloko	7.8	20	13	33	7.4	−0.4
Party of Russian Unity and Accord	6.8	18	9	27	6.1	−0.7
Democratic Party of Russia	5.5	14	7	21	4.7	−0.8
Others	13.3	0	60[a]	60	13.5	n.a.
Total	100.0	225	219[b]	444	99.9	

[a] 'Others' included the following: Civic Union for Stabilization, Justice and Progress 18; Movement for Democratic Reforms 8; Dignity and Mercy 3; Future of Russia 1; Independents 30.
[b] Six seats in the State Duma were left vacant after a boycott of the election in Chechnya, and postponements of the election in Tatarstan and Chelyabinsk.
Source: Keesing's Record of World Events.

while the LDPR was 7 per cent down on the proportion of seats it should have won if the system had been fully proportional.

The subsequent 1995 parliamentary elections revealed some additional quirks in the Russian MMM system (see Table 5.7). In comparison with 1993, when 13 parties fielded candidates, in the 1995 election 43 parties succeeded in registering for election (gathering the required 200,000 signatures). The number of candidates leaped to 5,675, three times more than in 1993. In some constituencies there were as many as 25 candidates, with a ballot paper the size of a broadsheet newspaper page. The effect of this large number of parties was to produce a highly disproportional result. Only four parties (LDPR, Communist Party, Yabloko and Our Home is

Table 5.7   The 1995 Russian election: State Duma

	List vote (%)	List seats	Const. seats	Total seats	Total seats (%)	Difference between list votes and total seats (%)
Russia's Democratic Choice	4.0	0	9	9	2.0	−2.0
LDPR	11.2	50	1	51	11.3	+0.1
Communist Party	22.3	99	58	157	34.9	+12.6
Agrarian Party	3.9	0	20	20	4.4	−0.5
Women of Russia	4.6	0	3	3	0.7	−3.9
Yabloko	6.9	31	14	45	10.0	+3.1
Our Home is Russia	10.1	45	10	55	12.2	+2.1
Power to the People	n.a.	0	9	9	2.0	n.a.
Congress of Russian Communities	4.3	0	5	5	1.1	−3.2
Party of Workers' Self-Management	4.0	0	0	0	0.0	−4.0
Communists/ Working Russia	4.6	0	0	0	0.0	−4.6
Others[a]	24.1	0	95	95	21.1	n.a.
Total	100.0	225	225	450	99.7	

[a] Independent candidates won 77 of the 225 single-member seats while a number of small parties won up to three seats each.
Source: Keesing's Record of World Events.

Russia) managed to cross the 5 per cent threshold required to win list seats. (For ease of comparison, the parties have been listed in the same order as in Table 5.6.) Between them, these four parties amassed 50.5 per cent of the vote: almost half of the voters supported parties that failed to win party list seats, causing the leaders of Yabloko to note, with some glee, how the electoral system succeeded in ensuring that 'microscopic intriguers with gigantic ambitions were eliminated' (cited in Orttung 1996: 6). As Robert Orttung (1996: 7) observes: 'The 5 percent barrier greatly benefited the four parties that managed to cross it, essentially doubling the value of every vote they won.'

Once again the constituency seats served to increase the vote–seat distortions in the Russian electoral system. The biggest beneficiary from this was the Communist Party which won 58 constituency seats, increasing its already inflated seat total to 34.9 per cent and giving it a 12.6 per cent surplus in its share of total parliamentary seats (when compared with its vote). Once again the LDPR lost out on its constituency seats, this time only managing to win one; however, this was in part compensated for by the inflation in its list seats caused by the exclusion of the smaller parties (for not passing the 5 per cent threshold), and as a result – and unlike the 1993 election – the LDPR total share of parliamentary seats (11.3 per cent) matched its vote share (11.2 per cent).

As the Russian case shows, the distinction between those mixed systems in which the list seats compensate for, or correct, the disproportionality of the constituency seats (that is, MMP) and those mixed systems where the two elections tend to operate as separate, parallel elections (that is, MMM) produces strikingly different results. This puts a very important gloss on exactly how we should categorize the mixed electoral systems generally, because while some are clearly proportional in their effect, others are not. Arguably it is only the former which can really be counted as following in the footsteps of the original version of the system established in postwar Germany. As Table 5.5 shows, therefore, apart from Germany there are currently only three other cases of MMP systems operating at the national level: Bolivia, New Zealand and Venezuela (see also Shugart and Wattenberg 2000a).

Having said that, it should be noted that both the Hungarian and Italian systems incorporate an element of proportional 'correction'. In Hungary's case, the operation of a two-tier system of allocation for the list seats helps to maximize the proportional effects of the list election. This, plus the fact that the upper-tier allocation also takes account of votes received by candidates defeated at the constituency level, provides a small degree of compensation for the dispropor-tionality of the constituency election (Benoit 2000). In Italy there is an element of linkage between the constituency and the seat elec-tions. But unlike German practice where this is based on seats, with a party performing well in the constituency election compensating by being awarded fewer list seats, in Italy the linkage is based on votes. Here before allocating list seats, a party's list votes are reduced by subtracting the votes received by those of its candidates who were elected in the single-seat consitutencies by the amount required by them to win the seats (Katz 2000). Because of this linkage between constituency and list votes, Massicotte and Blais (1999) include Italy in their category of 'corrective' (that is, MMP) systems. Shugart and Wattenberg (2000a) more accurately refer to Italy as a 'semi-parallel' system reflecting the fact that the element of correction is pretty limited, and for this reason it is more appropriate to catego-rize Italy as an MMM system.

5.4 Conclusion

As was pointed out in the introduction to this book, for a long time the field of electoral research was stagnant and unchanging, reflect-ing the fact that few countries were prepared to countenance elec-toral change. Events since the early 1990s have dramatically changed that picture, not only because of a general worldwide phenomenon of democratization, but also because of recent electoral reforms in three long-established democracies: Italy, Japan and New Zealand. What is most telling about these latter three cases as well as a large number of the newly democratizing countries is that they have all adopted mixed electoral systems.

There can be little dispute with the fact that mixed electoral systems are much in fashion at the beginning of the twenty-first century. The successful model of postwar (West) German politics is held up by many as at least part testimony to its achievements. However, now that the system is being used in other countries, par-ticularly in the context of seeking to reform corrupt (Italy, Japan) or electorally inequitable (New Zealand) systems, but also in a host of new democracies, there is an ideal opportunity to test once and for all whether this system has all the attributes that German experience has for so long suggested. Giovanni Sartori (1997: 75) is doubtful. He is particularly scathing with regard to the MMM variant, referring to it as a 'plurality–PR hybrid'. Sartori suggests that, while this system's advocates may believe 'that they are bringing together the best of two worlds', they are, in fact, more likely to obtain 'a bastard-producing hybrid which combines [the] defects' of PR and SMP.

6

The Single Transferable Vote System of Proportional Representation

The origins of the single transferable vote system of proportional representation (hereinafter STV) date back to the mid-nineteenth century. The two people credited most with its 'invention' – operating independently, and apparently without knowledge, of each other – are Thomas Hare (1806–92; an English lawyer) and Carl George Andrae (1812–93; a Danish mathematician and politician).[1] Of the two, it was Hare who played the larger role. As we saw in Chapter 2, Hare's *Treatise on the Election of Representatives, Parliamentary and Municipal* (1859) – and its subsequent amended editions – provided a considerable impetus to the debate about suffrage extension and the electoral system in Britain. Key figures, among them the philosopher John Stuart Mill, enthusiastically endorsed Hare's proposals (Hart 1992).

From the very beginning, STV has had its supporters. Indeed, if one were to carry out a headcount of the scholars writing about electoral systems at the beginning of the twenty-first century, it is likely that many of them would rate STV very highly. On the face of it, there appear to be good reasons for this. After all, here is a system which is both proportional *and* which facilitates constituency politicians. In contrast to the list systems of proportional representation, under the STV system the electors vote for candidates, not parties. Under STV, electors stand a better chance of seeing their preferred candidate elected; unlike in single member plurality (SMP) and the majoritarian systems, the voters have a choice between a number of constituency politicians.

STV appears attractive, and yet one is left with the nagging question: why is it so infrequently used? Why is it that after an extensive process of democratization across Southern, Central and Eastern Europe, the former soviet Union, and swathes of Latin America and Africa, with just the one small and temporary exception of Estonia from 1989 to 1992 (Taagepera 1996), STV was not the chosen electoral system? Why is it that, after a long period when few established democracies changed their electoral systems (France being possibly the sole exception), once a flurry of change does occur – in Italy, Japan and New Zealand – again STV is passed over? If STV is apparently so popular among the scholars, why is it avoided by the politicians?

There is a particular British angle to this question. As we saw in Chapter 2, throughout the twentieth century, STV featured repeatedly as the preferred system of pressure groups clamouring for reform of the British electoral system. It was very nearly adopted in the United Kingdom as a result of the 1917 Speaker's Conference. Ultimately it was used for some political elections in the UK: between 1918 and 1950 for four of the seven university seats; in the 1920s and again since 1973 for all elections other than Westminster elections in Northern Ireland. There is one additional reason why it could be argued that STV has a particular British resonance. This relates to the point made by Vernon Bogdanor almost two decades ago, when he noted that: 'Apart from a brief experiment in Denmark in the 1850s, STV has been used only in countries which have at some time been under British rule.' And, he added: 'It is the "Anglo-Saxon" method of securing proportional representation' (Bogdanor 1984: 76). At the time, Arend Lijphart (1987: 100) went so far as to suggest that 'we still have a perfect social science law without any major exceptions – very rare in the social sciences – linking political culture with forms of PR. When Anglo-American countries use PR, they always choose STV; in other countries, the choice is list PR.' With the exception of New Zealand (the first Anglo-Saxon country to adopt a form of list PR, in 1993) and also the temporary exception of Estonia (which is not Anglo-Saxon), this point still applies, though its status is now starting to look quite tenuous. STV is currently used by the following countries for their national elections: Australia (for elections to the Senate, the upper house), the Republic of Ireland (for all elections other than presidential elections), and Malta (for elections to the unicameral parliament). It is used at a regional level in several states in Australia (most notably in Tasmania; also by four other states and territories); it is used for local and European Parliament elections in Northern Ireland; it has been used for certain local elections in several states in the USA (where it is sometimes referred to as 'choice voting') (Farrell and McAllister 2000).

These cases all share one thing in common – their small size. Only Australia, with a population of just under 19 million, can lay claim to being a moderately large system. As we shall see below, in part to facilitate the use of STV in a larger system, Australia has adopted a particular variant of STV for its Senate elections. The fact is, however, that Australia's population is far smaller than Britain's, and, in any event, Australia does not use STV for its more important lower house elections. The only two countries which do – the Irish Republic (with a population of three and a half million) and Malta (with just 373,000) – are arguably far too small to provide adequate examples of what a larger country might expect if it switched to STV. This is one of the main problems for STV proponents to contend with; it also partially answers the question raised above about why STV is not popular among the politicians – because they see it as utopian, as suitable only for smaller countries where constituencies do not have to be too large.

There are, of course, other reasons why politicians have tended to reject STV: these are assessed later in the chapter. Given the fact that much of this chapter focuses on the Irish case, we start, in section 6.1, with a brief account of how Ireland ended up using STV. Section 6.2 deals with the operation of STV, the nuts and bolts of the system. This is followed, in section 6.3, with a discussion of the principal characteristics of STV, what distinguishes it from the other electoral systems, and its positive and negative features.

6.1   STV in Ireland

We saw in Chapter 2 how in the first part of the twentieth century, the proponents of PR had a tough – and ultimately unsuccessful – battle in trying to effect electoral reform in Britain. Ireland, however, presented a special case. From the moment that Home Rule appeared on the horizon, repeated references were made in the parliamentary debates to the need for some form of 'protection' for the 'loyal Irish minority' (Hart 1992: 104). There was some sympathy, therefore, for the idea that PR (specifically, STV) might be introduced in Ireland (and, for that matter, also in Scotland, Malta and parts of India – Hart 1992: 200). With the growing likelihood of Home Rule, and the belief that this would result in some form of partition of the island, there was a desire to placate the fears of southern Irish Unionists. In 1911, the president of the British PR Society, Lord Courtney, was invited to Dublin to give a public lecture on STV. This resulted in the same year, in the formation of the Proportional Representation Society of Ireland, which included in its membership Arthur Griffith, the founder of the secessionist party, Sinn Féin. He was on record for his praise of PR as ensuring 'that minorities shall be represented in proportion to their strength. It is the one just system of election under democratic government' (cited in O'Leary 1979: 6).

As Cornelius O'Leary (1979) observes, the original Irish Home Rule Bill of 1912 did not contain any provisions for PR. But in the ensuing debates, amendments were carried proposing the adoption of STV for a proportion of the seats in the proposed Irish House of Commons. The outbreak of the First World War caused the deferment of further debate (and any enactment) of Home Rule in Ireland for the time being. It was not until 1918 that STV appeared once more on the agenda, as a result of a private member's bill by an Irish Nationalist MP, Thomas Scanlon. He proposed the adoption of STV for municipal elections in his west of Ireland constituency of Sligo, arguing that this would encourage the Protestant minority to play a more active role in local politics. His bill was passed, and in December 1918 the first STV election for any part of the UK was held in Sligo, producing an impressive result for the Protestant minority. This result, as O'Leary (1979: 8) points out, was 'hailed as a triumph'. The (then) pro-Unionist *Irish Times* referred to STV as 'the *magna charta* of political and municipal minorities' (quoted in Proportional Representation Society 1919). The local *Sligo Champion* was gushing in its praise: 'The system has justified its adoption. We saw it work; we saw its simplicity; we saw its unerring honesty to the voter all through; and we saw the result in the final count; and we join in the general expression of those who followed it through with an intelligent interest – it is as easy as the old way; it is a big improvement and it is absolutely fair' (ibid.).

In the light of this result and its contrast with the dramatic electoral gains across all of southern Ireland by Sinn Féin in the 1918 general election (held under SMP), the Lloyd George government passed an Act proposing STV for all local authorities in Ireland, the intention being to try to limit some of Sinn Féin's electoral gains. Subsequently, in 1920, the first set of all-Ireland local elections with STV were held. Sinn Féin still managed to make big gains in southern Ireland, but in Northern Ireland the use of STV prevented Sinn Féin from gaining overall control of a number of councils.

Lloyd George's 1920 Government of Ireland Act (which ultimately was only ever enacted in Northern Ireland) contained a clause proposing STV for both parts of the partitioned island. (In the mid-1920s the new Northern Ireland administration replaced STV with SMP and this remained in operation until the 1970s.) The subsequent Anglo-Irish Treaty of 1921, establishing the Irish Free State in the 26 counties of southern Ireland, did not contain any explicit conditions relating to the electoral system for the new state; however, there was a notion that the rights of the minority Protestant community should somehow be protected. To an extent this would be achieved via the membership of the upper chamber of the new Irish parliament. It would also be achieved by the adoption of a PR system. O'Leary (1979: 14) suggests two other reasons why STV was adopted in the first Irish constitution of 1922: it followed a pattern in all new emergent states around that time, where PR was being adopted without debate; and the work of the British PR Society (including the Irish branch) ensured that PR was high on the agenda.

A curious feature of the Irish case is that, to an extent, it could be argued that the particular form of PR – namely STV – which was introduced may have had more to do with ignorance of other systems than a preference for one form of PR over another. The basic point of interest is that the 1922 constitution merely stated that the electoral system shall be 'PR'. It was not until the new constitution of 1937 that there was an explicit reference to 'STV' as the particular form of PR to be used in Ireland. In his detailed examination of the debates surrounding the adoption of the 1922 constitution, O'Leary (1979: 15) observes that there was little discussion of the particularities of the proposed electoral system, and, if anything, 'The speeches revealed a complete ignorance of the List systems'.

If STV was introduced into Ireland by accident, as it were, its retention as Ireland's electoral system has since been debated on two occasions in some detail and the decision to retain it has been quite deliberate. The current constitution of 1937 states that Ireland's electoral system is STV. To change this provision requires a referendum. In 1959 and again in 1968, there were attempts by the Fianna Fáil party to replace STV with SMP. The motivation on each occasion was to increase the party's chances of forming a single-party, majority government, for, despite the fact that by 1958 Fianna Fáil had been in power for 21 of the previous 27 years, it had only enjoyed an overall majority on four occasions. The party's founder, Eamonn de Valera, was due to retire soon and there was a fear that without him the party's chances of ever achieving an overall majority of seats would be greatly reduced. A referendum on electoral reform was called to coincide with the 1959 presidential election, in which de Valera, retiring as prime minister, was the Fianna Fáil candidate. This was seen as a cynical move designed to ensure the easy passage of the referendum bill. In the event, the bill was narrowly defeated (despite de Valera's easy victory), with 48 per cent voting in favour, 52 per cent against. The fact that Fianna Fáil's proposal was defeated by such a small margin (just 33,667 votes) encouraged the party to have another go, just nine years later, in 1968 (Sinnott 1999: 103). This time the proposal was resoundingly defeated, with 39 per cent voting in favour of replacing STV, 61 per cent voting against.

At the start of the new millennium electoral reform is once again on the agenda of Irish party politics. Senior government ministers have gone on record extolling the virtues of a mixed electoral system, and ongoing debates over root-and-branch constitutional reform (led by an all-party parliamentary Committee on the Constitution) have included discussions about electoral reform. As a result, a referendum proposal to change the electoral system in the near future cannot be ruled out.

6.2   How STV Works

STV differs from the other systems we have dealt with so far in terms of all three features of electoral systems (that is, district magnitude, ballot structure and electoral formula). Being a proportional system, STV operates with a district magnitude greater than one (thus distinguishing it from SMP and the majoritarian systems discussed in Chapters 2 and 3). In other words, more than one MP is elected per constituency (for example, in Ireland the range is between three and five MPs; in some parts of Australia there can be more than 20 MPs in a constituency). Hare had proposed that the whole of the UK should be one vast constituency; that electors should be able to choose between all candidates for the House of Commons. Obviously this proposal was never adopted, electoral engineers realizing that it would be hopelessly unrealistic to expect voters to choose between thousands of different candidates. As we shall see below, the fact that, for the most part, STV tends to operate with relatively small constituencies has important implications for the question of proportionality.

Another area of variation between STV and most other electoral systems is over the ballot structure, which is ordinal. Ordinal voting refers to the right of electors to vote for as many, or as few, candidates on the ballot paper as they wish; they can vote across party lines. Voters are advised to declare as many preferences as possible, so as to maximize the influence of their vote in the final election result. In Ireland electors need only mark one preference if they wish. In Australian elections, in order to have a valid vote, electors must vote a set minimum number of preferences. The precise number varies in different parts of Australia (for example, in Senate elections they must vote for all candidates).

Figure 6.1 provides an example of an Irish ballot paper for the Dublin North-Central constituency (three seats to be filled). Note how each of the large parties (Fianna Fáil and Fine Gael) have more than one candidate. Note also how the candidates are listed alphabetically. Ballot papers vary considerably across the different STV systems: all the other STV systems list the candidates under their different party groupings, as shown in Figure 6.2, which is a ballot paper for a general election in Malta.

STV also differs from other electoral systems with regard to electoral formula. Because STV operates in multi-member constituencies, some method is required to determine which candidates are elected and which are not. A quota, known as the 'Droop quota' – named after its nineteenth-century inventor, the mathematician and lawyer, H. R. Droop – is calculated, which ensures that exactly the correct number of candidates are elected in each constituency. Ordinarily, to be elected, a candidate must have as least as many votes as set by the quota. The quota is calculated as follows:

$$\text{`Droop quota'} = \left\{ \frac{\text{Total valid votes}}{(\text{Total number of seats}) + 1} \right\} + 1$$

Marcáil ord do rogha sna spáis seo síos. Mark order of preference in spaces below.	Marc Oifigiúl ➤ Official Mark
	BARLOW-COMMUNITY (Hannah Barlow-Community, of 67, Shantalla, Beaumont, Dublin. Alderman, Housewife, Midwife.)
	BELTON—FINE GAEL (Paddy Belton, of Ballivor, Howth, Co. Dublin. Director of Family Business.)
	BIRMINGHAM—FINE GAEL (George Birmingham, of "Denville", 498 Howth Road, Raheny, Dublin 5. City Councillor and Barrister-at-Law.)
	BRADY—FIANNA FÁIL (Vincent Brady, of 138, Kincora Road, Dublin 3. Company Director.)
	BROWNE—SOCIALIST LABOUR PARTY (Noel Browne, of Stepaside, Church Road, Malahide, Dublin. Medical Doctor)
	BYRNE—FINE GAEL (Mary Byrne, of 177, Seafield Road, Clontarf, Dublin 3 City Councillor.)
	CURLEY—THE COMMUNIST PARTY OF IRELAND (John Curley, of 44, Greencastle Road, Coolock, Dublin 5. Storeman.)
	DILLON (Andrew Dillon, of Drumnigh, Portmarnock, Co. Dublin. Solicitor.)
	DOHERTY (Vincent Doherty, of 76, Pembroke Road, Dublin. H Blocks Campaigner.)
	HAUGHEY—FIANNA FÁIL (Charles J. Haughey, of Abbeville, Kinsealy, Malahide, Co. Dublin. Taoiseach.)
	MARTIN—THE LABOUR PARTY (Michael Martin, of 28, Seafield Road. Insurance Agent.)
	O'HALLORAN—THE LABOUR PARTY (Michael O'Halloran, of 141, Ardlea Road, Artane. Public Representative and Trade Union Official.)
	TIMMONS—FIANNA FÁIL (Eugene Timmons, of 42, Copeland Avenue, Dublin 3. Public Representative.)

TREORACHA

I. Féach chuige go bhfuil an marc oifigiúil ar an bpáipéar.
II. Scríobh an figiúr 1 le hais ainm an chéad iarrthóra is rogha leat, an figiúr 2 le hais do dhara rogha agus mar sin de.
III. Fill an páipéar ionas nach bhfeicfear do vóta. Taispeáin *cúl an pháipéir* don oifigeach ceannais, agus cuir sa bhosca ballóide é.

INSTRUCTIONS

I. See that the official mark is on the paper.
II. Write 1 beside the name of the candidate of your first choice, 2 beside your second choice, and so on.
III. Fold the paper to conceal your vote. Show *the back of the paper* to the presiding officer and put it in the ballot box.

Figure 6.1   An Irish STV ballot paper

No. of Members to be elected .... Division		
Mark order of preference	**Badge of Candidate**	**Names of Candidates**
		PARTIT TAL-FJURI
		JONES, (John Jones, of 52 Old Bakery Street, Valletta, Merchant)
		MAGRO, (William David Magro, of 10 Tower Road, Sliema (Painter)
		MIFSUD, (Joseph Mifsud, of 16 Victoria Avenue, Sliema, Labourer)
		MUSCAT, (Francesco Muscat of 1 St. Paul's Str. Zabbar Driver)
		VELLA, (James Vella, of 5 Republic Street, St. Julians Architect
		WILLIAMS, (Francis Williams of 85 Genuis Street, Zurrieq Chemist)
		PARTIT TAL- GHASFUR
		AZZOPARDI, (Spiro Azzopardi, of 13 Marina Street, Zejtun, Printer)
		BORG, (Assuero Borg, of 69 Barbara Street, Mellieha, Clerk)
		CASSAR, (Lela Cassar, of "Dolores", Main Street, Cospiuca, Housewife)
		MIZZI, (Glormu Mizzi, of 70 Two Gates Str. Lija, Lawyer)
		ZARB, (Fortunat Zarb, of 15 Strait Street, Luqa, Clerk)
		PARTIT TAS-SIĠAR
		AZZOPARDI, (Reginald Azzopardi, of 165 St. Domenic Str., Qormi, Clerk)
		ZAMMIT, (Lawrence Zammit of "Josdor", 188 Bwieraq Str. Hamrun, Chemist)
		KANDIDATI INDIPENDENTI
		BUHAGIAR, (Louis Buhagiar, of 55 Republic Street, Zabbar, Merchant)
		GALEA, (Ninu Galea, of 67 B'Kara Lane, Qrendi, Worker)

Figure 6.2   A Malta STV ballot paper

The easiest way to understand how the Droop quota works is to imagine a scenario where the total number of valid votes is 100. As we know, STV works always with multi-seat constituencies: this is the principal characteristic distinguishing STV from the majoritarian systems dealt with in Chapter 3. In fact, the Droop quota can be easily applied to the alternative vote system used for Australian lower house elections. Since the alternative vote operates with single-seat constituencies (and hence is not proportional), the Droop quota is as follows: $(100/1 + 1) + 1 = 51$ votes. In other words, to be elected under the alternative vote system, a candidate needs at least 51 votes, or 51 per cent of the total vote, a majoritarian result. When there is more than one seat to be filled in a constituency, the minimum number of votes required to be elected is reduced. In a three-seat constituency a candidate requires 26 per cent of the vote; in a four-seat constituency, 21 per cent; in a five-seat constituency, 17 per cent. The greater the number of seats to be filled (that is, the larger the district magnitude) the lower the number of votes required to be elected. This fact has important implications for the issue of proportionality, as we shall see below.

Table 6.1 shows an example of an election count using STV. The Dublin South constituency in the 1997 election was a five-seat constituency. Fourteen candidates were fielded: three by Fianna Fáil, two by Fine Gael, one each by Labour, the Progressive Democrats and Greens, and there were an assortment of other minor party candidates and independents. The total number of valid votes (after subtracting the invalid votes) was 57,986, producing a quota of 9,665 votes.

The first count in an STV election involves the sorting of all the ballot papers according to the first preferences of the voters. If we were using a version of the plurality system in multi-seat constituencies (such as the block vote; see Chapter 2), the first five candidates with the greatest number of votes from the following list would be elected, providing a clean sweep for the three longest-established parties, Fianna Fáil, Fine Gael and Labour:

	Vote	*Distance from quota*
1. Tom Kitt (Fianna Fáil)	9,904	+239 Elected
2. Séamus Brennan (Fianna Fáil)	8,861	−804
3. Olivia Mitchell (Fine Gael)	8,775	−890

4. Alan Shatter (Fine Gael)   8,094   −1,571
5. Eithne FitzGerald (Labour)   6,147   −3,518
6. Liz O'Donnell (Progressive   5,444   −4,221
    Democrats)

However, since the electoral system being used here is STV, only those candidates with at least as many votes as the electoral quota are deemed elected. In this case just one candidate, Tom Kitt, met this requirement, and he was duly elected. Four seats were left to be filled, requiring the electoral count to move to the next stage. The next count, under STV, involves one of two things. If a candidate is elected, the next count usually consists of the transfer of all surplus votes – that is, of the number of votes by which they have exceeded the quota – transferring these votes to the remaining candidates based on the second-preference votes expressed by the electors. If no candidate has been elected (or if the surplus is too small to make any difference to the candidates left in the race), the next count entails the 'elimination' of the candidate with the least votes and the transfer of their votes to the remaining candidates, based again on the second preferences of the voters. Wherever the candidate to be eliminated has too few votes to make any difference to the rank order of the remaining candidates, in order to expedite matters, the returning officer can opt to eliminate two or more candidates at the same time. This transfer of the surplus votes of winning candidates or the votes of eliminated candidates – based, in turn, on second, third, fourth preferences, and so on – continues until such time as all the seats are filled.

In this Dublin South example, Kitt's surplus of 239 votes is too small to make any potential difference to the weaker candidates remaining in the race, so the reason for the next count consists of the elimination of the weakest candidate and the transfer of their second preferences. In this case, however, if we aggregate the votes of the four weakest candidates, Dolan (75 votes), Doody (80 votes), Lyons (115 votes) and Maher (624 votes) and throw in Kitt's 239-vote surplus, this totals 1,133 votes, which is less than the vote of the fifth weakest candidate, Christine Buckley (1,426 votes). This means that the returning officer was able to eliminate all four candidates in one go, because there was simply no way any of them could ever hope to catch up with the other candidates. As we can see, there are more credible catching-up distances between the next set of weaker candidates – Buckley (1,426 votes) and Greene (1,482 votes)

Table 6.1 Counting an Irish STV election: Dublin South in 1997

Seats 5 / Valid votes 57,986 / Quota 9,665	First count	Second count — Transfer of Dolan's, Doody's, Lyons's and Maher's votes	Third count — Transfer of Kitt's surplus	Fourth count — Transfer of Buckley's votes	Fifth count — Transfer of Greene's votes	Sixth count — Transfer of Ormonde's votes	Seventh count — Transfer of Brennan's surplus	Eighth count — Transfer of Boland's votes
Boland, G. (GP)	3,539	+241 / 3,780	+5 / 3,785	+356 / 4,141	+291 / 4,432	+150 / 4,582	+236 / 4,818	−4,818 / —
Brennan, S. (FF)*	8,861	+67 / 8,928	+113 / 9,041	+146 / 9,187	+352 / 9,539	+2,519 / 12,058 Elected	−2,393 / 9,665	
Buckley, C. (Ind)	1,268	+158 / 1,426	+4 / 1,430	−1,430 / —				
Dolan, G. (Ind)	75	−75 / —						
Doody, J. (Ind)	80	−80						
FitzGerald, E. (Lab)*	6,147	+125 / 6,272	+8 / 6,280	+205 / 6,485	+77 / 6,562	+105 / 6,667	+89 / 6,756	+1,402 / 8,158
Greene, R. (Ind)	1,431	+51 / 1,482 / —	+3 / 1,485 / −239	+100 / 1,585	−1,585 / —			

Kitt, T. (FF)*	9,904	9,904 −239 Elected	9,665					
Lyons, J. (NLP)	115		−115 –					
Maher, L. (SP)	624		−624 –					
Mitchell, O. (FG)	8,775	+54 8,829	+8 8,837	+178 9,015	+169 9,184	+158 9,342	+73 9,415	+721 10,136 Elected
O'Donnell, L. (PD)*	5,444	+47 5,491	+29 5,520	+149 5,669	+115 5,784	+809 6,593	+1,511 8,104	+966 9,070 Elected
Ormonde, A. (FF)	3,629	+54 3,683	+61 3,744	+93 3,837	+254 4,091	−4,091		
Shatter, A. (FG)*	8,094	+63 8,157	+8 8,165	+107 8,272	+80 8,352	+204 8,556	+103 8,659	+705 9,364 Elected
Non-transferable		34	–	96	247	146	381	1,024

* Sitting MPs.
Source: Nealon (1997).

– particularly when we add in the 1,133 votes which are already in the pool of transferable votes. Furthermore, votes of these sizes could make a material difference to the status of candidates ranked higher in terms of their first-preference votes.[2]

Having completed the transfer of Dolan's, Doody's, Lyon's and Maher's votes, no other candidates have yet been elected, so a third count is required. Now, attention is focused on the fate of the weakest two candidates, Christine Buckley (1,430 votes) and Richard Greene (1,485), each of whom has a sufficient tally of votes to make a potential difference for candidates placed higher in the rank order. Given that only 50 votes separate them, to decide the matter it now makes sense to transfer Kitt's surplus of 239 votes among the remaining candidates.

The important point here is that not all of Kitt's votes transfer, only that amount which is surplus to the quota; 9,665 votes must remain in his pile. As an illustration of how this is done, we can look at how the transfer of Kitt's votes to his running mate, Séamus Brennan, was calculated. When Kitt's ballot papers were sorted according to the number two preferences, a packet of votes were transferable to Brennan. The more mathematically-minded reader will be able to work out, after the event, that this packet amounted to some 4,683 votes, or 47.3 per cent of the total: that is, 4,683 of Kitt's 9,904 votes ranked Séamus Brennan as their number two choice. The issue now is how to translate this number down to a correct proportion based on the total figure of 239 votes which are available for transfer. The calculation of exactly how many of these 4,683 votes to transfer to Brennan is as follows:

$$
\begin{array}{ccc}
\text{Number of Kitt's votes to be transferred} & = & \dfrac{\text{Number of Kitt's surplus votes}}{\text{Number of Kitt's votes}} \times \text{Number of votes that would transfer to Brennan}
\end{array}
$$

If we apply this formula, we arrive at the following result: (239 ÷ 9,904) × 4,683 = 113 votes, that is, 47.3 per cent of Kitt's surplus (of 239 votes). This process is repeated for each of the remaining candidates, and the results are shown in the third column of Table 6.1. At this stage we notice one of the pleasures for the political scientist of the STV system. As Richard Sinnott (1995: 199) notes, STV is 'information-rich'. By studying the way in which votes are transferred between the candidates we can learn much about the relationships between candidates, about the links between parties, and about the coalitional tendencies of voters. We will look at this in more detail in a moment, but to illustrate the point, it is useful to look at how the Fianna Fáil votes (of Tom Kitt) transferred in this case: 174 votes (73 per cent of the total) went to his running mates, Séamus Brennan and Ann Ormonde; 16 votes (7 per cent) transferred to Fine Gael; 8 votes (3 per cent) went to Labour. Only the Progressive Democrat candidate received a decent proportion of 12 per cent of Kitt's transfers, consistent with the desire of both parties on this occasion to promote a potential post-election coalition deal.

The transfer of Kitt's surplus was not sufficient to place any of the other candidates over the quota, so the reason for the next count (count four) was the elimination of the candidate with the least votes, the Independent candidate, Christine Buckley (1,430 votes), and the transfer of all her votes based on the next declared preference on the ballot papers in question. Once again, this count did not result in the election of a candidate, and so the process of eliminating the weakest candidates continued, and did so again through counts five and six, by which time Séamus Brennan of Fianna Fáil had received a sufficient number of votes to be the second candidate elected (with 12,058 votes). But three more candidates still had to be elected, and the situation regarding the placement of candidates at the end of count six remained largely unchanged from that after count one. In other words, the top six candidates were arranged in the same order, as follows:

	Vote	Distance from quota
1. Tom Kitt (Fianna Fáil)	9,904	+239 Elected
2. Séamus Brennan (Fianna Fáil)	12,058	+2,393 Elected
3. Olivia Mitchell (Fine Gael)	9,342	−323
4. Alan Shatter (Fine Gael)	8,556	−1,109
5. Eithne FitzGerald (Labour)	6,667	−2,998
6. Liz O'Donnell (Progressive Democrats)	6,593	−3,072

Fine Gael was poised to win a seat; Olivia Mitchell required just 323 votes. Alan Shatter of Fine Gael looked a pretty sure bet for the fourth seat. The interesting battle was for the fifth seat. Only 74 votes separated FitzGerald (6,667) and O'Donnell (6,593). Given that Fianna Fáil and the Progressive Democrats had been talking up the issue of a possible coalition arrangement after the election, there was little surprise when, in count seven, the bulk of Brennan's surplus (1,511 votes; 63 per cent) transferred to Liz O'Donnell of the Progressive Democrats. Labour's Eithne FitzGerald received a derisory 89 votes.

The state of play after the seventh count was that Mitchell and Shatter were still poised to take the third and fourth seats. O'Donnell, with 8,104 votes, was now well ahead of FitzGerald, who had 6,756 votes. All would be decided by the next count, involving the elimination of Gerry Boland of the Green Party, and the transfer of his 4,818 votes. It was not inconceivable that the bulk of Boland's votes might have transferred to FitzGerald: a transfer from one left-of-centre party to another would appear more likely than from a left-of-centre party to a right-of-centre party. As we can see, FitzGerald did, indeed, receive a plurality of Boland's transfers (1,402 votes; 29 per cent). But this was nowhere near enough. FitzGerald's tally of 8,158 votes was almost one thousand short of Liz O'Donnell's 9,070 votes, and O'Donnell was declared the winner of the fifth seat. Note how O'Donnell was deemed elected without having actually reached the electoral quota – she was 595 votes short. The fact is, however, that there was no way that FitzGerald (the only other remaining candidate) could overtake her, so to carry out an extra count was unnecessary.

As this discussion suggests, an STV election count can take a long time; indeed, taking into account the possibility of recounts, it can sometimes take days before a final result is known. We have seen how the fortunes of candidates can change quite dramatically from one stage in the counting process to the next. There are two points worth noting about this. First, there is the fact that the STV system as used in Ireland (and Malta, though, as we shall see, not in Australia) contains an element of chance. Second, more generally the process of vote transfers can be crucial – indeed, this point is not lost on the party strategists seeking to maximize the gains for their parties.

The count in Dublin South-Central in 1992 provides a good illustration of the significance of the first point. On the final count (count thirteen) Ben Briscoe of Fianna Fáil was the fourth and final candidate to be elected with 6,526 votes (not reaching the quota of 8,049 votes). He had just five votes more than the candidate he beat, Eric Byrne (Democratic Left). Obviously the basic point is that Briscoe had more votes and therefore deserved to win. However, the reality is that Briscoe may quite possibly have been helped by an element of chance which is due to the way in which STV counts in Ireland (for lower house elections only) are administered. This relates to transfers of surplus votes. As we have seen, not all the votes are transferred, only those which are surplus to the quota. Once the returning officer has calculated which proportions of votes are to transfer to each of the remaining candidates, the problem then becomes one of determining which of the actual ballot papers are to be transferred and which are to remain in the pile. What happens at this stage varies between Ireland and Australia. In Ireland the returning officer simply picks the top ballot papers from each of the piles; in Australia the ballot papers are sorted according to all the remaining preferences and so the transfer (using fractions) takes adequate account of future vote transfers. The Irish case, therefore, incorporates an element of chance which could be significant whenever there is a close result (Gallagher and Unwin 1986).

As Sinnott (1995: 199) notes: 'transfer patterns have potentially a lot to tell us about Irish voting behaviour'. The transfer patterns revealed by STV counts can provide fascinating insights into the relationships between particular candidates, the degree of faction fighting within a party, and the views of voters towards certain coalition possibilities. In his seminal research on Irish transfer patterns from the 1920s to the 1970s, Michael Gallagher (1978) found a higher degree of voter 'loyalty' among Fianna Fáil supporters than among the supporters of the other parties. In other words Fianna Fáil voters were more likely to vote for all the party's candidates, rather than chopping and changing between candidates of other parties. This has important implications for vote management strategies, because a party needs to maximize the efficiency of its vote. Candidate chances are threatened whenever the party cannot rely on the consistency of the transfers between its candidates.

Gallagher (1978) also found that Fianna Fáil supporters tend to be more 'exclusive' than the supporters of the other parties: that is, they are more likely to plump only for Fianna Fáil candidates, not declaring any preferences for other candidates. On the one hand plumping is actually potentially damaging for the party involved because its supporters are not making maximum use of the possibility to influence the election outcome; the best way for a voter to 'use' STV is to declare as many preferences as possible. On the other hand, as Sinnott (1995: 212) notes:

> from a party point of view . . . it is possible to argue that any losses involved in failing to affect the outcome by not transferring beyond the party are more than compensated for by encouraging the party supporters to think exclusively of the party and not to contemplate the possibility of giving even lower order preferences to another party. The presumed effect of this would be to strengthen the voters' loyalty to the party and minimize leakage or defection in future elections.

The third set of patterns Gallagher identified in the period he studied related to transfers between candidates of different parties. In particular, given the fact that Fine Gael and Labour had formed coalition governments in the 1950s and again in the 1970s, it was interesting to examine the relationship between their respective supporters. In general there was some evidence of voter sympathy for the link between the two parties in the periods in question; however, the inter-party transfers tended to be higher from Fine Gael to Labour than vice versa.

Gallagher's (1993) examination of the transfer patterns in the 1992 election revealed a marked drop in the levels of voter 'loyalty' or 'solidarity' among Fianna Fáil supporters, down from 83 per cent in the 1980s to 70 per cent in 1992 – the party's worst result since 1927. This dropped still further in 1997, down to 67 per cent (RTÉ 1997). This decline reflects the fact that Fianna Fáil has been going through an unusually difficult period of internal indiscipline and faction fighting. Fine Gael's solidarity figure in 1992 was even lower, at 65 per cent its lowest since 1944. In 1997, the party held stable at 65 per cent.

The destinations of 'terminal' inter-party transfers in the 1997 election are shown in Table 6.2 (also Gallagher 1999: 137–41). This shows only those cases of vote transfers where the party in question had no more candidates in the race, providing a good indicator of levels of support for potential coalition arrangements. As expected, for instance, the table reveals high proportions of inter-party transfers from Fine Gael to Labour (50.2 per cent) and from Labour to Fine Gael (45.9 per cent), reflecting the fact that these parties had

Table 6.2 Destination of inter-party ('terminal') transfers in the Irish 1997 election

Transfers from	Fianna Fáil (%)	Fine Gael (%)	Labour (%)	Progressive Democrats (%)	Others (%)	Non-transferable (%)
Fianna Fáil	–	10.9	17.6	16.2	29.1	26.1
Fine Gael	16.6	–	50.2	3.7	12.8	16.7
Labour	18.6	45.9	–	2.0	16.6	16.9
Progressive Democrats	57.2	16.3	9.3	–	7.5	9.7

Note: 'Terminal' transfers relate to those cases where none of a party's candidates are left to receive any transfers (because they have either been elected or eliminated).
Source: RTÉ (1997).

been in government together and were campaigning on a shared platform.

Similarly, there is good evidence of transfers from the Progressive Democrats to Fianna Fáil (57.2 per cent), reflecting the expectation of a possible new coalition between these two parties. By contrast, however, Fianna Fáil supporters did not reciprocate: only 16.2 per cent of them transferred to the Progressive Democrats, slightly less than the proportion which transferred to Labour (17.6 per cent). Indeed, consistent with the Fianna Fáil practice of voting 'exclusively' for Fianna Fáil candidates, 26 per cent of the party's voters in 1997 did not transfer to any of the remaining parties, by far the highest proportion of all the major parties.

6.3 The Consequences of STV for the Political System

As we have seen, STV shares a number of features with the single member plurality system. The country is divided into territorial constituencies, electing constituency politicians. The voters are asked to choose between candidates not (as in most list systems) parties. On the other hand, STV differs from SMP in two significant respects: it is a proportional system; and there is more than one MP per constituency.

There are two themes we need to consider when assessing this (or other) electoral systems: how proportional it is, and what consequences it has for the political system generally. There has been much debate in the academic literature over how proportional STV is. This issue is dealt with in detail in Chapter 7. As we shall see, conclusions vary widely, some arguing that STV is one of the most proportional systems around, others suggesting that it is merely a semi-proportional system (Blondel 1969; Gallagher 1975; Lijphart 1986a, 1994a; Taagepera and Shugart 1989). For the most part, the former are dealing with theoretical comparisons between STV and list systems (in particular, ignoring the effects of a tendency for low district magnitudes in some STV systems), the latter with practical comparisons. In Chapter 7 the various electoral systems are assessed on the issue of proportionality; this section touches on a few of the themes of specific relevance to the STV system.

To repeat the exercise of earlier chapters, Table 6.3 lists the percentages of votes and seats for Irish parties in each election since 1951. As is evident from the columns listing the percentage differences between votes and seats, the system produces much more proportional results than is the case in SMP or majoritarian systems. The vote–seat differences are never in double figures; they are consistently smaller than in Tables 2.3, 3.3 or 3.4 (though generally not quite as small as in Tables 4.4, 4.5 or 5.2); smaller parties are, comparatively speaking, not systematically cheated by the system. Furthermore, there are few, if any, examples of the sorts of discrepancies over the formation of parliamentary majorities which were noted in Chapters 2 and 3. Indeed the only example worth noting is the case of the 1973 election when Fianna Fáil lost seats (and government) despite having gained votes.

When dealing with the issue of proportionality, the point of greatest significance – as indicated in the previous section – is constituency size (or district magnitude). If Hare's proposal of having all of the UK as one great constituency were followed, this would produce a highly proportional result, but at what cost? Imagine the unfortunate voter having to decide between thousands of candidates on a ballot paper which would be several metres long! An illustration of what this could mean is provided by an American example in the 1930s (Hermens 1984). For a brief period, New York state adopted STV for municipal elections. In one case, in Brooklyn, the constituency

Table 6.3 Irish general elections, 1951–97: percentage of votes and seats

	Fianna Fáil			Fine Gael			Labour		
	Vote (%)	Seat (%)	Diff. (%)	Vote (%)	Seat (%)	Diff. (%)	Vote (%)	Seat (%)	Diff. (%)
1951	46.3	46.9	+0.6	25.8	27.2	+1.4	11.4	10.9	−0.5
1954	43.4	44.2	+0.8	32.0	34.0	+2.0	12.1	12.9	+0.8
1957	48.3	53.1	+4.8	26.6	27.2	+0.6	9.1	8.2	−0.9
1961	43.8	48.6	+4.8	32.0	32.6	+0.6	11.6	11.1	−0.5
1965	47.7	50.0	+2.3	34.1	32.6	−1.5	15.4	15.3	−0.1
1969	45.7	52.1	+6.4	34.1	34.7	+0.6	17.0	12.5	−4.5
1973	46.2	47.9	+1.7	35.1	37.5	+2.4	13.7	13.2	−0.5
1977	50.6	56.8	+6.2	30.5	29.1	−1.4	11.6	11.5	−0.1
1981	45.3	47.0	+1.7	36.5	39.2	+2.7	9.9	9.0	−0.9
Feb. 1982	47.3	48.8	+1.5	38.0	48.8	+0.7	9.1	9.0	−0.1
Nov. 1982	45.2	45.2	–	42.2	45.2	+3.0	9.4	9.6	+0.2
1987	44.1	48.8	+4.7	30.7	48.8	+3.6	6.4	7.2	+0.8
1989	44.2	46.4	+2.2	33.1	46.4	+3.8	9.5	9.0	−0.5
1992	39.1	41.0	+1.9	24.5	27.1	+2.6	19.3	19.9	+0.6
1997	39.3	46.4	+7.1	28.0	32.5	+4.5	10.4	10.2	−0.2

	Progressive Democrats			Workers' Party/ Democratic Left			Green Party		
	Vote (%)	Seat (%)	Diff. (%)	Vote (%)	Seat (%)	Diff. (%)	Vote (%)	Seat (%)	Diff. (%)
1973				1.1	0.0	−1.1			
1977				1.7	0.0	−1.7			
1981				1.7	0.6	−1.1			
Feb. 1982				2.2	1.8	−0.4			
Nov. 1982				3.3	1.2	−2.1	0.2	0.0	−0.2
1987	11.8	8.4	−3.4	3.8	2.4	−1.4	0.4	0.0	−0.4
1989	5.5	3.6	−1.9	5.0	4.2	−0.8	1.5	0.6	−0.9
1992	4.7	6.0	+1.3	2.8	2.4	−0.4	1.4	0.6	−0.8
1997	4.7	2.4	−2.3	2.5	2.4	−0.1	2.8	1.2	−1.6

Note: Percentages may not add up to 100 because smaller parties and 'Others' have been excluded.
Sources: Mackie and Rose (1991); election results.

was so large that 99 candidates put their names forward for election. The ballot paper was more than four feet long.

In short, there is a trade-off in the use of STV. The constituency needs to be large enough to produce as proportional a result as possible (that is, to give candidates from all parties a fair chance), but it must not be so large that it makes the voter's job of choosing between candidates impossible. It is generally accepted that the optimal size for STV constituencies is at least five seats (Taagepera and Shugart 1989: ch. 11). In practice, in Malta and virtually all Australian STV elections, this requirement is met; in Ireland, however, a large proportion of the constituencies are three- or four-seater (Farrell and McAllister 2000).

The Australians have devised one way of getting round the problem of over-long ballot papers. In Australian Senate elections the ballot paper is divided in two by a line: above the line all the party labels are displayed horizontally with a box next to each one; below the line there are lists of party candidates, each one grouped under the appropriate party label. This is more akin to the Malta ballot paper than to the Irish one, though, as we can see in Figure 6.3, what distinguishes the Australian ballot paper is the fact that the party labels are grouped horizontally instead of vertically. The voter can either fill out preferences for all the candidates (remember that in the case of Australian Senate elections all preferences must be completed for a vote to be counted as valid), or, alternatively, the voter can opt to vote 'above the line', by making a 'ticket vote'. In this case the voter simply places a '1' in the box of their preferred party. This means the voter is (tacitly) accepting the preference ranking of candidates which has been agreed beforehand among the parties. In essence, what this amounts to is STV being treated as a list system. But it does mean that there can be large ballot papers. For instance, in the 1999 election to the 21-member legislative council of the Australian state of New South Wales, 80 parties fielded 264 candidates producing a ballot paper the size of a table-cloth. A candidate for the Outdoor Recreation Party was elected with only 0.2 per cent of the vote.

The issue of proportionality – to which we return in Chapter 7 – refers to the short-run or immediate effects of voting systems. Among the long-term effects which warrant attention are the numbers of parties, electoral competition between the parties, and representation by MPs. When considering the issue of electoral

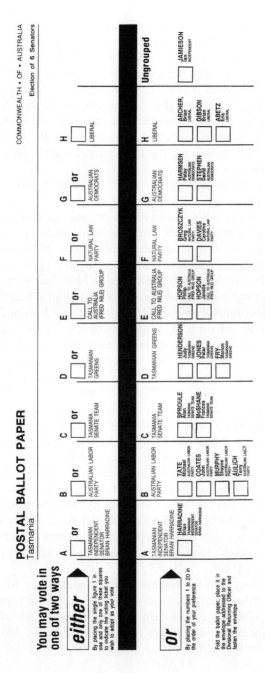

Figure 6.3   An Australian STV ballot paper

reform, it is usual practice to examine the operation of electoral systems elsewhere, to try to get an impression of the benefits and costs of the different systems. In the case of STV, Ireland is usually chosen as the case study, largely reflecting its long-established membership of the club of liberal democracies, its geographical location and its general familiarity. (Recent examples of where Ireland featured as the case study in considerations of electoral reform include the British Labour Party's Plant Working Party, the British Independent Commission on the Electoral System, and the New Zealand Royal Commission.)

The basic criticisms of STV in Ireland relate to apparent party system instability and to the clientelist emphasis of the parliamentarians. Let us deal with each in turn. First, the fact that a large proportion of Irish governments have either been coalition or minority governments (Farrell 1988) is seen to raise a question mark over governmental stability. And recent evidence suggests growing electoral instability. For instance, between 1932 and 1969 there were just four changes of government (that is, either Fianna Fáil was in power, or there was a coalition dominated by Fine Gael and Labour). By contrast, in the period since 1973, the government has changed hands (or at least had to change partners) in each of the nine elections up to 1997. Furthermore, there was a deeply unsettled period between 1981 and 1982, when three elections were held in just eighteen months. By the end of the 1980s, the previously unthinkable had happened: Fianna Fáil – which in the past had only ever formed single-party governments – crossed the Rubicon and (initially with deep reluctance) embraced coalition, first (in 1989) with the Progressive Democrats and then (in 1992) with Labour. Concomitant with the electoral shifts have been changes in the party system. What was once a textbook case of a 'two-and-a-half' party system (Fianna Fáil, Fine Gael and the small Labour Party) had, by the mid-1980s, become a multi-party system with the entry of the Workers' Party (later essentially replaced by the Democratic Left), the Progressive Democrats, and the Greens, all gaining Dáil (parliament) representation (Farrell 1999).

When dealing with the issue of electoral stability in Ireland, the first point to be stressed is that while there may have been a large number of coalition and/or minority governments over the years, these have for the most part been long-lasting (Farrell 1988). In fact, on average Irish governments have tended to last for three- to four-year terms (including two periods when Fianna Fáil was in power for 16 consecutive years, from 1932 to 1948, and again from 1957 to 1973). There may have been a phase of governmental instability in 1981–2, but the fact is that it was a phase. Subsequent elections produced more decisive results. And, of course, such occurrences are not unique to Ireland – as evidenced by the two 1974 British elections, and also in 1979 by the collapse of the minority British Labour government (which had been kept in office by a formal pact with the Liberals and various other less formal deals with minor parties).

As Table 6.3 shows, there may be more parties in the Irish system in the 1990s than there were in the 1970s, but the fact is that the three old parties remain predominant forces, and there is no certainty that the new parties will have a long-term future. Indeed, in 1998 we saw the demise of one of the new parties, Democratic Left, which merged with the Labour Party. In any event, why should we blame STV for this move towards multi-partyism? The fragmentation of the party system is a new feature to Irish politics, not a permanent fixture, yet the electoral system has remained unchanged since the 1920s. Furthermore, neither of the other countries where STV is used can be classified as multi-party. Malta has a two-party system (Zanella 1990). Similarly, Australia has a two-bloc party system (Labor versus the Liberal–National coalition), though smaller parties (notably the Democrats and the Greens) have managed to gain limited representation in the Senate (McAllister 1992).

The second apparent problem with STV relates to how political life in Ireland is predominated by a brokerage style of politics. Parliamentarians work their 'parish pumps', attracting votes by a heavy emphasis on constituency social work and localist concerns. (There is a large literature on this; see Carty 1981.) More time seems to be spent in the Dáil signing letters to constituents and raising constituency matters in question time than with the weightier matters of national legislation. Surveys of TDs (MPs) reveal a heavy constituency workload (Gallagher and Komito 1999; Roche 1982). Election campaigns are characterized by a similarly heavy emphasis on local issues and by regular faction fights between candidates of the same party. And there is good reason for the latter. Between 1951 and 1977, for example, roughly one-third of the incumbent TDs who lost their seats were displaced by running mates from the same party (Carty 1981: 114). In recent years that proportion seems to be rising (Gallagher 1990, 1993, 1999).

The emphasis on localism is also evident among Irish voters. There is a well-established literature which explores the 'friends and neighbours' voting tendencies of the Irish electorate (for a summary, see Carty 1981). Candidates are found to receive more votes in that part of the constituency where they live, and there is a clear localist bias in voting behaviour, affecting the rank ordering of candidates by the electorate. Since the 1980s the parties' headquarters have sought to exploit this 'friends and neighbours' tendency with elaborate vote-management strategies, whereby candidates are picked from different corners of the constituency and voters in each locale are actively encouraged to vary the ordering of their preferences so as to maximize the efficiency of the party vote. The basic idea is that the more equal the spread of first preferences across the different party candidates, the greater the chance that more will be elected (see Farrell 1994; for contrasts, see Bowler and Farrell 1996; Bowler *et al.* 1996; Farrell and McAllister 2000).

In each of these points about Irish localism, STV is usually credited with a key role: the heavy emphasis on constituency casework, faction-fighting between candidates from the same party, a focus on constituency, localist matters in election campaigns and parliamentary work, 'friends and neighbours' voting, are all seen as resulting – at least in large part – from the candidate-centred, preference voting of STV (Carty 1981; Farrell 1985; Katz 1980; Parker 1983).

To what extent is Irish brokerage politics caused by STV and to what extent is the apparent relationship coincidental? The fact is that Irish political culture is personified by a high degree of localism (Chubb 1982; Schmitt 1973) and it would be disingenuous to suppose that somehow this would dissipate if the electoral system were changed. It may be the case that multi-seat constituencies provoke competition between party candidates, but why need this take the form of competition over constituency work? As Michael Gallagher (1987: 32) has noted, there is nothing to prevent 'candidates of the same party trying fervently to establish reputations not as active constituency workers but as active parliamentarians'. Once again the international evidence does not support the linkage between STV and brokerage politics. A detailed comparison between Ireland and the Australian island state of Tasmania (the first place to use STV) finds little to support the claim that brokerage is caused by STV (O'Connell 1983). A comparison of attitudes and backgrounds of the membership of the two Australian houses of parliament finds, if anything, a higher constituency emphasis among lower house members (elected under the alternative vote) than among upper house members (elected by STV) (Farrell and McAllister 1995). Finally, a test of STV on London voters during the 1994 European Parliament election found little evidence of 'friends and neighbours' voting by the voters (Bowler and Farrell 1996).

There are two more technical matters which warrant attention when dealing with STV. First, there is the issue of what are known as 'ballot position effects', in which it is suggested that a candidate's chances of being elected are influenced by where their name is located on the ballot paper. Second, there is the point – much stressed by critics of STV (for example, Dummett 1997) – that STV can produce anomalous results. This latter point refers, in particular, to the issue of 'monotonicity', in which it is argued that, under STV, it is not necessarily always the case that a candidate's chances of being elected are helped by an increase in their share of the vote. We start with the first of these concerns.

Ballot position effects refer to the fact that voters are lazy or uninterested, that where possible voters may take short cuts to reduce the effort involved in voting. Evidently voting can be a non-taxing exercise in some systems. For instance, in a British election a voter simply marks an 'X' next to the name of one candidate. In a Spanish election, as we saw in Chapter 4, a voter chooses the ballot paper of their preferred party and simply pops it in the box. It is a quite different matter to require a voter to read through a list of, say, fifteen candidates and rank-order them. One obvious solution for the voter is to vote not in order of *preference*, but, instead, in order of *sequence*. The idea here is that voters read down (or possibly up) the list of candidate names and place a '1' next to the first name they recognize (or the first name from the party they support), a '2' next to the second, and so on. This is said to produce a biased result in favour of those candidates whose names start with letters at the beginning (or, at the other extreme, at the end) of the alphabet, and accordingly it is generally referred to as 'alphabetical' voting. It has also been given such titles as 'bullet' or 'donkey' voting.

Politicians have been known to take this issue very seriously. For instance, in a celebrated case in the Australian Senate elections of New South Wales in 1937, the Labor Party fielded four candidates whose surnames all happened to begin with 'A'; all four were elected. (Since 1940 the placement of Senate candidates has been determined by lot.) In Ireland, where politicians can quite easily change their name by deed poll, there were two cases in the 1980s of politicians who apparently sought to benefit from alphabetical voting, while at the same time attempting to advertise their particular issue concerns more widely. One candidate called Seán Loftus had his name altered to Seán Alderman Dublin Bay-Rockall Loftus; meanwhile a certain William Fitzsimon decided to change his name to William Abbey of the Holy Cross Fitzsimon. Of the two, Loftus was the only one to achieve any measure of success (briefly in 1981), but whether this had anything to do with the name change is a moot point.

Politicians are not the only ones to take ballot position effects seriously. Academics have been researching the issue for some time, and, while there may be doubts over the accuracy of a number of these studies on the grounds of methodological weaknesses (Darcy and McAllister 1990), there is nonetheless undoubted evidence that it does play a role in Australian and Irish elections (Kelley and McAllister 1984; Robson and Walsh 1974). However, if this is a problem (and a very small one at that), it is one with a simple solution – rotation of candidate names on the ballot paper (Darcy and Mackerras 1993). The idea is relatively simple. The ordering of candidate names is changed at a number of stages during the printing of the ballot papers to ensure that each candidate has an equal chance of appearing at the top (and bottom). This has been the practice in parts of the United States for over 40 years; Tasmania adopted it in 1980; and the Australian Capital Territory followed suit in 1994.

Among the criticisms of STV in the formal literature on voting theory, the most common is that it is 'non-monotonic', that 'more first-place votes can hurt, rather than help, a candidate' (Brams and Fishburn 1984: 151; Dummett 1997; Nurmi 1997). The basic point here is that in certain, very specific, circumstances STV can potentially produce a paradoxical result where a candidate can actually be harmed by a higher vote. Table 6.4 provides a hypothetical example of how a non-monotonic result could occur. Since the issue of non-monotonicity is shared by all preferential electoral systems, for the sake of simplicity the example refers to a single-seat constituency where a candidate requires a majority of votes in order to win the seat (that is, the alternative vote system used in Australia; see Chapter 3). In this example there are four candidates, Tom, Dick, Harry and Shirley, and an electorate of 21 voters. The voters have been grouped into four categories, based on the way in which they

Table 6.4   A hypothetical ordering of voter preferences in a preferential election

Category of voter	No. of voters in the category	Preference ranking of candidates
I	7	Tom, Dick, Harry, Shirley
II	6	Dick, Tom, Harry, Shirley
III	5	Harry, Dick, Tom, Shirley
IV	3	Shirley, Harry, Dick, Tom

Note: 11 votes required to win (i.e. majority).
Source: Based on Brams and Fishburn (1984: 150).

ranked each of the candidates. For example, the seven voters in category I ranked Tom as their first choice, Dick as their second, Harry as their third, and Shirley as their fourth.

Since none of the candidates has an overall majority of 11 votes, the count proceeds to the next stage, by the elimination of the candidate with the fewest votes – in this case, Shirley. Shirley's three votes all transfer to Harry whose vote tally now rises to eight. Still none of the remaining candidates has managed to accumulate a majority of the votes. It is now Dick's turn to be eliminated. All of his six votes transfer to Tom, giving him a grand total of 13 votes, and so he is elected.

But before Tom and his supporters can start celebrating, Dick asks for a recount. On re-sorting the ballot papers it is discovered that the ballot papers of the category IV voters were incorrectly sorted. In fact, they had all placed Tom as their first preference. Instead of ranking the candidates as Shirley, Harry, Dick and Tom, the category IV voters had ranked them as Tom, Shirley, Harry and Dick. At first glance, it looked to Tom and his supporters as if the recount was merely going to confirm his victory, because he now had a greater number of first-preference votes, an increase from seven to ten – just one short of an overall majority. In other words, the effect of the recount was to increase Tom's vote. Once the counting proceeded, however, it quickly became clear that, despite the fact that Tom's vote had risen, he was actually destined not to win the seat. Since Shirley was now found to have received no votes, the candidate with the fewest votes after count one was, in fact, Harry, with five votes. On his elimination, all five of his votes transferred to Dick, raising his vote tally to 11, an overall majority. This hypothetical example shows how the non-monotonic nature of preferential electoral systems (including STV) can work against a candidate. In this case, the increase of Tom's vote served to lose him the seat.

This issue of non-monotonicity was one of the reasons given by a British Labour Party working party on electoral reform in the early 1990s why STV would not be appropriate (Labour Party 1993; Plant 1991). A key figure advising the working party on this point was the academic, Michael Dummett, who is on record as describing STV as 'the second worst electoral system ever devised' after single member plurality (Dummett 1992). Nobody denies the non-monotonic nature of STV, or, for that matter, of other preferential systems. But the question is: just how important is this? There is no evidence to suggest that it is a common occurrence. Indeed, the Chief Electoral Officer of Northern Ireland is quite categorical in his view that 'the experience of the use of STV in Northern Ireland over the past 22 years, involving a range of election types and sizes, reveals no evidence to support *in practice* the lack of monotonicity' (Bradley, 1995: 47, emphasis in the original). Michael Gallagher (1999: 145–6) has found some small evidence of non-monotonic results in recent Irish Republic elections. A statistical test of the issue has produced the prediction that, were STV to be used in the UK, there would be 'less than one incidence every century of monotonicity failure' (Allard 1995: 49; though see Dummett 1997: 103). Furthermore, it should be pointed out that even if non-monotonicity can on some occasions produce an unfair STV election result, surely, on the scale of things, the overall election result is *always* going to be fairer than under non-proportional electoral systems.

6.4   Conclusion

STV has a lot to recommend it. Of all systems it goes furthest towards removing the power of the party elites to determine which of their candidates are elected. Under SMP a voter can only vote for the one party candidate nominated. Under closed list systems, the voter cannot even vote for candidates: the rank ordering is determined by the party elite who drew up the lists. In contrast, STV gives the voter great scope 'to choose between candidates on personal as well as party grounds, and his [*sic*] choice overrides that of any party organization' (Lakeman 1974: 150). In this sense it can be judged a highly democratic system.

STV incorporates a central role for constituency representation. More than that, in most cases it actually permits the possibility that voters for the main parties will have one (or two) constituency representatives they can approach – the problem of 'safe' seats should not arise. While STV counting procedures may be more complex and long-winded, the actual process of voting should not present any great difficulties for the average voter. For instance, with one exception, there is no significant evidence of any greater number of spoiled votes in STV systems. The exception is Australia which traditionally has had high numbers of spoiled, or 'informal', votes, and with good reason (McAllister and Makkai 1993). Australian voters have to contend with a confusing array of electoral systems for the different levels of elections, combined with a national tendency for regular electoral reform (perhaps only France alters its electoral system more frequently). Furthermore, the voters are expected, by law, to turn out to vote. And, prior to 1984, they were also forced to fill out every preference on the Senate ballot paper. The introduction of 'ticket voting' in 1984 – when voters were given the option of simply marking one preference against their favoured party, letting the rank ordering be decided by the party elite – did much to reduce the level of spoiled votes.

There are two other points in support of the argument that STV is not too confusing for voters. First, in the cases in Britain where it has been experimented with in 'mock-ballot surveys', or discussed in focus groups, the respondents appear to have had little difficulty in mastering it (Bowler and Farrell 1996; Farrell and Gallagher 1999; though see Dunleavy *et al.* 1998). Second, it has a popular following in those countries where it is currently being used. For instance, as we have seen, on two occasions the Irish voters were asked in a referendum whether they would like to replace STV with SMP. On both occasions, particularly the later, the answer was 'No'.

Evidently, there are many points that can be made in support of STV. However, it suffers from one major problem: the fact that 'it has been used in so few countries [means] that possible problem areas may remain untested' (Taagepera and Shugart 1989: 237). Technical problems (such as non-monotonicity) could turn out to be serious, though this is unlikely. There is also the question of constituency size. It might be argued that what works in Ireland and Malta (and, with some significant amendments, in Australia), may not necessarily work so well in, say, Britain, France or Germany. However, is there really any reason to suppose that population size should matter? Surely, STV can work just as easily in a system with 130 five-seat constituencies as it does in one with 30 five-seat constituencies, and therefore to invoke a size argument as one reason why not to employ STV in highly populated systems is a red herring.

Ultimately, of course, any judgements on this or any other electoral system must be based on a thorough examination of its consequences for the wider political system, an issue to which we now turn.

7

The Consequences of Electoral Systems

Electoral systems have consequences for the political systems in which they operate. The truth of this statement is revealed in the burgeoning literature on electoral systems which seeks to show precisely what these consequences are. This chapter explores the main findings of these studies, addressing the areas of disagreement between the authors. As we shall see, a number of consequences of electoral systems have been identified, among them the effects on proportionality, on numbers of parties, and on the representation of women and minorities. These are dealt with in the first three sections.

In addition to the *systemic* effects of electoral systems, which are all related in some way to their proportionality profiles, there has been increasing interest in the *strategic* effects of electoral systems, in terms of both how voters use them (for example, tactical and ticket-splitting) and how parties are affected by them (for example, variations in campaign style). Here, the attention is less on the question of proportionality (for the most part affected by district magnitude and electoral formula) and its consequences, and much more on the issue of the mechanics of the vote, which, for the most part, is affected by ballot structure. These strategic effects of electoral systems are considered in section 7.4.

7.1 Proportionality Profiles of Different Electoral Systems

How proportional are PR systems? The principal advantage which PR systems are supposed to have over non-PR systems is that, on average, they produce more proportional results: that is, they minimize the distortion between the number of votes a party wins and the number of seats it ends up with in parliament. The previous chapters provided evidence in support of this picture. When we looked at the percentage differences between votes and seats, the ranking between the different systems appeared to tally with expectations: that is, single member plurality and the majoritarian systems produced the largest percentage differences; single transferable vote, list and the mixed member proportional systems produced the smallest.

It is now time to produce more systematic evidence, to apply a more rigorous test across a large range of different electoral systems in various countries over a common period of time. This way we can get a true picture not only of whether, indeed, PR systems produce more proportional results than non-PR systems, but also about which of the different PR systems is the more proportional.

Of course, things are not as easy as they may seem. The comparative assessment of the proportionality of electoral systems has been dominated by a series of debates (sometimes rancorous) over methodology: first, on the issue of which factors most affect levels of proportionality, and second, on the issue of which is the most appropriate index to adopt. Given the disagreement over measuring techniques, there should be little surprise that this produces different rankings for the various electoral systems.

For the most part, questions about the factors influencing proportionality revolve around the three main dimensions of electoral systems which have been used throughout this study: electoral formula, district magnitude and ballot structure. The seminal work by Douglas Rae in the 1960s produced the finding that the electoral formula has some effect on proportionality, district magnitude has an even greater effect, and ballot structure has no effect. For a long time there was little disagreement with these general conclusions. However, recent research by Lijphart (1990, 1994a) indicates that ballot structure may also have some role. In addition, Lijphart adds a few other factors to the list of influences on proportionality, of which the most significant is assembly size, with larger parliaments being statistically associated with higher degrees of proportionality.

For a long time there has also been general agreement that district magnitude is 'the decisive factor' in determining proportionality (Taagepera and Shugart 1989: 112; also Lijphart 1994a). However, recent research by Richard S. Katz (1997a) suggests a more complex picture. His comprehensive analysis indicates that, if anything, the electoral formula is more important than district magnitude in separating proportional from non-proportional systems. According to Katz, it is only when we start trying to distinguish the different proportional electoral systems on their own that district magnitude features as the more important determinant. In these cases, 'differences among formulas are nearly irrelevant' (Katz 1997a: 137).

In general, there has been quite a degree of uncertainty over how to rank the different electoral formulas. In particular, there is a problem over how to include STV in any evaluation. As Lijphart (1986a) has observed, for this reason many simply ignore STV altogether and focus instead on the list systems. Here there is general agreement that the largest remainder systems are the most proportional, followed by Sainte-Laguë, with d'Hondt bringing up the rear (Lijphart 1986a; Loosemore and Hanby 1971; Rae 1967; see Chapter 4, pp. 71–9, for descriptions of these systems).

The problems with assessing the proportionality of STV are twofold. First, the relatively low level of district magnitude (at least as used in Ireland, which is the usual focus of attention, and whose constituencies are never more than five-seat), means that STV tends to be labelled as less proportional, or – as the phrase goes – 'quasi-proportional' (Taagepera and Shugart 1989: 207; Katz 1984). One way around this problem is simply to ignore district magnitude and instead focus on the theoretical aspects of how the different electoral formulas vary over proportionality. This is the approach adopted by Jean Blondel (1969); however, his conclusion that STV is the most proportional of the PR systems (and that largest remainder is the least) has not found general support.

The second problem with STV is that quintessentially it is a candidate-based system: unlike the list systems where voters are choosing between different parties, under STV voters choose between different candidates on the ballot paper. There are difficulties, therefore, in assessing STV with measures of proportionality which are based on vote and seat shares for *parties*. In consequence, as Rae (1967: 38) notes: 'It is not quite clear how this arrangement is likely to compare with other PR formulae'. And, rather than attempting a specific rank for STV, Rae (1967: 111) can only conclude that 'in general, [it] behaves like any other sort of proportional representation. It operates quite proportionally'. Lijphart (1994a: 159) suggests a way around the problem. He makes the 'simplifying assumption' that voters cast their votes entirely within party lines (which is pretty much the case in Malta), and that therefore the vote can be construed as a 'party-vote'. This leads to the following ranking of the main PR formulas, from most to least proportional:

- largest remainder Hare; Sainte-Laguë
- largest remainder Droop; single transferable vote; modified Sainte-Laguë
- d'Hondt; largest remainder Imperiali

This ranking is based on a theoretical assessment of the likely electoral outcomes from using each of these formulas. The problem next becomes one of how to assess the degree to which reality matches up with theory. *Prima facie*, it might appear a relatively straightforward exercise to plot the trends in proportionality for each of these formulas across a range of countries over time. In fact, it is not so simple, and for two main reasons. First, we need access to a suitable measure, or index, of proportionality. Second, we need a ranking which can take account of all the possible influences on proportionality, not just electoral formula, but also district magnitude and other lesser influences like assembly size. Both of these issues have featured prominently in the literature on electoral system effects (for a review, see Lijphart 1994a).

Over the years, a number of different measures of proportionality have been developed by Rae (1967), Loosemore and Hanby (1971), Gallagher (1991), and Lijphart (1994a – the largest-deviation index). This is not the place to go into the pros and cons of each of them. In his comprehensive overview, Lijphart (1994a: 67) finds that all four indices are 'highly and significantly correlated'; but he has a clear preference for Gallagher's index.[1] Table 7.1 makes use of the Gallagher index to rank the proportionality of electoral systems used in the 59 democracies listed in Table 1.2 during the 1990s. (Strictly speaking, the ranking is of levels of 'disproportionality': those countries with lowest levels of disproportionality are located towards the top.) Given the debates over the relative influences on proportionality of district magnitude and electoral formula, information on both factors are included in the table.

When we look first at the different electoral formulas, in some respects the rankings in Table 7.1 work pretty much as expected. For

Rank and country	New/old democracy[a]	Electoral formula[b]	District magnitude type[c]	Level of disproportionality[d]	Effective number of parliamentary parties[e]	Women MPs[f] (%)
1. South Africa	New	LR Droop[g]	C	0.24	2.18	30.0
2. Benin	New	LR Hare	B	1.00	6.8	6.0
3. Denmark	Old	LR Hare[g]	C	1.55	4.54	37.4
4. Netherlands	Old	d'Hondt	C	1.58	5.12	36.0
5. Uruguay	New	LR Hare	C	1.67	3.14	12.1
6. Austria	Old	LR Hare[h]	B	1.87	3.54	26.8
7. Israel	Old	LR Hare	C	1.96	6.23	11.7
8. Malawi	New	Plurality	A	2.00	2.7	8.3
9. Slovakia[i]	New	d'Hondt	C	2.12	4.75	12.7
10. Sweden	Old	M. Sainte-Laguë[g]	C	2.13	3.99	42.7
11. Slovenia[i]	New	LR Hare[h]	B	2.50	5.52	7.8
12. Colombia	Old	LR Hare	B	3.11	3.07	11.8
13. Belgium	Old	d'Hondt[g]	B	3.12	8.54	23.3
14. Germany	Old	LR-Hare[g]	C	3.38	3.31	30.9
15. Switzerland	Old	d'Hondt	B	3.62	5.82	22.5
16. Latvia[i]	New	Sainte-Laguë	B	3.71	5.49	17.0
17. Bulgaria[i]	New	d'Hondt	C	3.73	2.52	10.8
18. Venezuela[i]	Old	d'Hondt	B	3.76	4.74	12.1
19. Bolivia[i]	New	d'Hondt	B	3.86	5.36	11.5
20. Finland	Old	d'Hondt	B	3.91	5.09	37.0
21. Norway	Old	M. Sainte-Laguë[g]	B	3.92	4.20	36.4
22. New Zealand	Old[j]	Sainte-Laguë	C	4.36	3.76	29.2
23. Costa Rica	Old	n.c.	B	4.42	2.26	19.3
24. Portugal	Old	d'Hondt	B	5.07	2.47	18.7
25. Czech Republic[i]	New	d'Hondt	B	5.20	3.71	15.0
26. Brazil[i]	New	d'Hondt	B	5.34	9.35	5.7

Table 7.1 Continued

Rank and country	New/ old democracy[a]	Electoral formula[b]	District magnitude type[c]	Level of disproportionality[d]	Effective number of parliamentary parties[e]	Women MPs[f] (%)
27. Ireland	Old	STV	B	5.39	3.22	12.0
28. USA	Old	Plurality	A	5.43	1.95	13.3
29. Spain	Old	d'Hondt	B	6.36	2.70	21.6
30. Italy[j]	Old[j]	Plurality/LR-Hare	B	7.00	6.6	11.1
31. Mexico[i]	New	Plurality/LR-Hare	B	7.08	2.86	18.2
31. Greece	Old	LR-Droop[h]	B	7.08	2.29	6.3
32. Chile[i]	New	d'Hondt	B	7.09	5.19	10.8
33. India	Old	Plurality	A	7.22	4.72	8.4
34. Poland[i]	New	d'Hondt	B	9.79	2.95	13.0
35. Mozambique	New	d'Hondt	B	9.85	2.1	n.a.
36. Papua New Guinea[i]	Old	Plurality	A	9.86	10.83	1.8
37. Russia	New	Plurality/LR-Hare	B	10.00	9.10	10.2
38. Australia	Old	Majoritarian	A	10.31	2.46	22.4
39. Philippines[i]	New	n.c.	B	10.48	3.05	12.4
40. South Korea[i]	Old[j]	Plurality/LR Hare	B	10.62	3.13	3.7
41. Japan	New	Plurality/d'Hondt	B	10.78	2.9	4.6
42. Nepal[i]	New	Plurality	A	12.75	2.40	5.9
43. Lithuania[i]	New	Major./LR Hare	B	14.19	3.54	17.5
44. United Kingdom	Old	Plurality	A	15.19	2.20	18.4
45. Canada	Old	Plurality	A	15.49	2.66	20.6
46. Mongolia[i]	New	Plurality	A	16.33	1.85	7.9
47. France	Old	Majoritarian	A	21.37	3.20	10.9
48. Jamaica	Old	Plurality	A	26.27	1.34	13.3
Argentina	New	d'Hondt	B	n.a.	n.a.	28.0
Bangladesh[i]	New	Plurality	A	n.a.	2.51	9.1

Ecuador	New	LR Hare	B	n.a.	n.a.	17.4
Hungary[j]	New	Plurality/LR Droop	B	n.a.	3.43	8.3
Madagascar[i]	New	LR Hare	B	n.a.	4.00	8.0
Mali[i]	New	Majoritarian	A	n.a.	1.31	12.2
Panama[i]	New	LR Hare	B	n.a.	3.24	n.a.
Taiwan[i]	New	SNTV/LR Hare	B	n.a.	2.46	n.a.
Thailand[i]	New	Plurality	B	n.a.	4.32	5.6
Ukraine[i]	New	Plurality/LR Hare	B	n.a.	5.26	7.8

Notes: The countries are ranked by level of disproportionality. This table is based on the most recent information available from published sources and electoral systems specialists. In some cases sources conflict, and I have made a best guess. I would be grateful for any corrections from readers.

n.a. Not available.

n.c. Not (easily) classifiable.

[a] 'Old' = a democracy for at least 20 (uninterrupted years).

[b] In the cases of mixed member majoritarian systems (as defined in Table 5.5), both electoral formulas are included.

[c] This is a rough threefold classification, as follows: C = (effective) nationwide seat allocation; A = district magnitude of 1; B = all district magnitudes between these two extremes.

[d] The Gallagher (least squares) index of disproportionality. The higher the figure the greater the disproportionality. The Gallagher index is derived as follows: square the vote–seat differences for each party (ignoring 'others'); sum the results; divide the total by two; take the square root. In most cases, this shows average trends in the 1990s; where information is limited, disproportionality in the most recent election in the 1990s is reported (see note i below).

[e] The Laakso/Taagepera index of effective number of parliamentary parties (ENP). This is based on both the number of parties and their relative sizes. The index is derived as follows: one divided by the sum of the squared percentage seats for each party represented in parliament. In most cases, this shows average trends in the 1990s; where information is limited, ENP in the most recent election in the 1990s is reported (see note i below).

[f] Percentage of women MPs at the end of the 1990s.

[g] A two-tiered system using 'adjustment seats'. In this case the higher tier is decisive, so this has been selected (see Lijphart 1994a: Table 2.5).

[h] A two-tiered system using 'remainder transfers'. In this case the lower tier is decisive, so this has been selected (see Lijphart 1994a: Table 2.4).

[i] Trends reported based only on most recent election in the 1990s.

[j] Recently changed electoral system.

Sources: Gallagher *et al.* 2000; LeDuc *et al.* 1996; Lijphart 1994a; Mozaffar 1997; Shugart and Wattenberg (eds) 2000; International Foundation for Election Systems (www.ifes.org); Derksen's Elections Around the World (www.agora.stm.it/elections); Inter-Parliamentary Union (www.ipu.org/wmn-e/world.htm); personal communication with Michael Gallagher, Arend Lijphart and Matthew Shugart.

instance, the non-proportional systems (SMP and the majoritarian systems) are for the most part located towards the bottom of the table, as indeed are many of the mixed member majoritarian systems (indicated in the table by two electoral formulas; for more details, see Table 5.5). The only striking exception is Malawi whose average disproportionality in the 1990s was 2.00. Once we start trying to distinguish average disproportionality trends among the proportional electoral formulas, however, the picture becomes more complex, thus lending some support to Katz's contention (recited above) that, when examining PR systems on their own, 'differences among formulas are nearly irrelevant' (1997a: 137).

In an attempt to assess the validity of Katz's argument, and at the same time, to provide a 'real-world' test of Lijphart's ranking of different electoral formulas, the average levels of disproportionality for each of the electoral formulas are presented in Table 7.2. In some respects the electoral formulas are ranked appropriately. Certainly the location of the plurality (12.28) and majoritarian (15.84) systems at the bottom of the table, with double-digit disproportionality scores, is entirely as expected. Equally the location of largest remainder Hare at the top of the table (2.13), and largest remainder Droop (3.66), modified Sainte-Laguë (3.03) and, at a stretch, STV (5.39) at a sort of mid-point fits with Lijphart's ranking.

However, in some other respects, the electoral formulas arrayed in Table 7.2 do not quite fit Lijphart's rankings. In particular Sainte-Laguë (4.04) should really be located towards the top and certainly above modified Sainte-Laguë, while the positions of d'Hondt and STV should be reversed. There are two good reasons why the rankings in Table 7.2 do not quite fit those predicted by Lijphart. First, in some cases we are dealing with very few countries: we need to make allowance for the fact that some other factor might be affecting overall proportionality in those cases. Relatedly, but more generally, it could also be the case that variations in district magnitude (which, as discussed above, is seen generally – particularly by Katz (1997a) when distinguishing proportional systems – as having a greater effect on proportionality) may be distorting the trends.

The relationship between district magnitude and proportionality is shown quite clearly in Table 7.3 where the countries in Table 7.1 have been regrouped into ranges of district magnitude (DM) and the average disproportionality scores are given.[2] Again, we have to allow for some 'noise' from other electoral system factors, but the overall

Table 7.2   Relationship between electoral formula and proportionality

Electoral formula	Number of countries	Average disproportionality
LR Hare	8	2.13
Modified Sainte-Laguë	2	3.03
LR Droop	2	3.66
Sainte-Laguë	2	4.04
d'Hondt	15	4.96
STV	1	5.39
Plurality	9	12.28
Majoritarian	2	15.84

Sources: As for Table 7.1.

Table 7.3   Relationship between district magnitude and proportionality

District magnitude	Number of countries	Average disproportionality
A: 1	11	12.93
B: Greater than 1, less than 'nationwide'	28	6.08
C: 'Nationwide'	10	2.27

Sources: As for Table 7.1.

trends are as predicted – namely, the smaller the district magnitude the greater the disproportionality.

As Douglas Rae (1967) observes, the proportionality of different electoral systems relates to their short-term, or 'proximal' effects. Electoral systems also have 'distal', or long-run, effects, as revealed by the numbers of parties in the political system and the representation of women and minorities. The next two sections deal with these in turn.

7.2   Electoral Systems and Party Systems

We might expect – almost by definition, as it were – that electoral systems which are more proportional should coincide with more fragmented party systems. In the 1950s the French political scientist Maurice Duverger (1954) put forward the proposition that non-proportional electoral systems (he referred specifically to single member plurality) 'favour' two-party systems, while proportional electoral systems 'favour' multi-party systems. There are two parts to this argument, which can be summarized by looking at the case of non-proportional electoral systems. First, there is the fact that, because it is more difficult for smaller parties to win seats under non-PR systems, the *mechanics* of these systems are bound to result in fewer parties in parliament. Second, there is also a *psychological* aspect, in the sense that voters are aware of the fact that a vote for a smaller party is a wasted vote and therefore they are less inclined to bother voting for them, thereby further compounding the difficulties for smaller parties (Blais and Carty 1991).

Duverger's propositions have spawned a fascinating debate between political scientists over the issue of whether they should be considered to have lawlike status (for a sample, see Duverger 1986; Riker 1986; Sartori 1986). The principal point at issue is that of causality: is multi-partyism a consequence or a cause of proportionality? For instance, there are plenty of historical examples of multi-party systems which preceded the decision to opt for a PR electoral system; among them are Belgium, Denmark, Germany and Norway. In his comprehensive review of the debate between 'institutionalists' (like Duverger, who see multi-partyism as a consequence) and 'sociologists' (who see it as a 'cause'), Gary Cox (1997: 13–27) concludes that for all their shortcomings, Duverger's propositions are of value in assessing questions of strategic coordination under different electoral systems.

In short, then, while clearly there is a 'chicken and egg' problem over causality, this should not distract us from the fact that wherever there is a proportional electoral system there is a greater likelihood of finding more parties represented in the parliament, and wherever there is a non-proportional electoral system, we are more likely to find a two-party system. Obvious examples of the latter include the US Congress, dominated by the Republicans and the Democrats, and the UK House of Commons, dominated by the Conservatives and Labour.

Of course, given that in the British case there are clearly more than two parties in the parliament – in fact, at the time of writing there are nine – this indicates the need for appropriate 'counting rules' for parties. Markku Laakso and Rein Taagepera have devised an index which measures the 'effective' number of parliamentary parties (EPP), based on the number of parties in parliament and their different sizes.[3] Using this index, for instance, the current UK party system can be characterized as a '2.20-party system', reflecting the small presence of the Liberal Democrats and the various Nationalist parties.

Table 7.1 provides the EPP scores across a range of countries. While, in the detail, there are cases where we find more parties than would be expected (for example, non-proportional France with 3.20 parties) or fewer parties than expected (for example, proportional South Africa with 2.18 parties), for the most part the scores fit in well with expectations: those countries using non-proportional electoral systems average 3.18 parties, while the PR countries average 4.34 parties (see also Gallagher *et al.* 2000; Lijphart 1994a: 96).

In their test of Duverger's propositions, Taagepera and Shugart (1989: 142–55) produce convincing evidence that the relationship between the electoral system and the party system is not based simply on a dichotomy between non-proportional and proportional electoral systems; rather, they suggest a continuous relationship in which the number of parties becomes greater as the disproportionality of the system reduces. We can see this inverse relationship in Table 7.4, which reports summary averages. Countries with disproportional trends of less than 4 have an average of 4.60 parliamentary parties; by contrast, countries with far higher disproportionality

Table 7.4   The effects of electoral system proportionality on the numbers of parties and the proportion of women legislators

Disproportionality range	Number of countries	Average effective number of parliamentary parties	Average (%) women MPs
0.22–3.92	21	4.60	21.18
4.36–9.86	16[a]	4.19	13.63
10.00+	12	3.15	12.32

[a] The percentage of women MPs in Mozambique is not available, so for purposes of calculating average proportion of women MPs, N = 15.
Sources: As for Table 7.1.

trends (10+) average 3.15 parliamentary parties (the correlation is −0.28).

In a recent essay, Rein Taagepera (1997) refers to the possibility of Duverger's propositions operating quite differently in newer democracies. The reasoning behind this 'counter-Duvergerian psychological effect' is both simple and persuasive. In new democracies operating with proportional systems, small parties may be encouraged to run in the hope of picking up some parliamentary seats, thus artificially inflating disproportionality because many of them are unsuccessful. Taagepera suggests that 'The problem can be especially acute in recently established democracies, where lack of previous elections deprives party leaders of a realistic base line for evaluating their chances' (1997: 55). Similar (albeit somewhat more tenuous) reasoning might be thought to apply, in reverse, in the case of non-proportional systems, in which we may find disproportionality deflated by the decision of smaller parties not to bother running.

It is possible to test Taagepera's idea by comparing the disproportionality trends in old (at least 20 uninterrupted years) and new democracies, the suggestion being that in the latter case the disproportionality trends are affected by the numbers of parties in the race – more than usual in proportional systems, less than usual in non-proportional systems. The evidence in Table 7.5 provides some support for this: disproportionality is, indeed, higher than average in

Table 7.5   Testing Taagepera's 'counter-Duvergerian psychological effect'

	Number of countries	Average disproportionality
Proportional electoral systems		
New democracies	13	4.32
Old democracies	17	3.66
Non-proportional electoral systems		
New democracies	3	10.36
Old democracies	8	13.89

Notes: Proportional systems = all list, MMP and STV systems. Non-proportional systems = majoritarian and plurality systems. MMM systems are not included. 'New' and 'old' democracies are as defined in Table 7.1.
Sources: As for Table 7.1.

those new democracies using PR systems, and lower than average in those new democracies using non-PR systems.

7.3   Parliament as a 'Microcosm'?

In Chapter 1 we reviewed the debate between those who felt that the backgrounds and characteristics of members of a parliament should closely reflect the general population, and those who felt that what was more important was the abilities of the MPs and the nature of their decisions. The former view – that parliament should be a 'microcosm' of society – is held by proponents of PR; the latter – placing decisions of parliament above its composition – is held by opponents of PR. As we saw in Chapter 1, attempts to weigh the merits and demerits of either perspective ultimately come down to normative judgements: that is, if I *believe* that parliament *should* be a microcosm of society then I will *prefer* PR to non-PR systems. It is difficult to provide empirical evidence to support either perspective; although, as we shall see in Chapter 9, there may be empirical grounds for suggesting that PR systems on the whole have more beneficial effects on society than do non-PR systems.

One area where an empirical test can be applied is over the issue of whether indeed PR systems do produce a socially more representative parliament, that is, whether PR does fulfil its microcosmic role in producing a parliament whose composition more closely reflects society than is the case under non-proportional systems. Certainly it has long been the view of those scholars supporting PR that one of its principal merits is that it produces a socially more representative parliament. As we saw in Chapter 2, this has been one of the key points raised in ongoing US debates over electoral reform. In the light of US Supreme Court decisions since the early 1990s affecting the ability to use redistricting measures to help elect legislators from ethnic minority communities, attention has shifted to using electoral systems (such as cumulative or limited vote systems) as an alternative means of increasing the proportion of legislators from minority communities (Engstrom 1998; Ritchie and Hill 1999).

A similar debate has occurred over the representation of women. Scholars like Enid Lakeman (1982), Wilma Rule (1987), and Pippa Norris (1985) stress the role played by PR in promoting the greater representation of women in parliament. Certainly the evidence seems to support this case, as can be seen from the final column in Table 7.1. In general, the lowest representation of women is in those systems ranked low on the index of proportionality. The average representation of women in the 1990s (in the 46 countries for which information is available)[4] is 17.0 per cent: in PR systems this rises to 17.7 per cent; in non-PR system it plummets to 13.5 per cent. Table 7.4 shows clear evidence of the relationship between electoral system proportionality and the proportion of women in parliament: as disproportionality increases there is a downward trend in the proportion of women MPs (and the correlation is –0.32). Furthermore, recent research by Matland and Studlar (1996) suggests that this PR/non-PR dichotomy may be increasing over time.

Inevitably there are some countries where the representation of women is lower or higher than would be expected. For instance, the higher-than-average proportion of women legislators in non-proportional Britain (18.4 per cent) reflects the British Labour Party's use of party quotas before the 1997 election. Canada (20.6 per cent) is commonly also higher than the norm for non-PR systems, reflecting a high turnover in the membership of the parliament (Norris 1996). More generally, it is pretty clear that there is an element of regional patterning to the trends, as shown most clearly in the case of the Scandinavian countries, all of which are well above the average. This raises a question over whether it is actually the electoral system which affects the representation of women, or whether there are perhaps some other factors. On the whole, political scientists are in agreement that the electoral system does indeed play a very important role in affecting the proportion of women legislators in parliament, but other factors are also significant, such as economic development, region, and trends within the political parties (Beckwith 1992; Caul 1999; Darcy *et al.* 1994; Norris 1996; Rule 1987).

But exactly how does an electoral system affect the proportion of women in parliament? Clearly there must be more to this than simply the fact that one system produces a more proportional result than another. Ultimately the issue boils down to those features of the electoral system which influence the number and range of candidates being fielded by political parties. Therefore, where average district magnitude is large (that is, in multi-member regions), we should expect greater scope for parties to field more women candidates, allowing for a more balanced ticket, without fearing the upsetting of traditionalists. Similarly, under party list systems (particularly those which restrict the degree of preferential voting), we should expect greater scope for balancing the party ticket. On the whole, cross-national research supports these expectations: electoral systems incorporating large district magnitudes and PR list systems are associated with higher proportions of women MPs (Norris 1996; Rule 1987).

By implication, the attitudes of political parties and their 'selectorates' is crucial here. Certainly this has been seen as one reason why the STV's record on women's representation has been so poor. Given that the only two countries to use STV for lower house elections are Ireland (12.0 per cent women MPs) and Malta (9.2 per cent), both of which have relatively traditionalist political cultures, it is possible to lay some of the blame for the lower-than-average representation of women in their parliaments on 'the failure of party elites to recruit them in greater numbers' (Lane 1995: 152; see also Hirczy 1995; Rule 1994, 1996). In other words, it is not the electoral system which is at fault so much as the party selection committees (also Kelley and McAllister 1983).

In an attempt to tease out the precise role of district magnitude, there has been research focused on cases where there are significant variations in district magnitude in the same country, thus allowing the researcher to 'control' for other electoral system features, economic development and political culture. On the whole the research supports the argument that size of constituency matters, although there is some disagreement over the strength or consistency of the relationship (Darcy *et al.* 1994; Engstrom 1987; Welch and Studlar 1990). In the words of Studlar and Welch (1991: 465): 'the impact of multi-member districts on women's electability has neither been as universal nor as significant as the advocates of electoral reform sometimes assume. The case is still, in Scottish parlance, "not proven".'

If the objective is to seek to engineer a greater proportion of women or ethnic minorities in parliament, there are other ways of influencing the electoral laws (or party procedures) apart from switching to a PR system. For instance, in 1993 the British Labour Party introduced quota rules on the nomination of women candidates, forcing certain constituency parties to have all-women short-lists in the event of a vacancy. This was found to have a significant effect on the proportion of women entering the House of Commons in 1997 (Studlar and McAllister 1998). Similar steps have been taken by parties in other countries (Norris 1994), and Caul's research (1999) shows how the use of quotas has become more commonplace in recent years. A survey by the Inter-Parliamentary Union (1992) found that 22 parties used gender quotas for legislative elections, and 51 used them for elections to internal party posts. These measures were most common in Western Europe; tended to be adopted from the 1980s onwards; and were most associated with parties of the centre-left. Quota rules have also been used to ensure the better representation of minority groupings.

An alternative method is to provide a certain number of parliamentary seats for minorities, as is the case of the Maori seats in New Zealand (Lijphart 1986b). Another example is Ireland in the 1920s–30s when the upper house of the parliament included a number of seats for Protestants, designed as a means of placating the minority population in what was predominantly a Catholic state. As was suggested in Chapter 4, one other mechanical approach available in PR list systems (particularly with closed lists), is to place a certain number of women or minority candidates high on the party list (or to 'zip' the lists: man, woman, man and so on) and thereby ensure that more of them will be successfully elected (Darcy *et al.* 1994).

7.4   The Strategic Effects of Electoral Systems

In some senses, the debate on the proportionality and party system effects of electoral systems is pretty much complete; it is difficult to see what there is left to say about these issues. Accordingly, attention has started to shift to other aspects of possible electoral system influence, with particular attention given to ballot structure. It could be argued that all the issues dealt with in the previous sections share in common a concern with the macro-level effects of electoral systems, in terms of how they influence the electoral process in a global sense. An alternative perspective is to assess the micro-level effects of electoral systems. Here the concern is less with the *systemic* effects of electoral systems and more with their *strategic* effects (Cox 1997).

When considering ballot structure, so far we have tended to draw a distinction between 'categorical and 'ordinal' ballot papers. As we have seen throughout this book, this distinction is particularly useful for separating electoral systems in terms of how much 'choice' is given to voters in the system. For instance, in single member plurality (SMP) systems such as used in the UK or the closed list system used in Spain, voters have a categoric (either/or) choice to vote for one candidate (in the UK) or one party (in Spain). By contrast, under STV as used in Ireland the voters have greater flexibility to vote 'ordinally'. To an extent this latter category can also be said to include open list systems, such as used in Finland, on the grounds that the voter has free rein to determine the rank order of a party's candidates (see p. 173 below). Implicitly, it is also possible to talk of *degrees* of ordinality: STV offers greater choice to voters (where voters have as many options as there are candidates on the ballot paper) than, say, the German mixed systems (where votes have just two options).

Another way in which we might distinguish electoral systems based on ballot structure is between those systems where voting is candidate-based (such as SMP or STV) and those systems where voting is party-based (such as the list systems) (Bowler and Farrell 1993). As we shall see, such a distinction affects the degree of emphasis placed on candidates both in the campaigns of the parties and in the voting decisions of electors, among other things. In Figure 7.1 we can see how the two dimensions of distinction (relating to extent of choice and nature of choice on the ballot paper) produce four main types of electoral systems.

Given these important distinctions between different types of electoral system based on the extent and nature of choice given to voters, it can be expected that both the politicians and the voters will be influenced in their behaviour according to each type. We begin with the politicians. The variations in electoral choice can affect the role and activities of politicians in three areas: election campaigning, style of party organization and forms of parliamentary representation. In the first instance, where the system allows high levels of intra-party choice (as best represented by STV), there is a tendency for parties to campaign in a decentralized fashion; there is more emphasis on the campaigns of individual candidates; and, on occasions, this can result in faction-fighting between candidates of the same party. By contrast, if the system is categoric there is no scope for faction-fighting between candidates. And if the system is party-based, there is far less emphasis on the candidates: the campaign is run from, and about, the centre. In short, then, there are significant

Extent of choice

		Categoric	Ordinal
Nature of choice	Candidate-based	Single member plurality (UK)	Single transferable vote (Ireland)
	Party-based	Closed list (Spain)	Open list (Finland)

Figure 7.1   A typology of electoral systems based on ballot structure characteristics

differences in the nature of a party's campaign depending on the electoral system (Katz 1980).

It may also be surmised that there are effects on the nature of party organization, though to date the academic evidence is more anecdotal than systematic. In candidate-based systems there appears to be more emphasis on grassroots links, on the need for constituency parties and on internal party democracy. The centre is not so well resourced and is less in control of the party as a whole (for example, on Ireland, see Farrell 1994). In party-based systems, by contrast, the organization is traditionally much more top-down, with tighter controls imposed on branches and members (for example, on Spain, see Holliday 2001). Since the 1980s, with the process of campaign and organizational professionalization, these distinctions have been breaking down (Farrell and Webb 2000), though it is still possible to identify remnants of strong organization at the local level in candidate-based systems.

Ballot structure distinctions can also affect the nature of parliamentary representation. The debate, reviewed in Chapter 1, over the 'principal–agent' and 'microcosm' conceptions of representation, focused specifically on the question of representation in the *aggregate*, in terms of the collective assembly of parliament. An alternative perspective is to focus on the representative role of *individual* MPs. In his famous address to the voters of Bristol in 1774, Edmund Burke set out two competing concepts of the role of the representative in their constituency: as a *delegate* of the voters, or as a *trustee*.

According to the first type, MPs are said to listen closely to the views of the voters. There are even suggestions that they are 'mandated' by the voters to take certain decisions. According to the second type, the trustee role – favoured by Burke – MPs are elected to act on behalf of the constituency as a whole. They are better placed than anyone to weigh up the often conflicting views of their voters and come to a considered decision, without needing to always check back with the voters.

In party-based electoral systems, where the voter is choosing between parties and not candidates, there is little scope for mandating the politicians (apart, that is, from the mandate given to the parties), and therefore we can expect a greater tendency for politicians to act as trustees. Indeed, in such systems, the principal 'voting constituency' of the individual politician is not the voters, but rather the 'selectorates' who determine whether the politician will appear on the list, and in which rank position (Bowler *et al.* 1996). By contrast, in candidate-based electoral systems, where the MPs are clamouring for precious personal votes (in some cases, such as under STV, in direct competition with fellow party candidates), we can expect a greater tendency for MPs to act as delegates.

Evidence in support of this argument is provided by a survey of the activities of Members of the European Parliament. Given that there is a large range of different electoral systems used to elect the MEPs, the European Parliament provides a useful laboratory to test the influence of electoral systems on parliamentary representation. This study found that MEPs elected under candidate-based electoral systems – and particularly systems which were constituency-based (namely the UK and Ireland) – were more inclined to have regular contact with individual voters. By contrast, the MEPs elected under party-based systems were prone to have closer links with organized interests. The study concluded that 'individual voters are better – or at least more frequently – served by representatives elected under district based systems and where voters can choose candidates' (Bowler and Farrell 1993: 64; for an alternative perspective, see Katz 1997b).

Ballot structure can also have an effect on the strategic calculations of voters (Cox 1997: Part II). In a categoric system where voters can make only a single decision on which candidate (in the case of SMP), or party (in the case of closed list), to support, the voting exercise is relatively straightforward. The voter selects the appropriate candidate or party and votes accordingly. There is, however, some limited scope for 'tactical' voting under the SMP electoral system. Take the scenario of a voter who likes a particular candidate but knows full well that this candidate does not stand a chance of being elected. This could be a situation where the candidate in question is expected to come in a bad third in the constituency race. The voter has one of three options: to vote for the candidate anyway despite the fact that this vote will be wasted; not to bother voting; or to vote for the candidate expected to come second, on the grounds that *anyone* would be better than the sitting MP. This last option opens up the possibility of what is referred to as tactical voting. Survey evidence reveals that in the UK an increasing number of voters have been making use of this option in recent elections (Evans *et al*. 1998; Niemi *et al*. 1992).

The scope for strategic voting increases once we start to complicate the electoral process, and, in particular, when we take account of more complex electoral systems.[5] For instance, where there are different levels of election occurring at the same time, the voter can take advantage of this situation and vary their support for the different parties. This phenomenon of 'ticket-splitting' is particularly acute in the USA, where voters increasingly split their votes between the Republicans and the Democrats, providing one indicator of the extent to which American parties are 'in decline'. According to Martin P. Wattenberg (1998: 23), 'Ticket-splitting has assumed massive proportions compared to the rate just two decades ago, and only a small minority of the electorate now believes that one should vote strictly on the basis of party labels'. Ticket-splitting can be expected wherever there are two or more levels of election coinciding (for example, on the Australian case, see Bowler and Denemark 1993). It is also a feature of mixed systems. As the evidence presented in Chapter 5 revealed (see Table 5.4), over the years, the German Free Democrats have successfully exploited ticket-splitting to cushion themselves against the danger of falling below the 5 per cent threshold.

There are clear limits to the strategic options available to voters in the systems discussed so far. What is unique about preferential electoral systems – such as the alternative vote, STV, and certain types of open list systems – is that they provide such large scope for voters to express more complex and nuanced preferences. Voters can switch and change between one candidate and another at will (and, in STV, between one party and another). There is plenty of scope to retain loyalty for party X, while at the same time giving a preference to a candidate from party Y whose policies appear attractive (Bowler and Farrell 1991a, 1991b). In short, then, under preferential electoral systems (characterized by an ordinal ballot structure) there is great scope for voters to act strategically (Bowler 1996; Bowler and Farrell 1996; Darcy and Marsh 1994).

This focus on ballot structure and the strategic consequences of electoral systems suggests the potential for a very different hierarchy of electoral systems to that discussed in section 7.1. A good starting point is Shaun Bowler's (1996) discussion about the 'menu-dependence' of electoral choice. He cites the example of diners being offered a choice of three different desserts, but while they are still making their minds up the waiter informs them that one of the desserts is no longer available. A different version of this episode has the waiter suddenly inform the diners that not only are all three desserts still available but a fourth 'special' dessert is now also on the list. As Bowler observes: 'It seems clear that in either instance the choices people make are conditioned by the alternatives open to them' (1996: 114). Equally, as we have seen above, the choices are also conditioned by the *extent* of choice available to the diners: for instance, what if they are allowed to mix desserts for the same price as one?

According to Bowler (1996; also Grofman and Bowler 1996; Farrell and Gallagher 1998), it is possible to develop an entirely new categorization of electoral systems 'according to the degree of complexity they impose upon voters', in this sense thinking of electoral systems 'not so much from the parties' point of view, but from that of the voters' (1996: 118–19). In short, the emphasis here is on 'voter choice', and this could produce a ranking such as the following:

- STV: can rank all candidates from all parties
- Panachage: can vote for candidates from more than one party
- Open list: 'personal' votes determine ranking of candidates
- Mixed member: two votes – one for candidates, one for party
- Alternative vote: can rank all candidates, but only one gets elected
- Closed list: can only vote categorically for one party
- SMP: can only vote categorically for one candidate of one party

This ranking (based on Farrell and Gallagher 1998: 9) is merely illustrative. Even if we might quibble over the details, and suggest alternative rankings, the point still stands, however, that rankings based solely on the proportionality profiles of electoral systems (such as discussed in section 7.1) provide a distorted picture of the effects of electoral systems, and produce a very lopsided hierarchy. Grofman and Bowler (1996) have developed this point further, arguing:

> once we recognise that electoral systems have multiple effects it becomes a certainty that there will be no system that is best with respect to all possible criteria of evaluation. Once this is admitted, then the field of normative debate about electoral system choice is significantly broadened and the nature of the debate should be less polemic, as we move to debate the nature of appropriate trade-offs among multiple competing criteria, all of which have something to recommend them. (1996: 47; also Bowler and Grofman 2000)

7.5 Conclusion

Electoral systems have important systemic and strategic consequences. In the first case, we can distinguish between electoral systems with regard to degrees of proportionality, and in the longer term with regard to the numbers of parties in parliament and the degree to which the parliament is socially representative. In these terms, both the supporters and the opponents of PR have plenty of ammunition with which to fight their corners. Furthermore, we can produce a credible ranking of electoral systems in terms of their systemic characteristics. But, as we have seen, a very different ranking of electoral systems can be produced when we take account of their strategic effects on the political system. Here the stress is placed on the nature and extent of choice given to voters under different systems.

At the basis of these discussions of the consequences of electoral systems are questions over system stability, particularly centred around conflicting views over whether PR contributes to a strengthening or a weakening of our representative institutions. These issues are dealt with in the concluding chapter. Before getting to that, we turn, in the next chapter, to the question of choices in the adoption (and/or reform) of electoral systems.

8

Electoral Reform and the Choice of an Electoral System

In the last chapter we saw how there has been some shift in the literature on electoral systems towards studying their strategic consequences, as opposed to their systemic consequences. Another growing trend in the literature has been to deal with electoral systems in their own right, as opposed to trying to explain their consequences. Given the rush of new democracies, each of which has had to make choices over electoral system design, and the recent fashion for electoral reform in established democracies, it is understandable why political scientists should want to reverse the order of causality and seek to understand the basis for electoral system choice. In other words, the new emphasis is on looking at electoral systems themselves, rather than at their consequences, or, to use the political science jargon, treating electoral systems as 'dependent variables' rather than 'independent variables'.

Once we begin to assess electoral systems as dependent variables this opens up a range of interesting questions, three of which warrant attention here. We start, in the first section, with an assessment of why countries end up with the electoral systems they have. As we shall see, for the most part, this is affected by the proclivities of the political elite, and the choices they make in favour of certain electoral systems. Section 8.2 considers a different, more normative angle, namely, given a choice, what electoral system should a country choose? Here it is interesting to review the advice of scholars over the merits and demerits of different electoral systems. Finally, section 8.3 raises the question of whether voters should have a say over electoral system design. Do they understand enough about the complexities of electoral systems to be able to form a coherent view and, if so, what factors seem most important to them?

8.1   The Politics of Electoral System Design

Given the plethora of different electoral systems in operation throughout the world, it is difficult to escape from the conclusion that each one ultimately is the product of particular national circumstances, of the whims of particular actors. Despite the best efforts of learned electoral system specialists to offer kindly words of advice to 'electoral engineers' on specific features of existing electoral systems that might warrant incorporation (Lijphart 1994a; Taagepera and Shugart 1989; Sartori 1997), it appears difficult to disagree with Pippa Norris's (1995b: 4) observation that 'electoral systems are rarely designed, they are born kicking and screaming into the world out of a messy, incremental compromise between contending factions battling for survival, determined by power politics'.

In a recent paper exploring electoral system design in new democracies, Ben Reilly and Andrew Reynolds (1999) refer to three main 'waves', which correspond closely to Samuel Huntington's influential thesis on the 'waves of democratization' (Huntington 1991). According to Huntington, the first wave, from the 1820s to the 1920s, featured the processes of democratization in the USA and across much of Europe. The second wave was a phenomenon of post-Second World War decolonization and the rebuilding of democracies like West Germany. The ongoing third wave, starting in the 1970s, features the burgeoning new democracies of Latin America, southern Africa, Central and Eastern Europe and the former Soviet Union. Reilly and Reynolds argue persuasively that debates over electoral system adoption vary quite distinctly across these three waves, both in terms of the types of electoral systems selected, and also in terms of the ways in which the electoral systems were chosen.

In the cases of first-wave democracies, the tendency was for electoral systems to emerge gradually, very much in line with the gradual evolution of the democracies themselves. As we have seen in earlier chapters (see Chapters 2 and 4), two patterns are apparent, though here we are painting in rather broad-brush strokes (see also Carstairs 1980). First, there are the cases of Anglo-American democracies which are characterized by relatively homogenous societies, based around a single partisan cleavage and a simple two-party system (Lijphart 1999a). There was a desire by the established elite to retain maximum hold over the system, seeking to constrain the influence of minor groups and parties. Relatively early on there was a focus on territorial links, tied in with the desire of local elites to hold on to their power bases. Once the countries had settled on single member plurality systems (SMP), there was little desire for change. For the most part, attention was focused on questions regarding constituency boundary divisions and the gradual reform of the administration of elections.

Quite a different pattern occurred in the early continental European democracies, which tended to be characterized by more plural societies, lacking a single dominant group (Lijphart 1999a). In these cases, relatively early on there was recognition of the need to accommodate different groupings in the political system. At the turn of the twentieth century, the writings of prominent scholars (like d'Hondt, or Sainte-Laguë) influenced a shift towards the adoption of list systems. (As Carstairs (1980) shows, in many cases this shift from SMP to list was via a two-round majoritarian system.)

In this first wave, therefore, the evidence clearly points to a gradual, evolutionary process in the adoption of an electoral system. The system is designed by the indigenous elite. According to Reilly and Reynolds, the choice of electoral system in this first wave is characterized by some kind of mix of 'conscious design' and 'accidental evolution'. In some cases the decision is deliberate, such as Australia's decision to adopt AV in 1918 to try and prevent splits among the parties of the Right in the face of an emerging Labor Party, or the decision of the Irish Free State in the 1920s to adopt PR to help protect the minority community in the south. It is also worth drawing attention to the central importance of party politics in influencing the type of electoral system adopted, thereby lending support to the argument (referred to in the previous chapter, see p. 162) that Duverger's propositions might need to be looked at in reverse. But, of course, not all electoral systems were deliberately chosen: 'Often, choices are made through a kaleidoscope of accidents and miscommunications leading to a multitude of unintended consequences' (Reilly and Reynolds 1999: 26), such as Ireland's decision to keep STV in part, as we have seen (p. 125), due to ignorance of other PR systems, or the adoption of SNTV in 1993 by Jordan which, if anything, has contributed to the rise of Islamic fundamentalism (Reynolds and Elklit 1997).

Huntington's second wave is much shorter than the other two: it is focused on the postwar decades which saw the reestablishment of some democracies and the process of decolonization, which produced a spate of new democracies. According to Reilly and Reynolds (1999), two central features of electoral system design in this wave were 'colonial inheritance' and 'external imposition', both obviously involving a significant role played by external elites. Shaheen Mozaffar (1997) concurs. Both sets of authors find a clear set of regional patterning in the selection of electoral system, coinciding with historical colonial links. For instance, according to Reilly and Reynolds, 37 out of the 53 former British colonies use SMP. (It is also worth noting over the years the influence of British electoral reformers in the adoption of STV in some other former British colonies; see Farrell 2000). The plurality (11/27) of francophone territories use French two-round systems, and most of the remainder use PR list (also used for certain elections in France). Former Spanish and Portuguese territories tend to use list systems. Mozaffar also refers to the role of South Africa in influencing the adoption of PR list by countries within its sphere of influence.

Needless to say, of course, the electoral system adopted in these former colonies may not actually be very appropriate to meet the needs of the particular country, 'as the begetting colonial power was usually very different socially and culturally from the society colonized' (Reilly and Reynolds 1999: 24). The same criticism need not apply in those cases where an electoral system has been imposed on a country by an external power in order to meet a specific purpose. The best example of electoral system design resulting from 'external imposition' is postwar (West) Germany, in which the allied powers played an important role in the adoption of the mixed system, which was designed to avoid the apparent mistakes of the Weimar period when extreme proportionality was said to have influenced the instability of the system, and also to incorporate some of the supposed 'strengths' of the Anglo-American constituency-based system. Reilly and Reynolds (1999) refer also to the case of Namibia in the 1980s where PR was adopted rather than SMP as a means of trying to calm warring factions.

The ongoing third wave of democratization has produced some new patterns of electoral system adoption. A central feature of this wave has been conscious design. According to Reilly and Reynolds, this wave has 'seen a new appreciation of the necessity for and utility of well-crafted electoral systems as a key constitutional choice for new democracies' (1999: 25). They refer to the cases of democratic transition in Hungary, Bolivia, South Africa, Korea, Taiwan and Fiji, among a host of other cases, where there has been extensive discussion and debate about the merits of particular electoral systems. This is not to deny the fact, however, that such a process involves close bargaining between competing elites (Nohlen 1997) and that the system which emerges may, indeed, have required some 'messy compromise' (Norris 1995b; Taagepera 1998). Furthermore, there is also the point that many of these third-wave countries have far from completed the process of democratization (Rose and Chull Shin 1999), and therefore further electoral reform in the future cannot be ruled out (Reilly and Reynolds 1999; Taagepera 1998).

Once we start to consider the question of reforming existing electoral systems, this introduces a relatively recent 'fourth wave' of cases of electoral system design. Electoral reform in established democracies used to be a rarity. For a long time, only France seemed to be prone to pretty regular change of its electoral systems; there were few other cases. In this context, Dieter Nohlen was quite correct in his observation that electoral reform was very uncommon, occurring only in 'extraordinary historical circumstances' (1984: 218). Of course, given the 'messy' nature of electoral reform (as stressed by Pippa Norris 1995b), it seems fair to ask what would cause a country with a long-established electoral system to go down this route? Up until relatively recently it appeared as if it would require something very significant to force electoral reform: the bias was very much in favour of keeping the existing electoral system regardless of its faults. The abiding principle was: 'Familiarity breeds stability' (Taagepera and Shugart 1989: 218). According to Dunleavy and Margetts (1995: 11), such a view reflected an 'orthodoxy' in the literature favouring the *status quo*, and, they continue, 'Seen against this type of argument, 1993–94 appears as an *annus mirabilis* in which three established liberal democracies – Italy, Japan, and New Zealand – radically changed their voting systems.'

It is difficult to establish exactly what has caused electoral reform to become so high on the agenda of politics. In a review of the debates in Israel, Italy, Japan, New Zealand and the UK, Pippa Norris (1995b: 7) discerns three long-term factors which these countries (or some combination of them) share in common, and which, at least in part, appear to have played a role in triggering demands for electoral reform: (1) electoral change (and, in particular, the weakening of electoral alignments); (2) 'political scandals and/or government failures which rock public confidence in the political system'; and (3) the ability of voters (in Italy and New Zealand) to use referendums to force the hands of politicians. Norris comments: 'Long-term conditions created the potential for change, and electoral reform is seen as completing a process of democratization which would put an end to deep-rooted failures in the political system.'

Dunleavy and Margetts (1995) distinguish between 'plurality rule' countries and PR countries, and they suggest that the specific motivations for change have been influenced by the nature of the existing electoral system in each case. In the case of plurality countries, the process of electoral change – and, specifically, the rise of new parties – increased the disproportional tendencies of the electoral system, as well as the amount of attention to these disproportional tendencies. As has been discussed in Chapter 2, the SMP system can operate quite proportionally in a two-party system, such as the USA. But as the system becomes more fragmented (for example, as shown by the increased vote of the Liberals/Liberal Democrats in the UK), the inherent disproportional tendencies of the electoral system become evident.

In PR countries, the push for electoral reform has had different root causes. Here, by definition, there is less concern about the proportionality of the system. According to Dunleavy and Margetts (1995), there is, instead, a concern about questions of accountability and parliamentary representation, relating either to the large electoral districts in PR list systems, or the degree of party control over the candidate lists. They refer to four cases: Italy, Japan, Israel and the Netherlands. While in general this is a credible argument, one can take issue with certain aspects of detail. For instance, the (now replaced) Japanese SNTV system could hardly be categorized as 'proportional' (see Chapter 2, p. 47), and the catalyst for change in Italy and Japan had rather more to do with issues of political corruption generally than with the specifics of parliamentary accountability.

What is apparent from the recent wave of electoral reform in established democracies is two things they share in common: (1) a preference for some form of mixed system (Shugart and Wattenberg

2000b), and (2) evidence that, to varying degrees, the mass public has had some input into the process of electoral system selection: that is, the choice of which electoral system to adopt was not the sole decision of the political elite.

8.2 Conflicting Academic Advice to Electoral Engineers

Electoral reform is now a much more realistic proposition than it was in the early 1990s. Some countries have changed their system, and others are considering it. It is therefore both relevant and important to review academic debates over electoral system design. Scholars tend to break down into two main camps, those who suggest that it is inappropriate for political scientists to advise on electoral system design, and those who are quite prepared to proffer such advice. The latter, in turn, are divided between those who believe the aim should be for 'simple' electoral systems, and those who tend to favour more complex electoral systems.

Prominent among those arguing that there is no place for political scientists in advising on electoral system design is Richard S. Katz, whose recent tome on *Democracy and Elections* places heavy stress on the contingent nature of electoral system design. This leads Katz to conclude that the choice on which is the best electoral system for a given country ultimately 'depends' on 'who you are, where you are, and where you want to go' (1997a: 308). In his most recent essay on this topic, Katz (1999) develops this point further, arguing for caution in predicting the likely consequences of the transference of a given electoral system from one country to another.

In his essay on 'the tailor of Marrakesh' (who suggested to his clients that a poorly fitting suit was alright providing it was fashionable), Rein Taagepera (1997, 1998) takes issue with the view that there is no place for political scientists in advising on electoral system design. Taagepera's mantra is to be cautious in electoral system design, recognizing that, like a good suit, electoral system design needs to be adaptive to a given political environment. Taagepera is not alone in seeing a role for political scientists as advisers to political engineers. In fact, among the current brood of scholars writing on electoral systems, the greater bulk of them are at some point prepared to stick their neck out and express a preference for a specific electoral system. There is, however, some disagreement between those favouring simple (perhaps incremental) change and those who support complex electoral rules.

Among the proponents of simple electoral system design is Giovanni Sartori (1997) who favours the (French) two-round majoritarian system. Other scholars expressing sympathy for majoritarian systems include Blais and Massicotte (1996: 74–5) and, specifically for AV, Horowitz (1991) and Reilly (1997a). A key argument in favour of majoritarian systems is the idea that when choosing between electoral systems, a guiding principle should be 'simple is best'. While agreeing with this principle, Taagepera and Shugart (1989: 236) tend, however, to hedge their bets, stating that they have 'no emotional attachment to any electoral system'. Their starting point is that electoral systems are best left alone: 'Keeping the ills we know of may be better than leaping into the unknown'. However, in the circumstances of adopting electoral rules in a newly democratizing country, Taagepera and Shugart (1989: 236) indicate a preference for small, multi-member constituencies, with some kind of proportional electoral formula. But they stress the need to keep it simple; there should be 'no complexities such as adjustment seats, thresholds, multi-stage elections, or multi-tiered seat allocations'. Ultimately, in the closing sentence of their book they express a guarded preference for STV. In his review of options for southern African democracies, Andrew Reynolds also shows some sympathy for STV (1999). Taagepera's most recent work on this topic sets out four key recommendations: (1) keep the system as simple as possible; (2) be aware of trends in other countries; (3) keep the same rules for at least three elections; (4) be prepared to make small, incremental changes.

In contrast to these authors, Arend Lijphart shows no apparent concern about the complexity of certain electoral systems. In his advice to would-be electoral reformers, he stresses the virtues of such features as two-tier districting, national legal thresholds, vote transferability and *apparentement* (Lijphart 1994a: 145). While Lijphart (p. 151) does tend to agree with Taagepera and Shugart that in the case of existing electoral systems the preference should be for 'incremental improvements, not revolutionary upheaval', his advice for 'electoral engineers in the new democracies' is to examine 'all the options' (p. 152). Dunleavy and Margetts are even more explicit in making a virtue of electoral system complexity. They suggest that the reforms of the early 1990s (in Italy, Japan and New Zealand) reflect an 'apparent convergence of liberal democracies' (Dunleavy and Margetts 1995: 26) towards 'mixed' electoral systems, which, they assert, combine 'the accountability strengths of plurality rule in single-member constituencies with the offsetting proportional qualities of regional or national lists' (see also Shugart 2000).

Even in this short, and admittedly incomplete, review, we can see that there is little agreement between the various specialists: Blais and Massicotte, Horowitz, Reilly and Sartori favour majoritarian systems; Reynolds, and Taagepera and Shugart reveal a sympathy for STV (though this appears more a case for Taagepera than for Shugart: compare Taagepera 1998 with Shugart 2000); Lijphart favours list systems with two-tier districting; Dunleavy and Margetts see a 'convergence' towards mixed systems. If the specialists cannot agree on which is best, it is hardly so surprising that the politicians have come up with such a wide range of different electoral systems.

8.3   Measuring Voter Attitudes towards Electoral Systems

We saw in the previous chapter how there has been a recent interest in studying the strategic consequences of electoral systems, both with respect to how politicians operate under different electoral systems, and also in terms of the strategic calculations of voters. This latter perspective has led to some interest in trying to measure public attitudes towards electoral systems. Another reason for the recent interest in measuring attitudes towards electoral systems is a reaction to the processes of electoral reform in a number of established democracies, prompting enquiries into what the voters think of the new system.

For a long time (and as implied by the discussion of the previous two sections), the electoral systems literature tended to treat the domain of electoral systems as part of the grand strategy of elite politicians and electoral engineers (Sartori 1997). After all it is politicians who set laws, and electoral laws should be seen as no exception. In his elite-led model, Lijphart (1977) goes so far as to make electoral system design one of the core features of 'consociationalism'. In many cases the assumption has been that the politicians impose electoral systems on the passive voters. This ignores the many instances of where voters have had great influence over electoral system design, such as Ireland in 1959 and 1968, or Italy and New Zealand in the early 1990s.

The fact is that, in many cases, the voters influence electoral system design; in all cases the voters are the political actors actually using the electoral system. It is important to know, therefore, what the voters think about electoral systems. But there are problems with measuring public attitudes in this area. First, it is pretty clear that few people actually understand much about electoral systems, and therefore it is difficult to take seriously their responses to any questions posed. Second, electoral system specialists need to give some thought to which aspects of electoral systems are of direct relevance to the voters, and which therefore warrant some effort to try and measure attitudes towards them. The fact is that, while the proportionality of an electoral system may be of crucial importance in determining who wins and who loses at a systemic level, at the individual level the voter is likely to be even more interested in questions relating to the act of voting and how some systems may allow voters more flexibility and choice than others.

One rather circuitous way of measuring public support for electoral systems is to examine attitudes towards the greater political system. In Chapter 7, we reviewed some of the main systemic consequences of electoral systems, in terms of proportionality, numbers of parties and representation of women and minorities. These factors, in turn, have important consequences for questions relating to styles of government and forms of representation, and even more fundamentally relating to system stability. For instance (and as shall be explored in more detail in Chapter 9), PR systems are more likely to produce coalition governments; there is likely to be greater congruence between legislators and their representatives (Huber and Powell 1994); the political system is likely to operate in a more consensual fashion (Lijphart 1999a). In the light of such consequences, it can be expected that this will influence levels of support for the political system. In general, the research shows higher levels of attachment to, and support for, the political system in PR countries than in non-PR countries (Anderson and Guillory 1997; Lijphart 1994a) – something we return to later (see Chapter 9, pp. 205–6). This approach to measuring levels of support for electoral systems does usefully skirt around the problems associated with low levels of knowledge of the actual electoral system itself, by providing only indirect measures; however, there are limitations on exactly how much can be read into the results in terms of levels of support for electoral systems. Furthermore, this research cannot pick out attitudes towards specific electoral systems, nor can it isolate what exactly are the issues which matter for voters.

Some effort has been made to get around the problem of low levels of public knowledge of electoral systems. In the past, the main cause of all this has been a lack of available data. For a long time, it was necessary to rely on secondary analysis of existing data sets, in which the single electoral system question was little more than an aside in a larger project, and was asking the public's view of electoral systems in the abstract. A case in point is Peter Kellner's review of British poll evidence in the early 1990s, which led him to conclude, pretty definitively, that 'reform is less popular with the public than its advocates supposed' (Kellner 1992: 10). As Patrick Dunleavy and his colleagues argue, research like this has many shortcomings because of the use of 'biased, crude or overly complex single questions' (1993: 179).

Dunleavy and his collaborators have sought to get around this problem through more sophisticated measures of public attitudes towards electoral reform. As part of their testing of alternative electoral systems on a sample of British voters in the 1992 general election, Dunleavy *et al.* posed a series of election system-relevant statements, asking their respondents whether they agreed or disagreed with the following: (i) 'This country should adopt a new voting system that would give parties seats in Parliament in proportion to their share of the votes', (ii) 'We should retain the current voting system as it is more likely to produce single-party government'. The findings reveal that 43 per cent of voters consistently supported PR, while 32 per cent did not. This evidence leads Dunleavy *et al.* to conclude (*pace* Kellner) that 'We find no evidence of any across-the-board shift against electoral reform' (1993: 181). Despite the best efforts of Dunleavy and his colleagues, however, they were still open to the charge of presuming too much of their respondents. For instance, how many respondents knew enough of the existing system to form an impression of its worth? The point is that this survey was still asking questions about relatively complex matters in the abstract.

A much bigger stride towards solving this problem was taken by Dunleavy *et al.* in their subsequent mock-ballot survey of British voters in the 1997 general election (1997; see also Bowler and Farrell

1996). Respondents were first required to complete a series of mock ballots for reruns of the election using four alternative electoral systems: alternative vote, supplementary vote, single transferable vote and additional member system (AMS, that is, the 'mixed' system). On the basis of their experience of using these different systems, the respondents were then asked what they thought about them. The results are summarized in Table 8.1. Dunleavy *et al.* conclude that on the basis of the attitudes expressed in the table, and the general performance of the different systems in their simulations, 'AMS is the system which is likely to prove the most acceptable candidate for the "reform" option' in Britain (1997: 5). Having selected AMS as the preferred option, Dunleavy *et al.* next carried out a mock referendum on their sample of voters, offering them a choice between the existing SMP system and AMS. This produced an even balance, with 41 per cent backing SMP, and 44 per cent backing AMS.

The Dunleavy *et al.* research has gone some way towards meeting the first problem of measuring public opinion towards electoral reform, namely the low level of understanding of the issues involved. However, even then questions need to be asked over just how much a voter can learn of the different systems on offer from a series of one-off election simulations being thrust at them in quick succession. Evidently some effort was made to explain the different systems, but only so much can be achieved in the little time available to the investigators in what was essentially a quantitative exercise involving a large sample of voters.

Table 8.1   Measuring British attitudes towards alternative electoral systems in 1997 (%)

Question: 'How much would you like to vote this way in the future?'

	Like	*Neutral*	*Dislike*
Mixed (AMS) system	54	25	21
Supplementary vote	53	25	22
Alternative vote	37	27	35
Single transferable vote	24	23	53
N = 1901			

Source: Dunleavy *et al.* 1997.

Clearly, one way of getting round this problem of low levels of understanding of different electoral systems is to measure voter attitudes after actual electoral reform has taken place. Such exercises have been carried out in those established democracies which have recently undergone fundamental electoral reform – Italy, Japan and New Zealand (see, for example, Reed 1999; Vowles *et al.* 1998a, 1998b). In the USA, there has also been research, by Richard Engstrom and his colleagues (for example, Brischetto and Engstrom 1997; Engstrom *et al.* 1997), measuring attitudes towards the adoption of cumulative voting (CV; for discussion, see pp. 45–6) in southern US states.

In general, these studies show some quite impressive ability on the part of voters in developing an understanding of the new system, and learning how to operate it. But when it comes to measuring degrees of satisfaction with the new system, the evidence is less positive. Indeed, with possibly the only exception being the ethnic minority communities in the southern US states – who are conscious of the fact that CV has been designed to protect their interests – the general reaction quite quickly becomes unfavourable.

We already know what the general pattern of opinion is likely to be from the summary of the arguments of electoral specialists above (see p. 183), namely, that after a brief groundswell of support for the new system, its first use is likely to disappoint, causing public support to dip quite dramatically (for instance, just such a path was predicted accurately for Japan by Reed 1994; also Reed 1999). Figure 8.1 shows this trend very clearly in the case of New Zealand, causing Bowler and Karp (1999) to speculate over what this trend could reveal regarding general levels of public support for New Zealand democracy.

The advice of electoral systems specialists is that it is important to give a new electoral system some time (certainly more than three elections) to embed itself, thereby allowing the political system time to adapt to it sufficiently, and for the voters (as well as the politicians and political commentators) to grow accustomed to it. So far, the policy-makers in Japan and New Zealand appear to be following this advice. In Italy, by contrast, recent efforts have been made to change the electoral system once again, this time to 'full-blown' SMP. However, proposals were defeated (if only by a technicality) in referendums held in 1999 and 2000, and the country looks destined to continue using its mixed system for some time to come.

For all its strengths, the research to date tends to focus predomi-

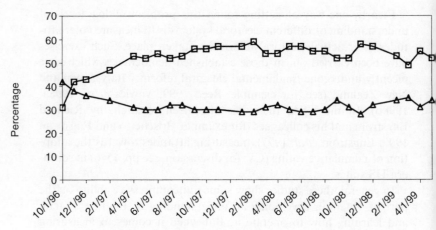

Figure 8.1 Support for MMP and SMP in New Zealand, October
            1996–May 1999

Note: Voters were asked: 'Now that we have had experience of the MMP
system and the first-past-the-post [SMP] system which do you prefer?'
        □ = SMP
        △ = MMP

Sources: *UMR-Insight*. Published in Vowles *et al.* (1998b), and updated by
Shaun Bowler and Jeffrey Karp.

nantly on macro-level questions, relating to such themes as levels of
support for the system (Brischetto and Engstrom 1997; Engstrom *et
al.* 1997), levels of satisfaction with democracy (Bowler and Karp
1999; Vowles *et al.* 1998a), or the age-old issue of proportionality
(Dunleavy *et al.* 1997). In all this research no effort has been made
to glean voter attitudes towards more micro-level questions surrounding the different electoral systems, such as over the ability of
some systems to allow more tactical voting, or the problems of
'wasted votes'. In other words, one could argue that much of the
attention of this research is to some extent miscast, failing to pay
attention to those aspects of electoral systems which most directly
affect voters.

The point is that quantitative, survey research of public opinion
towards electoral systems can only take us so far. Given the complexities surrounding electoral systems, and the low levels of interest in and knowledge of electoral systems among the mass public,

arguably a far more effective means of assessing attitudes towards electoral systems is to make use of qualitative research techniques (more generally, see Devine 1995).

This was the motivation behind a focus-group exercise on groups of British voters in 1998, which was designed to coincide with the deliberations of the Jenkins Commission (see p. 36 above) (Farrell and Gallagher 1998, 1999). The principal objective of this research was to attempt to understand underlying attitudes towards this complex issue of electoral reform, and to tease out the principal features of electoral systems which mattered most to the voters involved in the exercise. Among the main conclusions of this research were the following two points. First, it was evident that, at the start of the proceedings, very little was known about the subject area. To a person, nobody was able to correctly define the existing SMP system, nor was anyone able to offer a credible alternative to it. As a consequence, it was not surprising to find that the bulk of the respondents favoured retaining the existing electoral system. During the course of the two-hour discussions, during which each group was introduced to four alternative electoral systems (AV, STV, list and a mixed system), the mood shifted sharply in favour of change from SMP, though without any clear support for any one of the other electoral systems: that is, the groups were divided over the four systems (with list appearing the least popular).

Second, and in contrast to the focus of electoral systems scholars, proportionality *per se* did not feature as a major concern in the focus groups – though it was raised. By far the most important criteria related to the need to minimize electoral system complexity, the desirability of greater 'voter choice' (though not so much as to make the system too complex), and the fear of losing the constituency link (a feature stressed more perhaps in Britain than in other countries, and therefore possibly a cultural phenomenon).

The findings of this focus-group research suggest some promising new avenues of study in the field of electoral systems, making use of more qualitative research techniques. Two points, in particular, are worth drawing out from this research. First, the fact that few voters either care or know much about the question of electoral systems need not be a block to researching their attitudes towards them: qualitative research techniques offer one means of providing voters an opportunity to learn the fundamentals of electoral systems, and then to explore their attitudes to them. Second, there is some evidence to suggest that electoral systems scholars may not be focusing sufficiently on those features of electoral systems which matter most to the voters, who after all are, by definition, the people actually using the electoral systems. If anything, it seems that voters are particularly interested in the *strategic* consequences of electoral systems, which as we saw in the previous chapter have only relatively recently become a subject of interest among the scholarly community. By contrast, the subject of intense debate among the scholarly community relating to the *systemic* consequences of electoral systems does not appear to feature that highly on the scale of interest among voters.

8.4   Conclusion

There is an impression of a paradigm shift in the field of electoral systems. Based on our review, in this chapter, of three areas in the study of electoral systems as dependent variables, there is some evidence of convergence on a common theme – namely, that there is more to the study of electoral systems than the question of 'proportionality' (and its associated effects). Our review of the 'four' waves of electoral system design, in section 8.1, shows this quite clearly, particularly by the way in which recent moves towards electoral reform in established democracies have demonstrated a willingness on the part of electoral engineers to embrace relatively complex, mixed, electoral systems, which by their nature are concerned with influencing much more than proportionality. It is clear that debates relating to such issues as constituency representation and voter choice have had some influence in the adoption of such systems.

While, as we saw, the academic community remains divided over the merits of the different systems on offer, even here there is, nonetheless, a constituency of opinion favouring the adoption of more complex electoral systems, again to take account of a broader set of issues than proportionality (for example, Bowler 1996; Dunleavy and Margetts 1995; Grofman and Bowler 1996; Lijphart 1994a; Reynolds 1999; Shugart and Wattenberg 2000a). Finally, and most significantly, it is pretty apparent that voters themselves are less concerned with proportionality than they are with other (potential or actual) consequences of electoral systems, and this warrants much more investigation.

All this brings us back to a central question relating to what the consequences are of different electoral systems for the greater political system. In Chapter 7 we examined the main themes in terms of the systemic and strategic consequences of electoral systems. This discussion has wider implications for the political system generally, particularly with regard to the question of system stability – the topic of our concluding chapter.

9
Electoral Systems and Stability

Electoral engineers are spoilt for choice. As we have seen, there is no shortage of 'off-the-shelf' electoral systems to choose from, and, indeed, as the last chapter demonstrated, in recent times electoral engineers have not been averse to experimenting with new 'mixed' designs, thereby adding to the available pool of electoral systems. Chapter 7 reviewed the main systemic and strategic consequences of electoral systems, demonstrating the need to take due care when selecting a new electoral system for a country. Depending on that decision, a political system can be affected in any number of ways, but most notably in terms of the numbers of parties in the parliament, the degree of social representation (in terms of numbers of women and possibly ethnic minority MPs), the tendency to have more (or less) coalition governments, the nature of parliamentary representation, the style of party campaigning (and party organization), and the degree of electoral choice given to voters.

As has been demonstrated throughout this book, the principal distinction is between proportional and non-proportional systems. It is easy enough to see how a proponent of PR could develop a case: PR systems are fairer to smaller parties and to supporters of smaller parties; PR provides better social representation; certain PR systems provide voters with greater electoral choice, and so on. But do all these benefits come at a cost? For instance, while few would dispute that having a more representative assembly is a good thing, there is considerable disagreement over the degree to which such an assembly can operate effectively. The issue is usually presented in terms of a trade-off: either you can have a representative parliament which elects a similarly representative government, or you can have strong and stable government; you cannot have both at the same time. This is perhaps best summarized by Samuel Beer as follows: 'representative government must not only represent, it must also govern' (Beer 1998: 25).

This is a very persuasive argument, and it involves a number of interrelated points which, for the sake of convenience, can be grouped into three main areas: government longevity and accountability; party political extremism; system complexity and voter confusion. We start, in section 9.1, with a review of the arguments relating to the stability of governments under PR. There are two main streams of argument here. First, it is suggested that PR produces coalition governments which are unstable by virtue of being made up of several parties, and therefore governments tend to change more often. Second, the point is often made that coalition governments are not accountable, having been formed on the basis of backroom deals between party leaders after the election; the parties' manifesto promises are forgotten in the rush to gain power; the voters' wishes are ignored.

Section 9.2 addresses the theme of whether and how PR promotes the rise of political extremism. Here the argument is that PR systems ensure the easy entry of small and extremist parties into parliament, threatening the stability of the government, particularly in those cases where the extremists hold the balance of power in the parliament. Section 9.3 considers the question of whether the complexity of (some) PR systems may affect voter activity (or lack thereof) in the system. In this case, the issue is that, because some PR systems are more complex than non-PR systems, they add an extra burden to the voters, thus raising the question of whether voters really understand what is going on. Finally, in section 9.4, we review the debates over whether the supposed trade-off between proportionality and stability really exists. As we shall see, if anything the more accurate picture to draw of the relationship between proportionality and measures of stability appears to be of a virtuous circle.

9.1 PR and Government Stability and Accountability

The stability of government varies from one political system to the next. Anecdotally comparisons are often drawn between the stability of governments in Britain, where prime ministers usually appear unassailable, and the highly precarious position of governments in countries like Israel or Italy, where terms of government office appear more appropriately counted in months rather than years. One of the major features behind such arguments is the type of electoral system employed. Put simply, the suggestion is that PR electoral systems have a greater tendency to produce coalition governments which, by their nature, are bound to be less stable than the single-party majority governments more normally associated with non-PR systems.

Of course, to rigorously assess the stability of government in terms of how long it stays in office is fraught with difficulties (see, for example, Laver and Schofield 1991). What defines a change of government: an election, a new prime minister, a cabinet reshuffle, a partial change of cabinet membership? For instance, according to some definitions, the British Conservatives' replacement of Margaret Thatcher by John Major in 1990 constituted a change of government. Furthermore, allowance must be made for systems like Germany where it is difficult to unseat a government in mid-term, or Switzerland where a government cannot be touched in mid-term.

Arend Lijphart's (1999a) review of the evidence is the most up to date. He distinguishes two main definitions of 'cabinet duration': one associated with Lawrence Dodd (1976), in which cabinets are deemed to have changed only if the party composition changes; and the more commonly accepted definition (employed, for instance, by Gallagher *et al.* 2000) which takes account of a range of possible features, including an election, a change in the prime ministership, and a change in the status of the cabinet (for example, whether a party leaves the cabinet). Lijphart employs both definitions, taking an average of the two, and producing the range of figures reported in the final column of Table 9.1.[1] Consistent with the practice in Chapter 7, the table includes information on the countries' electoral systems and the degree of disproportionality of these systems. Given that Lijphart's analysis covers the postwar period (or, in some cases, the period since the relevant country became a democracy), the table reports the postwar average disproportionality scores provided by Lijphart (also using the Gallagher index), which produces a slightly different ranking to that shown in Table 7.1 (particularly in the cases of Italy, Japan and New Zealand, since it refers to their previous electoral systems). Table 9.1 also reports the proportion of time a country had one-party governments, as opposed to coalitions.

Table 9.1 Proportionality and government stability

	Electoral system	Level of disproportionality	One-party governments (%)	Average government duration (years)
Switzerland	List	2.53	0.0	8.59
Jamaica	SMP	17.75	100.0	5.99
United Kingdom	SMP	10.33	100.0	5.52
Austria	List	2.47	33.8	5.47
Australia	AV	9.26	69.2	5.06
Canada	SMP	11.72	100.0	4.90
USA	SMP	14.91	89.1	4.45
Spain	List	8.15	100.0	4.36
Costa Rica	List	13.65	100.0	4.31
New Zealand	SMP	11.11	99.7	4.17
Colombia	List	10.62	52.9	3.48
Sweden	List	2.09	70.4	3.42
Norway	List	4.93	79.4	3.17
Ireland	STV	3.45	53.9	3.07
Greece	List	8.08	96.4	2.88
Germany	MMP	2.52	1.7	2.82
Venezuela	List	14.41	83.1	2.72
Netherlands	List	1.30	0.0	2.72
Japan	SNTV	5.03	46.2	2.57
France	2-R	21.08	53.1	2.48
Denmark	List	1.83	42.9	2.28
Portugal	List	4.04	43.0	2.09
India	SMP	11.38	41.4	2.08
Belgium	List	3.24	8.3	1.98
Israel	List	2.27	0.1	1.58
Papua New Guinea	SMP	10.06	0.0	1.57
Finland	List	2.93	10.9	1.24
Italy	List	3.25	10.3	1.14

Notes: The countries are ranked by 'average government duration'. Disproportionality is as reported by Lijphart (using the Gallagher index). This produces slightly different results to those reported in Table 7.1 given that Lijphart's figures are aggregates of all relevant postwar elections (and, in the cases of Italy, Japan and New Zealand, refer to their previous electoral systems). The 'one-party governments' measure shows the proportion of time the government in that country was single-party rather than coalition. The 'average government duration' measure shows, in years, how long the same government remained in office on average.
Source: Lijphart (1999a: Tables 6.3, 7.1, 8.2).

As expected, SMP countries like Britain and Jamaica, both of which are characterized by continuous one-party government, have very stable governments, while PR countries like Israel and (pre-reform) Italy, where coalitions predominate, have far less stable governments. The fact is, however, that for each example one can find to support the proposition that PR electoral systems are associated with government instability, it is possible to find a counter example. Countries like Austria, Sweden and Norway, with highly proportional systems and regular coalition governments, also enjoy high degrees of government stability. By contrast, non-proportional countries like Japan, India and Papua New Guinea are located towards the lower half of the table, with relatively unstable governments. In other words, the evidence in Table 9.1 suggests that while having a non-proportional electoral system helps to promote government duration (and hence at least one indicator of stability), it is quite possible for proportional systems to have the same result (also Gallagher *et al.* 2000; Lijphart 1999a).

Coalition governments are also often criticized, by opponents of PR, for being 'undemocratic' (for example, Hain 1986; Pinto-Duschinsky 1999; Norton 1997). There are a number of parts to this argument, three of which can be recited here. First, coalitions are produced after the election as a result of secret meetings between party leaders. The voters' 'word' on which party or parties should form the government is peripheral to the outcome; what matters is who can strike the better deal. In consequence, 'there is little connection between elections and the creation of governments' (Pinto-Duschinsky 1999: 121; also Katz 1997a: 165–7). As always it is easy to find examples of coalition governments being formed in this way. But equally there are examples of coalition bargains between parties being struck *before* the election, so voters know what they are voting for. For that matter, in systems where coalitions are the norm, voters may be very well aware of the likely coalition arrangements that will emerge after the election. In short, the whole process of coalition formation can be entirely predictable: 'Thus we should not get too bewitched by an image of the political future of most European states being settled not by the electorate but by the wheeling and dealing of party leaders' (Gallagher *et al.* 2000: 341; also Vowles 1999: 140). Furthermore, as Geoffrey K. Roberts (1975: 221) has noted: 'British experience in 1974 demonstrates that even the plurality system is no guarantee that post-election manoeuvres may not be required as a preliminary to the formation of a government.'

Second, coalitions are also said to be undemocratic because they make a mockery of manifesto pledges. At least in the case of single-party governments, a voter can hold the government to account if it does not fulfil campaign pledges. The evidence shows that, on the whole, British governments have a good record of implementing manifesto proposals (Rallings 1987; Rose 1980). To date, there have been few studies of the record of coalition governments elsewhere in Europe. Gallagher and his colleagues cite one Dutch study of the 1980s–90s which does, indeed, show that over the period Dutch parties have a worse record than British parties in fulfilling campaign pledges. In general, they surmise, 'The expectation in a coalition system is that fewer pledges will be fulfilled, because of the policy compromises between parties that must be made in order to form a government' (Gallagher *et al.* 2000: 383; though, see Klingeman *et al.* 1994). Of course, such a situation need not arise wherever coalition arrangements are agreed before the election, allowing the partners to coordinate their policy proposals.

A final charge against PR systems and the perpetual coalitions they engender is that the governments formed under such systems are very difficult to dislodge; in Pinto-Duschinsky's (1999) words, it is difficult to 'send the rascals packing'. At the heart of this, once again, is the issue of how governments are made and unmade not as a direct result of the popular vote, but rather as a result of the wheeling and dealing that goes on between party leaders. In particular, attention is often focused on the 'pivotal' role of tiny parties, such as most notably the German Free Democrats who, as we saw in Chapter 5, have enjoyed long uninterrupted periods in government despite having a tiny vote. In large part this is raking back over the discussion relating to Table 9.1, only this time the focus is specifically on which parties are in government at any one time, rather than which individuals of which parties. If the relevant definition of 'cabinet change' is the former, then it is, indeed, possible to find examples (such as Germany or Switzerland) of PR systems where the same parties appear to be able to stay in government almost in perpetuity, regardless of how they fared in the polls. However, as discussed above, if the definition of cabinet change includes partial replacements (for example, such things as whether one party leaves or enters a coalition of several parties, or changes in the personnel in the government), then this produces quite a different picture. As Lijphart observes: 'In the Netherlands, for instance, there has never been a complete cabinet turnover since 1945, but that does not mean that the same parties were in power all the time: centre-left cabinets have alternated with centre-right cabinets, generally in response to electoral verdicts' (Lijphart 1999b: 134; Powell 1999; Shugart 1999; Vowles 1999).

Furthermore, to what extent can non-PR Britain be held up as a good example of where the rascals can be easily turfed out, especially given the recent 18-year period of successive Conservative administrations being returned to power despite never once achieving anything remotely approaching a majority of the vote? To put this point more generally, while non-proportional electoral systems may have a good record in producing safe legislative majorities and therefore in facilitating the implementation of manifesto promises, there is a question mark over the extent to which these are sufficient indicators of government stability. The government may be stable because it has a majority of seats, but how *representative* is it? In other words, to what extent is it stable in terms of proportion of votes? The UK government elected in 1997 had the support of just 43.2 per cent of those who voted. By contrast, other governments elected in proportional systems around the same time were far more representative of public opinion by virtue of the fact that they comprised coalitions of several (in some cases, many) parties. In general, as Katz concludes: 'Apparently, the price one pays for the electoral simplification engendered by single-member plurality and its resulting high likelihood of single-party legislative majorities is a correspondingly high likelihood that those legislative majorities will not be based on electoral majorities' (1997a: 164).

A final aspect of government stability which is worth noting is the issue of continuity of government policies. The adversarial nature of British politics is characterized by sharp shifts in policy as governments change (Finer 1975). By contrast, the more 'consensual' nature of coalitional systems – due to the need to strike deals between parties – ensures a far greater degree of policy consistency over time (Lijphart 1999a).

9.2   PR and the Rise of Extremist Parties

A second main area of criticism of proportional electoral systems is that, by making it easier for smaller parties to win seats in parlia-

ment (which was demonstrated in Chapter 7), these systems facilitate the rise of extremist parties. This not only increases the risk of
hung parliaments, with governments being hostage to the vagaries
of extremist politicians, more generally it also affects the stability of
the political system by giving undue representation to politicians and
parties whose views are abhorrent to the majority of citizens. The
débâcle of Weimar Germany and the rise of Hitler is often held up
as an example. More recently, in February 2000 this point was
demonstrated forcibly by the decision of the Austrian People's Party
to form a coalition with the extremist Freedom Party, led by its
populist leader, Jörg Haider, despite the huge international (and
domestic) outcry. In its defence, the People's Party leadership argued
that the only alternative would have been a fresh set of elections with
every indication that the Freedom Party would have picked up more
votes.

Undoubtedly extremist parties are more commonly found in proportional systems (certainly this is shown by the fact that virtually
all the cases in Table 9.2 are proportional systems); however, extremist parties can also achieve prominence in non-proportional systems,
in particular wherever they can take advantage of a geographical
concentration in their support base. This is exemplified by the case
of France, where Jean-Marie Le Pen and his National Front have
made shock waves in a majoritarian-based system, winning 14.9 per
cent of the vote in the 1997 legislative elections. The other point
worth remarking on in Table 9.2 is the lack of any apparent relationship between the degree of proportionality of the electoral
system (as shown by the disproportionality rank) and the relative
success of extreme right parties.

There is little doubt, however, that proportional systems can make
life easier for extremist politicians and parties. One could always
develop a defence of PR along the lines that, in a democracy, all
views and opinions should have equal rights of expression and that
morally, therefore, such parties should be facilitated, not blocked.
One could even make the argument that, by allowing extremists into
the parliament, the electoral system might be playing a moderating
role, encouraging such parties to work within the system, rather than
seeking to overthrow it. It might also help stem their electoral appeal
as 'anti-establishment' parties.

Of course, such arguments may have a moral force, but they do
not really answer the criticism that PR facilitates the entry of extrem-

Table 9.2 The electoral performance of the extreme Right in Western Europe in the 1990s

	Disprop-ortionality rank	Latest election result (%)	Election	Party(ies)
Austria	6	26.9	1999	Freedom Party
Italy	30	15.7	1996	National Alliance
Norway	21	15.3	1997	Progress Party
France	47	14.9	1997	National Front
Belgium	13	11.4	1999	Flemish Bloc Belgian National Front
Germany	14	3.0	1998	Republicans German People's Union
Switzerland	15	2.7	1999	Swiss Democrats Freedom Party
Denmark	3	2.4	1998	Progress Party
Netherlands	4	0.6	1998	Centre Democrats
Greece	31	0.2	1996	National Political Union/National Party

Notes: The countries are ranked based on size of vote for relevant party/ies. See Table 7.1 for information on disproportionality ranking.
Sources: Election returns (information supplied by Elisabeth Carter); Table 7.1.

ism. If the objective is to try to prevent extremist parties and politicians from being elected, then what can proportional systems do to meet it? In fact, there are two ways of meeting this objective. One is to apply quota rules (see pp. 17–18), such as the German 5 per cent rule, which ensures that smaller parties are excluded from parliament, and, since extremist parties usually are smaller, this affects them (certainly it would affect half the cases in Table 9.2). The second method is to pass a law banning certain categories of parties, as used in Germany to prevent the rise of neo-Nazi parties.

At this point, the critic of proportional electoral systems might raise the following set of objections: these legal blocks on parties are hardly cast-iron guarantees against the danger of extremists 'breaking through'; non-proportional systems provide a more effective, and simpler, means of achieving the same result; and, in any event, operating such legal restrictions is somewhat against the principle of proportionality and is, therefore, contradictory. Each of these points has some validity. The only counter to them is to remind ourselves that, to date, the entry of extremist parties has not exactly been a mad rush (as demonstrated by Table 9.2), and this places a question mark over the degree to which we need to be unduly concerned about them.

9.3 System Complexity, Voter Confusion and Electoral Behaviour

It is worth addressing one final area of criticism of PR systems – namely that, because they are more complex, they are more likely to confuse voters. The voters may not be entirely certain of what their vote means, and of how the final election result has been calculated. After all, it is far easier to understand how a politician has been elected because they had more votes than anyone else than it is to make sense of how modified Sainte-Laguë produced a certain number of seats for your preferred party. If the voters are more uncertain, more confused, then perhaps there is a greater likelihood of their being alienated by the complexities of the system.

One problem with such an argument is that it reveals a rather low expectation of voters. Why should they be more confused under PR systems? And, for that matter, why should it matter that the voters do not understand precisely how the final election result has been produced? Surely, the fact that the result is more proportional should have a higher priority than whether the complexities of the system are understood. Setting aside these objections, it is useful to examine the evidence of voter trends under different electoral systems. The issues of voter confusion and/or alienation could be said to manifest themselves in terms of greater numbers of invalid votes (also referred to as 'spoiled' or 'informal' votes), or in terms of lower voter turnout. Table 9.3 provides some indication of how these have varied across the different systems in the 1990s. Needless to say, invalid votes and low turnout can have many causes, such as the rise of anti-party sentiment generally, or the fact that, in some systems (notably Switzerland and the USA), voters are called upon to vote too often. In some cases where laws are operating which require voters to turn out to vote (notably Australia, Belgium, Greece and Luxembourg, but also in a number of newer democracies), it is to be expected that the turnout figures are artificially inflated.

There are several points worth making about Table 9.3. First, there is little by way of striking evidence to support the assumed negative relationship between the proportionality of the electoral system

Table 9.3 Voter turnout and invalid votes under different electoral systems in the 1990s

Rank and country		Level of disproportionality	Turnout (%)	Invalid votes (%)
26	Brazil	5.34	76.8*	18.8
35	Mozambique	9.85	66.4	11.7
30	Italy	7.00	87.4*	7.8
12	Colombia	3.11	29.2	7.8
13	Belgium	3.12	83.2*	7.5
11	Slovenia	2.50	75.5	5.9
32	Chile	7.09	81.9*	5.5
47	France	21.37	59.9	4.9
43	Lithuania	14.19	50.0	4.9
19	Bolivia	3.86	50.0*	4.8
5	Uruguay	1.67	96.1	4.7
31	Mexico	7.08	50.0*	4.2
34	Poland	9.79	48.8	3.9
38	Australia	10.31	95.3*	3.8
18	Venezuela	3.76	72.7*	3.8
23	Costa Rica	4.42	73.7*	3.0
33	India	7.22	61.1	2.5
2	Benin	1.00	73.7	2.4
8	Malawi	2.00	67.7	2.4
6	Austria	1.87	78.6	2.3
40	South Korea	10.62	65.3	2.3
15	Switzerland	3.62	35.7	2.3
7	Israel	1.96	84.7	2.2
31	Greece	7.08	83.9*	2.0
24	Portugal	5.07	79.1	1.9
37	Russia	10.00	62.8	1.9
9	Slovakia	2.12	75.9	1.6
10	Sweden	2.13	83.6	1.5
42	Nepal	12.75	83.6	1.5
29	Spain	6.36	80.6	1.5
1	South Africa	0.24	68.0	1.5
27	Ireland	5.39	66.7	1.5
45	Canada	15.49	63.9	1.4
14	Germany	3.38	72.4	1.3
48	Jamaica	26.27	48.8	0.9
3	Denmark	1.55	83.1	0.8
17	Bulgaria	3.73	66.9	0.8
20	Finland	3.91	71.1	0.6
21	Norway	3.92	76.9	0.5
4	Netherlands	1.58	75.2	0.5
22	New Zealand	4.36	83.0	0.4

Table 9.3 *Continued*

Rank and country	Level of disproportionality	Turnout (%)	Invalid votes (%)
25 Czech Republic	5.20	76.7	0.4
46 Mongolia	16.33	73.6	0.4
44 United Kingdom	15.19	75.4	0.1
36 Papua New Guinea	9.86	98.8	n.a.
39 Philippines	10.48	68.4	n.a.
16 Latvia	3.71	50.6	n.a.
28 USA	5.43	49.1	n.a.
41 Japan	10.78	44.9	n.a.

Notes: This table reports the disproportionality, turnout and invalid vote trends for the most recent election (for which information is available) in the 1990s. The countries have been ranked in terms of percentage invalid votes. For details on disproportionality index and ranking, see Table 7.1.
* Countries operating compulsory voting rules.
n.a. Not available.
Sources: International IDEA Website on Global Voter Turnout (http://www.idea.int/turnout/voter_turnout.html); Table 7.1.

(which, in this instance, can be taken to mean its 'complexity') and numbers of invalid votes or size of turnout. Some of the most proportional systems have both high turnout and low numbers of invalid votes (for example, Denmark, Germany and the Netherlands).

In the case of turnout, if we take the 39 countries listed in Table 9.3 (where voting is not compulsory), Britain – with one of the simplest electoral systems – has a pretty good record of turnout. In its 1997 election, 75.4 per cent of voters turned out to vote. Only two other SMP countries did better in their most recent elections: Nepal (83.6 per cent) and Papua New Guinea (98.8 per cent). However, a further 12 countries also scored better than Britain in terms of turnout at the most recent election, all of which use proportional representation (Austria, Czech Republic, Denmark, Israel, New Zealand, Norway, Portugal, Slovakia, Slovenia, Spain, Sweden and Uruguay). Across our sample cases (excluding those countries where voting is compulsory), turnout in the most recent election averaged 68.2 per cent in non-proportional systems and 70.8 per cent in proportional systems (the correlation between the two is –0.26). This tallies with Lijphart's more comprehensive analysis (1994b: 6–7; also Lijphart 1999a: 284–6) which reveals that average voting partici-pation is about 9 percentage points higher in PR systems than in non-PR systems.

One also has to look quite hard to find evidence of electoral system complexity affecting the ability of voters to use the system properly. For instance, among one of the worst performers in terms of the proportion of invalid votes is France (4.9 per cent) with its 'simple' majoritarian system; among one of the best performers is New Zealand (0.4 per cent) with its, still relatively new, 'complex' MMP system. It cannot be denied, however, that, on the whole, non-proportional systems fare better than proportional systems in terms of the average proportion of invalid votes: across our sample cases in Table 9.3, they average 1.8 per cent in non-proportional systems and this rises to 2.5 per cent in proportional systems. But this dif-ference of 0.7 per cent is hardly earth-shattering (and the correlation is only −0.03 and not significant).

With the exceptions of Mozambique (11.7 per cent) and Brazil (18.8 per cent) – the latter case operating compulsory voting – none of the other countries have anything approaching double-digit pro-portions of invalid votes, perhaps one reason why this issue has yet to attract any attention in the academic literature. It seems pretty clear that the complexity of the electoral system has a very limited role in determining the numbers of invalid votes – a point which was reinforced by our examination of voter attitudes to electoral systems in the previous chapter (see pp. 183–90). What would seem to matter more are such questions as the economic development and rates of literacy in the country, and, of course, whether the voters have been forced to turn out. We would expect higher proportions of invalid votes in compulsory turnout systems, where voters are forced to vote against their will (for example, McAllister and Makkai 1993), and this is demonstrated in Table 9.3 where, in the cases of compulsory vote systems, the proportions of invalid votes range between 2.0 and 18.8 per cent.

9.4   Is There a Trade-Off between Proportionality and Stability?

On the basis of the evidence reviewed in this chapter, the supposed trade-off between the proportionality of an electoral system and measures of governmental or system stability appears, for the most part, conspicuous by its absence. On the contrary, it would seem more accurate to conclude from this discussion that, if anything, proportional electoral systems are associated with greater degrees of stability.

Given the current wave of interest in institutionalist explanations in political science, it should be no surprise to find that scholars have started to address the question of the relationship between electoral systems and the quality of democracy. Two main approaches have been adopted, each the subject of some debate: (1) analysis of individual-level data measuring public support for democracy, and (2) use of aggregate indicators of socioeconomic development, social quality and political stability.

To date, the use of individual-level data has produced quite mixed findings. Arend Lijphart's well-known dichotomy between 'majoritarian' and 'consensus'[2] democracies has been employed by some scholars to assess the effects of political institutions on levels of satisfaction with democracy, making use of survey evidence of individual-level attitudes. As is well-known, the electoral system is one of the principal features separating the two models of democracy (Lijphart 1999a). Anderson and Guillory (1997) employ Eurobarometer data to examine trends in western democracies, showing clear evidence that, in all cases, levels of satisfaction are highest among those who form the political majority, and lowest among those in the minority. The differences are narrowed significantly, however, in consensus systems (which use proportional electoral systems): 'The more consensual the democracy, the more likely it is that losers are satisfied with the functioning of democracy and the less likely it is that winners are satisfied' (1997: 78).

Given that Anderson and Guillory were examining trends in Western Europe only, they were open to the charge that their findings might not be generalizable to a wider context. More recently, Pippa Norris has employed other data sets, involving a wider range of countries, and this produces quite different findings. If anything, her evidence leads her to conclude that 'majoritarian institutions tended to produce greater institutional confidence than consociational arrangements', and, she continues, 'majoritarian electoral systems and moderate multi-party systems, in particular, tend to generate slightly higher levels of institutional confidence than alternative arrangements' (Norris 1999: 233, 234).

The studies which make use of aggregate indicators have produced less ambiguous findings. One of the earliest such studies was by Arend Lijphart, whose comprehensive analysis of the postwar records of different systems in terms of the performance and effectiveness of democracy led him to conclude:

> the conventional wisdom is wrong in positing a trade-off between the advantages of plurality and PR systems. The superior performance of PR with regard to political representation is not counterbalanced by an inferior record on governmental effectiveness; if anything, the record of the PR countries on macro-economic management appears to be a bit better than that of the plurality systems – but not to the extent that the differences are statistically significant. The practical conclusion is that PR is to be preferred over plurality since it offers both better representation and at least as effective public policy-making. (1994b: 8)

While such conclusions have not been entirely free from criticism (for example, Castles 1994), Arend Lijphart continues to stand by them. In his most recent *Patterns of Democracy*, Lijphart reaches much the same conclusion, observing that 'contrary to conventional wisdom, there is no trade-off at all between governing effectiveness and high-quality democracy' (Lijphart 1999a: 302). On this occasion his analysis relates to the consensus–majoritarian distinction, but, even here, he attaches 'crucial indirect importance' (p. 303) to the electoral system.

Undoubtedly, the jury is still out on whether, and to what degree, the use of a proportional representation electoral system can have a beneficial effect on democracy. On balance, the evidence presented in this chapter and the majority of the academic studies to date would appear to point to the conclusion that PR does, indeed, have a largely positive affect on democracy, according to a range of measures. As we have seen, however, there are some scholars whose research would lead them to demur from such a conclusion. But even if we accept their qualifications, we still have travelled quite a distance from the initial standpoint of those who posited a *trade-off* between proportionality and stability. On this issue, then, there appears to be a growing consensus – proportional representation does not have to be associated with political instability.

9.5 Conclusion

The study of electoral systems can reveal much about political behaviour. The proportionality of the system plays a significant role in deciding who wins and who loses in the election game, on the con-stellation of parties in parliament (and therefore also in govern-ment), and on the characteristics of the individual MPs. In turn, this raises questions relating to the degree of stability of the government and political system; though, as we have seen, the evidence in support of the argument that proportionality produces instability is tenuous. In this respect, then, we have a conclusion which favours propor-tional electoral systems, because apparently we can have our cake and eat it. We can have a proportional electoral system and, at the same time, a stable political system.

As to whether we can be more specific about which proportional system is 'best' is a moot point. We may all have our 'favourite' elec-toral systems (the current author's happens to be STV), but in truth it would stretch credulity to attempt to argue that one electoral system is 'best' or 'ideal' for all circumstances. The fact is that one country's circumstances can vary dramatically from another's, and a judgement on which electoral system is best for a given country should be made in the light of that country's history, social compo-sition and political structures. What we have seen in this book is that electoral systems do not operate in a random fashion. Their opera-tion and effects can be systematically studied and evaluated, and given the right advice, a country should be able to choose the correct system for its particular circumstances.

Glossary

Note: Cross-entries are in **bold** type

Apparentement

To get around the problem for smaller parties of 'wasted' votes in list systems – that is, where they just fail to win seats – two or more parties may opt to formally link their lists, contesting the election as an alliance, and thereby increasing the prospect of having candidates elected. *Apparentement* is used most commonly in **d'Hondt** systems to compensate for the relatively low disproportionality of the result (compared with other list systems).

Ballot Structure

The nature and degree of choice available to the voter in an election. The basic distinction is between a categoric ballot structure (such as under single member plurality and certain list systems), where the voter can declare a preference for just one candidate (or party), and an ordinal ballot structure (such as under preferential electoral systems and some list systems), where, to varying degrees, the voter can rank-order candidates in order of preference.

Cube Rule

This suggests that the single member plurality electoral system has a built-in mechanism to produce single-party parliamentary majorities, and thereby ensure 'strong' and stable governments. It can be formalized as follows: if the ratio of votes that two parties receive is A:B, then this will result in the following ratio of seats, $A^3:B^3$. In other words, the party which receives the most votes wins by far the most seats in parliament. Recent evidence indicates that this rule no longer applies in the UK case.

d'Hondt

Named after Victor d'Hondt, and referred to in the USA as the Jefferson method, this is the most common divisor used in the **highest average** system, and (together with **largest remainder** Imperiali) is regarded as one of the least proportional of the list systems. It operates with the following divisors: 1, 2, 3, 4 and so on.

District Magnitude

Literally the size of the constituency in terms of numbers of MPs (for example, a single-seat constituency has a district magnitude, or DM, of one). Generally the single member plurality and majoritarian electoral systems have a DM of one, while the proportional systems have DMs greater than one. The size of the DM has a very important bearing on the overall proportionality of a PR system: the larger the DM the more proportional the system.

Droop Quota

Named after H. R. Droop, and often referred to as the Hagenbach-Bischoff quota, this is used in **largest remainder** list systems and in the single transferable vote electoral system to determine the allocation of seats. It is regarded as less proportional than **Hare**, but more proportional than **Imperiali**. It is calculated as follows: first, the total valid vote is divided by one plus the number of seats, and then one is added to the total (ignoring decimal points).

Electoral Formula

The counting rules which apply in a given electoral system. This is generally the way in which one distinguishes between the different electoral systems, such as: single member plurality (where a candidate requires a plurality of votes to be elected), majoritarian systems (where a candidate requires an overall majority), single transferable vote (where the **Droop** quota is used to determine how many votes a candidate requires), and the list systems (which separate, in turn, into **largest remainder** and **highest average** systems). The electoral formula has an important bearing on overall proportionality (though not as important as **district magnitude**).

Electoral Law

The family of rules governing the process of elections: from the calling of the election, through the stages of candidate nomination, party campaigning and voting, and right up to the stage of counting votes and determining the actual election result.

Electoral System

One part of the **electoral law** which specifically deals with the final determination of who is elected. Electoral systems determine the means by which votes are translated into seats in the process of electing politicians into office.

Gerrymandering

The practice of redrawing constituency boundaries with the intention of producing an inflated number of seats for a party, usually the governing party. Named after Governor Gerry of Massachusetts in 1812 who produced a constituency boundary which resembled a salamander, giving rise to the term 'gerrymander'.

Hare Quota

Named after Thomas Hare (who devised the single transferable vote electoral system), and often referred to as the 'simple quota', this is the most common quota used in the **largest remainder** system to determine the allocation of seats and tends to produce highly proportional results. It is calculated as follows: total valid vote divided by the number of seats.

Highest Average

This is one of the **electoral formulas** used by list systems to arrange the translation of votes into seats, and is far more common than the alternative, the **largest remainder** system. It operates by use of divisors, of which there are two main forms in use: **d'Hondt** (by far the most common) and **modified Sainte-Laguë**. Each party's votes are divided by a series of divisors to produce an average vote. The party with the 'highest average' vote after each stage of the process wins a seat, and its vote is then divided by the next divisor. The process continues until all the seats have been filled.

Imperiali Quota

Used in Italy until 1993, this is regarded as the least proportional of the **largest remainder** systems. It is calculated as follows: total valid vote divided by two plus the number of seats.

Largest Remainder

Referred to in the USA as the Hamilton method. This is one of the **electoral formulas** used by list systems to arrange the translation of votes into seats (the other is **highest average**). It operates by use of an electoral quota, the most common of which are **Hare** and **Droop.** The counting process is in two stages: (1) those parties with votes exceeding the quota are awarded seats, and the quota is subtracted from their total vote; (2) those parties left with the greatest number of votes (the 'largest remainder') are awarded the remaining seats in order of vote size.

Malapportionment

A situation in which there are imbalances in the population densities of constituencies which favour some parties over others (for example, such as happens when constituency boundaries are not redrawn to take account of rural depopulation).

Modified Sainte-Laguë

Named after A. Sainte-Laguë, and associated most with Scandinavian countries, this **highest average** divisor tends to produce more proportional results than the more common **d'Hondt** divisor. It operates with the following divisors: 1.4, 3, 5, 7, and so on. The 1.4 divisor was brought in to reduce the overall proportionality of the original pure Sainte-Laguë system which was seen as too proportional. Referred to in the USA as the Webster method, pure Sainte-Laguë uses the following divisors: 1, 3, 5, 7. It was adopted by New Zealand in 1993.

Monotonicity

If a candidate's vote increases this should improve the prospects of winning a seat. As pointed out in the formal literature on voting theory, it is possible under preferential electoral systems (such as alternative vote or single transferable vote) for a candidate's prospects to be hindered, not helped, by an increase in first-preference votes. This potential for a non-monotonic result is seen by some as a flaw of preferential electoral systems; others point out that it is difficult to find examples of it ever actually occurring.

Panachage

This is the most 'open' form of **ballot structure** available in list systems, and is operated in Luxembourg and Switzerland. The ballot paper allows voters to give preferences to candidates from more than one party.

Two-Tier Districting

Most of the list systems carve up a country into regions or constituencies, thereby reducing the size of the **district magnitude** and therefore the overall proportionality of the result. To help increase proportionality, a certain number of seats are allocated in a second tier such as across the nation as a whole. All remaining votes from the first tier which have not been used to fill seats are pooled and the distribution of the remaining seats is determined in the second tier.

Überhangmandate Seats

Literally surplus mandates or surplus seats. In the German mixed system, where the number of constituency seats a party wins is subtracted from the number of list seats it is being allocated, it is possible for a party to win more constituency seats in one *Land* (or state) than the total to which its share of the vote would entitle it. Whenever this happens the party is allowed to retain these extra seats and the size of the Bundestag is temporarily enlarged.

Notes and References

1 The Study of Electoral Systems

1. For annual updates on publications in the field of electoral systems and representation, see http://www.indiana.edu/~playpol/REShome.html.
2. According to Reilly and Reynolds' survey of 98 'free' countries, the majoritarian systems are used in nine countries (Reilly and Reynolds 1997: 20); according to Massicotte and Blais's wider sweep of 170 countries, majoritarian systems are used in 23 of them (1999: 345).

2 The Single Member Plurality System and its Cousins

1. For examples of other ballot papers, see http:/www.aceproject.org/.
2. For recent debate over whether the 'North–South' divide still holds at the end of the 1990s, see Curtice and Park (1999), McAllister (1997) and Rossiter *et al.* (1999b).
3. Rob Ritchie and Steven Hill are directors of the Center for Voting and Democracy, an organization committed to promoting electoral reform in the USA (http://www.igc.org/cvd/).

3 Majoritarian Electoral Systems: Two-round Systems and the Alternative Vote

1. The minimum of 12.5 per cent was set in 1978. Between 1962 and 1978, it was 10 per cent; between 1958 and 1962 it was just 5 per cent.
2. In the USA this system is referred to as 'instant run-off voting' by electoral reform campaigners seeking to distinguish this system from existing two-round (run-off) voting systems.

4 The List Systems of Proportional Representation

1. Another variant, referred to as the Hagenbach-Bischoff system, involves the use of the highest average *combined with* a quota in the first round.

213

This is used in Belgium, Luxembourg and Switzerland. In this section, for the sake of simplicity, we will deal only with highest average without a quota.

2. This discussion relies heavily on Kimmo Kuusela's (1995) excellent account of the Finnish electoral system.

3. Given the unique situation of German unification, a special exception was made to the electoral law to allow the electoral threshold for parties to be calculated separately in the east and the west of the country. The Green Party won 6 per cent of the vote in the east and accordingly was allocated eight Bundestag seats (Boll and Poguntke 1992).

4. In Denmark the parties are free to choose between Belgian and Finnish forms of open list: that is, they can decide on whether they want personal votes to determine the overall ranking of the candidates. Generally most of the parties opt for the more open Finnish version (Danish Ministry of the Interior 1996).

5   Mixed Electoral Systems

1. This system is referred to in Germany as the 'Niemeyer method'. Prior to 1985 the list seats were determined by the highest average system using d'Hondt divisors. In other words, Germany adopted more proportional counting rules in 1985, making it easier for small parties to win seats.

2. In fact a number of the *Land* electoral systems compensate for surplus seats, so that the other parties are also granted extra seats (Nohlen 1989: 231–3). No such compensation applies for Bundestag elections.

3. I am grateful to Matthew Shugart from having drawn my attention to this reference.

6   The Single Transferable Vote System of Proportional Representation

1. Arguably the origins of STV can be traced back even further, to the writings of Thomes Wright Hill (1763–1851; a mathematician). However, the system he proposed lacked many of the features of STV (Hart 1992: 6–9).

2. This process of multiple eliminations has become more common in recent elections as a result of amendments to the electoral law in 1992 (Sinnott 1999: 123–4).

7   The Consequences of Electoral Systems

1. The Gallagher index is calculated as follows: square the vote–seat differences for each party (ignoring 'others' – usually parties with less

than 0.5 per cent of the vote); sum them; divide the total by two; and then take the square root (Gallagher 1991). The principal advantage of this index over the others is that it is not so easily distorted by the presence of small parties (a particular problem with the Rae index); nor has it too many problems with systems containing large numbers of parties (a particular problem with the Loosemore–Hanby index).

2. Nationwide average district magnitude is notoriously difficult to calculate. In their respective analyses, Taagepera and Shugart (1989) and Lijphart (1994a) argue that the best measure to use is 'effective' district magnitude, whose calculation requires information on a country's 'legal threshold' (where relevant) as well as precise details on upper-level tiers (where relevant). Given the major gaps in available information on the 59 democracies being considered in this book, it has been decided to classify district magnitude into three broad categories: effective nationwide seat allocation; district magnitude of one; all district magnitudes between these two extremes. There are obvious shortcomings with this approach, particularly with the last of these categories, but at least this classification allows for some demarcation between extremes of district magnitude.

3. The index of 'effective' number of parliamentary parties is calculated as follows: 1 divided by the sum of the squared percentage seats for each party. A similar index of *electoral* parties can be derived based on the percentage votes received by each party in the election.

4. That is where the electoral system can be classified and we have information on the proportion of women in the national parliament. Note for the purposes of this exercise, the MMM systems are excluded from the calculations.

5. Here I part company from social choice perspectives on strategic voting, which tend to examine it in terms of 'insincere' voting (for example, Dummett 1997) or 'co-ordination failure' (Cox 1998). An example of where this occurs is in the case of an SMP election in which voters vote tactically for their second preferred candidate (B) because she has a better chance of defeating the least preferred candidate (C) than does their most preferred candidate (A). In this case the vote for B is 'insincere'. The alternative perspective being put forward in this section relates to the possibility for voters to use certain (preferential) electoral systems to express a complex strategic vote, such as in the case of voting for a set of parties that might form a coalition. The vote can be both sincere (in the sense that the voters are supporting their most preferred candidates) *and* strategic.

9   Electoral Systems and Stability

1. Lijphart takes this a stage further, in developing his 'index of executive dominance', by taking account of certain peculiarities of particular

political systems. This measure is less suitable for our purposes because his adjustments are designed principally to assess the degree of executive dominance which requires him to stress cabinet change over nonchange.

2. Some scholars replace Lijphart's 'consensus' type with his earlier model of 'consociational' democracy, which strictly speaking is incorrect.

Bibliography

Allard, Crispin (1995), 'Lack of Monotonicity – Revisited', *Representation* 33:48–50.

Amy, Douglas J. (1993), *Real Choices, New Voices: The Case for Proportional Representation Elections in the United States*, New York: Columbia University Press.

Anderson, Christopher and Christine Guillory (1997), 'Political Institutions and Satisfaction with Democracy: A Cross-National Analysis of Consensus and Majoritarian Systems', *American Political Science Review* 91:66–81.

Andeweg, Rudy B. and Galen A. Irwin (1993), *Dutch Government and Politics*, London: Macmillan.

Baker, Gordon E. (1986), 'Whatever Happened to the Reapportionment Revolution in the United States?', in Bernard Grofman and Arend Lijphart (eds), *Electoral Laws and Their Political Consequences*, New York: Agathon Press.

Bean, Clive (1986), 'Electoral Law, Electoral Behaviour and Electoral Outcomes: Australia and New Zealand Compared', *Journal of Commonwealth and Comparative Politics* 24:57–73.

Bean, Clive (1997), 'Australia's Experience with the Alternative Vote', *Representation* 34:103–10.

Beckwith, Karen (1992), 'Comparative Research and Electoral Systems: Lessons from France and Italy', *Women and Politics* 12:1–33.

Beer, Samuel (1998), 'The Roots of New Labour: Liberalism Rediscovered', *The Economist*, 7 February.

Benoit, Kenneth (2000), 'Evaluating Hungary's Mixed-Member Electoral Systems', in Matthew S. Shugart and Martin P. Wattenberg (eds), *Mixed-Member Electoral Systems: The Best of Both Worlds?*, Oxford: Oxford University Press.

Berghe, Guido van den (1979), 'Belgium', in G. Hand, J. Georgel and C. Sasse (eds), *European Electoral Systems Handbook*, London: Butterworth.

Birch, Sarah (1997), 'Ukraine: The Perils of Majoritarianism in a New Democracy', in Andrew Reynolds and Ben Reilly (eds), *The International IDEA Handbook of Electoral System Design*, Stockholm: International Institute for Democracy and Electoral Assistance.

Blackburn, Robert (1995), *The Electoral System in Britain*, London: Macmillan.

Blais, André (1988), 'The Classification of Electoral Systems', *European Journal of Political Research* 16:99–110.

Blais, André and R. K. Carty (1991), 'The Psychological Impact of Electoral Laws: Measuring Duverger's Elusive Factor', *British Journal of Political Science* 21:79–93.

Blais, André and Louis Massicotte (1996), 'Electoral Rules', in Lawrence LeDuc, Richard G. Niemi and Pippa Norris (eds), *Comparative Democratic Elections*, Thousand Oaks, Calif.: Sage.

Blondel, Jean (1969), *An Introduction to Comparative Government*, London: Weidenfeld & Nicolson.

Bogdanor, Vernon (1981), *The People and the Party System: The Referendum and Electoral Reform in British Politics*, Cambridge: Cambridge University Press.

Bogdanor, Vernon (1983), 'Introduction', in Vernon Bogdanor and David Butler (eds), *Democracy and Elections: Electoral Systems and Their Political Consequences*, Cambridge: Cambridge University Press.

Bogdanor, Vernon (1984), *What is Proportional Representation? A Guide to the Issues*, Oxford: Martin Robertson.

Boll, Bernhard and Thomas Poguntke (1992), 'Germany: The 1990 All-German Election Campaign', in Shaun Bowler and David Farrell (eds), *Electoral Strategies and Political Marketing*, Houndmills, Basingstoke: Macmillan.

Bolongaita, Emil P. (1999), 'A Political Economy of Electoral Reforms of Democratizing Southeast Asian Countries: Notes on the Philippines and Indonesia', American Political Science Association annual meeting, Atlanta, Georgia, 3–5 September.

Bowler, Shaun (1996), 'Reasoning Voters, Voter Behaviour and Institutions', in David Farrell, David Broughton, David Denver and Justin Fisher (eds), *British Elections and Parties Yearbook, 1996*, London: Frank Cass.

Bowler, Shaun and David Denemark (1993), 'Split Ticket Voting in Australia: Dealignment and Inconsistent Votes Reconsidered', *Australian Journal of Political Science* 28:19–37.

Bowler, Shaun and David Farrell (1991a), 'Party Loyalties in Complex Settings: STV and Party Identification', *Political Studies* 39:350–62.

Bowler, Shaun and David Farrell (1991b), 'Voter Behavior under STV-PR: Solving the Puzzle of the Irish Party System', *Political Behavior* 13:303–20.

Bowler, Shaun and David Farrell (1993), 'Legislator Shirking and Voter Monitoring: Impacts of European Parliament Electoral Systems upon Legislator–Voter Relationships', *Journal of Common Market Studies* 31:45–69.

Bowler, Shaun and David Farrell (1996), 'Voter Strategies under Preferential Electoral Systems: A Single Transferable Vote Mock Ballot Survey of London Voters', in Colin Rallings, David Farrell, David Broughton and David Denver (eds), *British Elections and Parties Yearbook, 1995*, London: Cass.

Bowler, Shaun and Bernard Grofman (2000), 'Introduction: STV as an Embedded Institution', in S. Bowler and B. Grofman (eds), *Elections in Australia, Ireland and Malta Under the Single Transferable Vote:*

Reflections on an Embedded Institution, Ann Arbor, Michigan: University of Michigan Press.

Bowler, Shaun and Jeffrey Karp (1999), 'Coalition Government and Satisfaction with Democracy: An Analysis of New Zealand's Reaction to Proportional Representation', photocopy.

Bowler, Shaun, David Denemark and David Farrell (2000), 'Party Strategy and Voter Organization under Cumulative Voting in Victorian England', *Political Studies* XLVII:906–17.

Bowler, Shaun, David Farrell and Ian McAllister (1996), 'Constituency Campaigning in Parliamentary Systems with Preferential Voting: Is There a Paradox?', *Electoral Studies* 15:461–76.

Bradley, Patrick (1995), 'STV and Monotonicity: A Hands-On Assessment', *Representation* 33:46–47.

Brams, Steven J. and Peter C. Fishburn (1984), 'Some Logical Defects of the Single Transferable Vote', in Arend Lijphart and Bernard Grofman (eds), *Choosing an Electoral System: Issues and Alternatives*, New York: Praeger.

Brischetto, Robert R. and Richard L. Engstrom (1997), 'Cumulative Voting and Latino Representation: Exit Surveys in Fifteen Texas Communities', *Social Science Quarterly* 78:973–91.

Butler, David (1963), *The Electoral System in Britain Since 1918*, 2nd edn, Oxford: Clarendon Press.

Butler, David (1983), 'Variants of the Westminster Model', in Vernon Bogdanor and David Butler (eds), *Democracy and Elections: Electoral Systems and Their Political Consequences*, Cambridge: Cambridge University Press.

Cain, Bruce E. and Kenneth P. Miller (1998), 'Voting Rights Mismatch: The Challenge of Applying the Voting Rights Act to "Other Minorities"', in Mark E. Rush (ed.), *Voting Rights and Redistricting in the United States*, Westport, Conn.: Greenwood Press.

Cain, Bruce, John Ferejohn and Morris Fiorina (1987), *The Personal Vote: Constituency Service and Electoral Independence*, Cambridge, Mass.: Harvard University Press.

Carstairs, Andrew McLaren (1980), *A Short History of Electoral Systems in Western Europe*, London: George Allen & Unwin.

Carty, R. K. (1981), *Party and Parish Pump: Electoral Politics in Ireland*, Waterloo: Wilfrid Laurier University Press.

Castles, Francis G. (1994), 'The Policy Consequences of Proportional Representation: A Sceptical Commentary', *Political Science* 46:161–71.

Caul, Miki (1999), 'Women's Representation in Parliament: The Role of Political Parties', *Party Politics* 5:79–98.

Chubb, Basil (1982), *The Government and Politics of Ireland*, 2nd edn, London: Longman.

Cole, Alistair and Peter Campbell (1989), *French Electoral Systems and Elections Since 1789*, Aldershot: Gower.

Cole, Philip (1995), 'Bonus Seats in the German Electoral System', *Representation* 33:9–10.

Cox, Gary (1997), *Making Votes Count: Strategic Coordination in the World's Electoral Systems*, Cambridge: Cambridge University Press.

Curtice, John (1992), 'The Hidden Surprise: The British Electoral System in 1992', *Parliamentary Affairs* 45:466–74.

Curtice, John and Alison Park (1999), 'Region: New Labour, New Geography?', in Geoffrey Evans and Pippa Norris (eds), *Critical Elections: British Parties and Voters in Long-Term Perspective*, London: Sage.

Curtice, John and Michael Steed (1982), 'Electoral Choice and the Production of Government: The Changing Operation of the Electoral System in the United Kingdom Since 1955', *British Journal of Political Science* 12:249–98.

Danish Ministry of the Interior (1996), *Parliamentary Elections and Election Administration in Denmark*, Copenhagen: Ministry of the Interior.

Darcy, Robert and Ian McAllister (1990), 'Ballot Position Effects', *Electoral Studies* 9:5–17.

Darcy, Robert and Malcolm Mackerras (1993), 'Rotation of Ballots: Minimizing the Number of Rotations', *Electoral Studies* 12:77–82.

Darcy, Robert and Michael Marsh (1994), 'Decision Heuristics: Ticket-Splitting and the Irish Voter', *Electoral Studies* 13:38–49.

Darcy, Robert, Susan Welch and Janet Clark (1994), *Women, Elections and Representation*, 2nd edn, Lincoln, Nebr.: University of Nebraska Press.

Denemark, David (2000), 'Choosing MMP in New Zealand: Explaining the 1993 Electoral Reform', in M. S. Shugart and M. Wattenberg (eds), *Mixed-Member Electoral Systems: The Best of Both Worlds?*, Oxford: Oxford University Press.

Devine, Fiona (1995), 'Qualitative Analysis', in David Marsh and Gerry Stoker (eds), *Theory and Methods in Political Science*, London: Macmillan.

De Winter, Lieven (1988), 'Belgium: Democracy or Oligarchy?', in Michael Gallagher and Michael Marsh (eds), *Candidate Selection in Comparative Perspective: The Secret Garden of Politics*, London: Sage.

Dodd, Lawrence (1976), *Coalitions in Parliamentary Government*, Princeton, NJ: Princeton University Press.

Donovan, Mark (1995), 'The Politics of Electoral Reform in Italy', *International Political Science Review* 16:47–64.

Dummett, Michael (1992), 'Towards a More Representative Voting System: The Plant Report', *New Left Review* 194:98–113.

Dummett, Michael (1997), *Principles of Electoral Reform*, Oxford: Oxford University Press.

Dunleavy, Patrick and Helen Margetts (1995), 'Understanding the Dynamics of Electoral Reform', *International Political Science Review* 16:9–29.

Dunleavy, Patrick, Helen Margetts and Stuart Weir (1993), 'The 1992 Election and the Legitimacy of British Democracy', in David Denver, Pippa Norris, David Broughton and Colin Rallings (eds), *British Elections and Parties Yearbook, 1993*, Hemel Hempstead, Herts: Harvester Wheatsheaf.

Dunleavy, Patrick, Helen Margetts and Stuart Weir (1998), 'Making Votes Count 2', *Democratic Audit Paper* No. 14.

Dunleavy, Patrick, Helen Margetts, Brendan O'Duffy and Stuart Weir (1997), 'Making Votes Count', *Democratic Audit Paper* No. 11.

Duverger, Maurice (1954), *Political Parties: Their Organization and Activity in the Modern State*, London: Methuen.

Duverger, Maurice (1986), 'Duverger's Law: Forty Years Later', in Bernard Grofman and Arend Lijphart (eds), *Electoral Laws and Their Political Consequences*, New York: Agathon Press.

Elgie, Robert (1997), 'Two-Ballot Majority Electoral Systems', *Representation* 34:89–94.

Engstrom, Richard L. (1987), 'District Magnitudes and the Election of Women to the Irish Dáil', *Electoral Studies* 6:123–32.

Engstrom, Richard L. (1998), 'Minority Electoral Opportunities and Alternative Election Systems in the United States', in Mark E. Rush (ed.), *Voting Rights and Redistricting in the United States*, Westport, Conn.: Greenwood Press.

Engstrom, Richard L., Jason Kirksey and Edward Still (1997), 'One Person, Seven Votes: The Cumulative Voting Experience in Chilton County, Alabama', in Anthony A. Peacock (ed.), *Affirmative Action and Representation: Shaw v. Reno and the Future of Voting Rights*, Durham, NC: Carolina Academic Press.

Erickson, Lynda (1995), 'The October 1993 Election and the Canadian Party System', *Party Politics* 1:133–44.

Evans, Geoffrey, John Curtice and Pippa Norris (1998), 'New Labour, New Tactical Voting?', *British Elections and Parties Review* 8.

Farrell, Brian (1985), 'Ireland: From Friends and Neighbours to Clients and Partisans', in Vernon Bogdanor (ed.), *Representatives of the People?*, Aldershot: Gower.

Farrell, Brian (1988), 'Ireland', in Jean Blondel and Ferdinand Müller-Rommel (eds), *Cabinets in Western Europe*, London: Macmillan.

Farrell, David (1994), 'Ireland: Centralization, Professionalization and Campaign Pressures', in Richard Katz and Peter Mair (eds), *How Parties Organize: Adaptation and Change in Party Organizations in Western Democracies*, London: Sage.

Farrell, David (1999), 'Ireland: A Party System Transformed?', in David Broughton and Mark Donovan (eds), *Changing Party Systems in Western Europe*, London: Pinter.

Farrell, David (2000), 'The United Kingdom Comes of Age: The British Electoral Reform "Revolution" of the 1990s', in Matthew S. Shugart and Martin P. Wattenberg (eds), *Mixed-Member Electoral Systems: The Best of Both Worlds?*, Oxford: Oxford University Press.

Farrell, David and Michael Gallagher (1998), *Submission to the Independent Commission on the Voting System*, London: McDougall Trust.

Farrell, David and Michael Gallagher (1999), 'British Voters and their Criteria for Evaluating Electoral Systems', *British Journal of Politics and International Relations* 1:293–316.

Farrell, David and Ian McAllister (1995), 'Legislative Recruitment to Upper Houses: The Australian Senate and House of Representatives Compared', *Journal of Legislative Studies* 1:243–63.

Farrell, David and Ian McAllister (2000), 'Through a Glass Darkly: Understanding the World of STV', in Shaun Bowler and Bernard Grofman (eds), *Elections in Australia, Ireland and Malta Under the Single Transferable Vote: Reflections on an Embedded Institution*, Ann Arbor, Michigan: University of Michigan Press.

Farrell, David and Paul Webb (2000), 'Political Parties as Campaign Organizations', in Russell Dalton and Martin P. Wattenberg (eds), *Parties Without Partisans*, Oxford: Oxford University Press.

Farrell, David, Ian McAllister and David Broughton (1994), 'The Changing British Voter Revisited: Patterns of Election Campaign Volatility Since 1964', in David Broughton, David Farrell, David Denver and Colin Rallings (eds), *British Elections and Parties Yearbook, 1994*, London: Frank Cass.

Finer, S. E. (ed.) (1975), *Adversary Politics and Electoral Reform*, London: Anthony Wigram.

Fisichella, Domenico (1984), 'The Double-Ballot System as a Weapon Against Anti-System Parties', in Arend Lijphart and Bernard Grofman (eds), *Choosing an Electoral System: Issues and Alternatives*, New York: Praeger.

Flanagan, Tom (1998), 'The Alternative Vote: An Electoral System for Canada', *Inroads* 7:73–8.

Franklin, Mark and Philip Norton (eds) (1993), *Parliamentary Questions*, Oxford: Clarendon Press.

Gallagher, Michael (1975), 'Disproportionality in a Proportional Representation System: The Irish Experience', *Political Studies* 23:501–13.

Gallagher, Michael (1978), 'Party Solidarity, Exclusivity and Inter-Party Relationships in Ireland 1922–1977: The Evidence of Transfers', *Economic and Social Review* 10:1–22.

Gallagher, Michael (1987), 'Does Ireland Need a New Electoral System?', *Irish Political Studies* 2:27–48.

Gallagher, Michael (1990), 'The Election Results and the New Dáil', in Michael Gallagher and Richard Sinnott (eds), *How Ireland Voted 1989*, Galway: Centre for the Study of Irish Elections/PSAI Press.

Gallagher, Michael (1991), 'Proportionality, Disproportionality and Electoral Systems', *Electoral Studies* 10(1):33–51.

Gallagher, Michael (1993), 'The Election of the 27th Dáil', in Michael Gallagher and Michael Laver (eds), *How Ireland Voted, 1992*, Dublin: Folens/PSAI Press.

Gallagher, Michael (1999), 'The Results Analysed', in Michael Marsh and Paul Mitchell (eds), *How Ireland Voted, 1997*, Boulder, Colo.: Westview Press.

Gallagher, Michael and Lee Komito (1999), 'The Constituency Role of TDs', in John Coakley and Michael Gallagher (eds), *Politics in the Republic of Ireland*, 3rd edn, London: Routledge/PSAI Press.

Gallagher, Michael and A. R. Unwin (1986), 'Electoral Distortion under STV Random Sampling Procedures', *British Journal of Political Science* 16:243–68.

Gallagher, Michael, Michael Laver and Peter Mair (2000), *Representative Government in Modern Europe*, 3rd edn, New York: McGraw-Hill.

Gladdish, Ken (1991), *Governing From the Centre: Politics and Policy-Making in the Netherlands*, London: Hurst & Co.

Goldey, David B. (1993), 'The French General Election of 21–28 March 1993', *Electoral Studies* 12:291–314.

Grofman, Bernard and Shaun Bowler (1996), 'STV's Place in the Family of Electoral Systems: The Theoretical Comparisons and Contrasts', *Representation* 34:43–8.

Hain, Peter (1986), *Proportional Mis-Representation: The Case Against PR in Britain*, Hants: Wildwood House.

Hand, Geoffrey, Jacques Georgel and Christoph Sasse (eds) (1979), *European Electoral Systems Handbook*, London: Butterworth.

Harris, Paul (1992), 'Changing New Zealand's Electoral System: The 1992 Referendum', *Representation* 31:53–7.

Harris, Paul (1993), 'Electoral Reform in New Zealand', *Representation* 32:7–10.

Hart, Jennifer (1992), *Proportional Representation: Critics of the British Electoral System, 1820–1945*, Oxford: Clarendon Press.

Hermens, Ferdinand A. (1984), 'Representation and Proportional Representation', in Arend Lijphart and Bernard Grofman (eds), *Choosing an Electoral System: Issues and Alternatives*, New York: Praeger.

Hirczy, Wolfgang (1995), 'STV and the Representation of Women', *PS: Political Science and Politics* 28:711–13.

Holliday, Ian (1994), 'Dealing in Green Votes: France, 1993', *Government and Opposition* 29(1):64–79.

Holliday, Ian (2001), 'Spain', in Paul Webb, David Farrell and Ian Holliday (eds), *Political Parties at the Millennium*, Oxford: Oxford University Press.

Horowitz, Donald L. (1991), *A Democratic South Africa? Constitutional Engineering in a Divided Society*, Berkeley, Calif.: University of California Press.

Horowitz, Donald L. (1997), 'Encouraging Electoral Accommodation in Divided Societies', in Brij V. Lal and Peter Larmour (eds), *Electoral Systems in Divided Societies: The Fiji Constitution Review*, Canberra: National Centre for Development Studies, Research School of Social Sciences, Australian National University (Pacific Policy Paper 21).

Huber, John and G. Bingham Powell (1994), 'Congruence Between Citizens and Policymakers in Two Visions of Liberal Democracy', *World Politics* 46:291–326.

Huntington, Samuel P. (1991), *The Third Wave: Democratization in the Late Twentieth Century*, Norman: University of Oklahoma Press.

Inter-Parliamentary Union (1992), *Women and Political Power*, Geneva: Inter-Parliamentary Union.

Irvine, William F. (1979), *Does Canada Need a New Electoral System?*, Kingston, Ontario: Institute of Intergovernmental Relations, Queen's University.

Jeffery, Charlie (1999), 'Germany: From Hyperstability to Change?', in David Broughton and Mark Donovan (eds), *Changing Party Systems in Western Europe*, London: Pinter.

Jeffery, Charlie and Dan Hough (1999), 'The German Election of September 1998', *Representation* 36:78–84.

Jesse, Eckhard (1988), 'Split-Voting in the Federal Republic of Germany: An Analysis of the Federal Elections from 1953 to 1987', *Electoral Studies* 7:109–24.

Johnston, R. J., Charles Pattie, David Rossiter, Danny Dorling, Iain MacAllister and Helena Tunstall (1999), 'New Labour's Landslide and Electoral Bias: An Exploration of Differences between the 1997 UK General Election Result and the Previous Thirteen', *British Elections and Parties Review* 9:20–45.

Jones, Mark (1995), 'A Guide to the Electoral Systems of the Americas', *Electoral Studies* 14:5–22.

Jones, Mark (1997), 'A Guide to the Electoral Systems of the Americas: An Update', *Electoral Studies* 16:13–16.

Karlan, Pamela S. (1998), 'The Impact of the Voting Rights Act on African Americans: Second- and Third-Generation Issues', in Mark E. Rush (ed.), *Voting Rights and Redistricting in the United States*, Westport, Conn.: Greenwood Press.

Katz, Richard S. (1980), *A Theory of Parties and Electoral Systems*, Baltimore, Md: Johns Hopkins University Press.

Katz, Richard S. (1984), 'The Single Transferable Vote and Proportional Representation', in Arend Lijphart and Bernard Grofman (eds), *Choosing an Electoral System: Issues and Alternatives*, New York: Praeger.

Katz, Richard S. (1986), 'Intraparty Preference Voting', in Bernard Grofman and Arend Lijphart (eds), *Electoral Laws and Their Political Consequences*, New York: Agathon Press.

Katz, Richard S. (1989), 'International Bibliography on Electoral Systems', revised and expanded edition, *International Political Science Association*, Comparative Representation and Electoral Systems Research Committee.

Katz, Richard S. (1992), 'International Bibliography on Electoral Systems', 3rd edn, *International Political Science Association*, Comparative Representation and Electoral Systems Research Committee.

Katz, Richard S. (1996), 'Electoral Reform and the Transformation of Party Politics in Italy', *Party Politics* 2:31–53.

Katz, Richard S. (1997a), *Democracy and Elections*, Oxford: Oxford University Press.

Katz, Richard S. (1997b), 'Representational Roles', *European Journal of Political Research* 32:211–26.

Katz, Richard S. (1998), 'Malapportionment and Gerrymandering in Other Countries and Alternative Electoral Systems', in Mark E. Rush (ed.), *Voting Rights and Redistricting in the United States*, Westport, Conn.: Greenwood Press.

Katz, Richard S. (1999), 'Electoral Reform and its Discontents', *British Elections and Parties Review* 9:1–19.

Katz, Richard S. (2000), 'Reforming the Italian Electoral Law, 1993', in Matthew S. Shugart and Martin P. Wattenberg (eds), *Mixed-Member Electoral Systems: The Best of Both Worlds?*, Oxford: Oxford University Press.

Kelley, Jonathan and Ian McAllister (1983), 'The Electoral Consequences of Gender in Australia', *British Journal of Political Science* 13:365–77.

Kelley, Jonathan and Ian McAllister (1984), 'Ballot Paper Cues and the Vote in Australia and Britain: Alphabetic Voting, Sex, and Title', *Public Opinion Quarterly* 48:452–66.

Kellner, Peter (1992), 'The-Devil-You-Know-Factor', *Representation* 31:10–12.

Kendall, M. G. and A. Stuart (1950), 'The Law of Cubic Proportion in Election Results', *British Journal of Sociology* 1:183–97.

Klingemann, Hans-Dieter, Richard I. Hofferbert and Ian Budge (1994), *Parties, Policies, and Democracy*, Boulder, Colo.: Westview Press.

Kuusela, Kimmo (1995), 'The Finnish Electoral System: Basic Features and Developmental Tendencies', in Sami Borg and Risto Sänkiaho (eds), *The Finnish Voter*, Tampere: The Finnish Political Science Association.

Laakso, M. and R. Taagepera (1979), 'Effective Number of Parties: A Measure with Application to West Europe', *Comparative Political Studies* 12:3–27.

Labour Party (1993), *Report of the Working Party on Electoral Systems, 1993*, London: Labour Party.

Lakeman, Enid (1974), *How Democracies Vote: A Study of Majority and Proportional Electoral Systems*, 4th edn, London: Faber & Faber.

Lakeman, Enid (1982), *Power to Elect: The Case for Proportional Representation*, London: Heinemann.

Lal, Brij V. and Peter Larmour (eds) (1997), *Electoral Systems in Divided Societies: The Fiji Constitution Review*, Canberra: National Centre for Development Studies, Research School of Social Sciences, Australian National University (Pacific Policy Paper 21).

Lancaster, T. and W. Paterson (1990), 'Comparative Pork Barrel Politics: Perceptions from the West German Bundestag', *Comparative Political Studies* 22:458–77.

Lane, John C. (1995), 'The Election of Women under Proportional Representation: The Case of Malta', *Democratization* 2:140–57.

Laver, Michael and Norman Schofield (1991), *Multiparty Government: The Politics of Coalition in Western Europe*, Oxford: Oxford University Press.

LeDuc, Lawrence, Richard G. Niemi and Pippa Norris (1996), 'Introduction: The Present and Future of Democratic Elections', in Lawrence LeDuc, Richard G. Niemi and Pippa Norris (eds), *Comparing Democracies: Elections and Voting in Global Perspective*, Thousand Oaks, Calif.: Sage.

Lijphart, Arend (1977), *Democracy in Plural Societies: A Comparative Exploration*, New Haven, Conn.: Yale University Press.

Lijphart, Arend (1984), *Democracies: Patterns of Majoritarian and Consensus Government in Twenty-One Countries*, New Haven, Conn.: Yale University Press.

Lijphart, Arend (1985), 'The Field of Electoral Systems Research: A Critical Survey', *Electoral Studies* 4:3–14.

Lijphart, Arend (1986a), 'Degrees of Proportionality of Proportional Representation Formulas', in Bernard Grofman and Arend Lijphart (eds), *Electoral Laws and Their Political Consequences*, New York: Agathon Press.

Lijphart, Arend (1986b), 'Proportionality by Non-PR Methods: Ethnic Representation in Belgium, Cyprus, Lebanon, New Zealand, West Germany and Zimbabwe', in Bernard Grofman and Arend Lijphart (eds), *Electoral Laws and Their Political Consequences*, New York: Agathon Press.

Lijphart, Arend (1987), 'The Demise of the Last Westminster System? Comments on the Report of New Zealand's Royal Commission on the Electoral System', *Electoral Studies* 6:97–103.

Lijphart, Arend (1990), 'The Political Consequences of Electoral Laws, 1945–85', *American Political Science Review* 84:481–96.

Lijphart, Arend (1994a), *Electoral Systems and Party Systems: A Study of Twenty-Seven Democracies, 1945–1990*, Oxford: Oxford University Press.

Lijphart, Arend (1994b), 'Democracies: Forms, Performance, and Constitutional Engineering', *European Journal of Political Research* 25:1–17.

Lijphart, Arend (1999a), *Patterns of Democracy: Government Forms and Performance in Thirty-Six Countries*, New Haven, Conn.: Yale University Press.

Lijphart, Arend (1999b), 'First-past-the-post, PR and the Empirical Evidence', *Representation* 36:133–6.

Lijphart, Arend, Rafael Lopez Pintor and Yasunori Sone (1986), 'The Limited Vote and the Single Non-Transferable Vote: Lessons from the Japanese and Spanish Examples', in Bernard Grofman and Arend Lijphart (eds), *Electoral Laws and Their Political Consequences*, New York: Agathon Press.

Loosemore, John and Victor J. Hanby (1971), 'The Theoretical Limits of Maximum Distortion: Some Analytic Expressions for Electoral Systems', *British Journal of Political Science* 1:467–77.

McAllister, Ian (1992), *Political Behaviour: Citizens, Parties and Elites in Australia*, Melbourne: Longman Cheshire.

McAllister, Ian (1997), 'Regional Voting', in Pippa Norris and Neil Gavin (eds), *Britain Votes, 1997*, Oxford: Oxford University Press.

McAllister, Ian and Toni Makkai (1993), 'Institutions, Society or Protest? Explaining Invalid Votes in Australian Elections', *Electoral Studies* 12:23–40.

McAllister, Ian and Stephen White (1995), 'Democracy, Political Parties and Party Formation in Post-Communist Russia', *Party Politics* 1:49–72.

Mackerras, Malcolm (1996), *The Mackerras 1996 Federal Election Guide*, Canberra: Australian Government Publishing Service.

Mackie, Thomas T. and Richard Rose (1991), *The International Almanac of Electoral History*, 3rd edn, London: Macmillan.

Mackie, Thomas T. and Richard Rose (1997), *A Decade of Election Results: Updating the International Almanac*, Glasgow: Centre for the Study of Public Policy.

McLean, Iain (1991), 'Forms of Representation and Systems of Voting', in David Held (ed.), *Political Theory Today*, Cambridge: Polity Press.

McLean, Iain (1992), 'Why Does Nobody in Britain Seem to Pay Any Attention to Voting Rules?', in Pippa Norris, Ivor Crewe David Denver, and David Broughton (eds), *British Elections and Parties Yearbook, 1992*, Hemel Hempstead: Harvester Wheatsheaf.

Mair, Peter (1986), 'Districting Choices under the Single Transferable Vote', in Bernard Grofman and Arend Lijphart (eds), *Electoral Laws and Their Political Consequences*, New York: Agathon Press.

Margetts, Helen and Patrick Dunleavy (1999), 'Reforming the Westminster Electoral System: Evaluating the Jenkins Commission Proposals', *British Elections and Parties Review* 9:46–71.

Marsh, Michael (1985), 'The Voters Decide? Preferential Voting in European List Systems', *European Journal of Political Research* 13:365–78.

Massicotte, Louis and André Blais (1999), 'Mixed Electoral Systems: A Conceptual and Empirical Survey', *Electoral Studies* 18:341–66.

Matland, Richard and Donley T. Studlar (1996), 'The Contagion of Women Candidates in Single-Member Districts and Proportional Representation Electoral Systems: Canada and Norway', *Journal of Politics* 58:707–33.

Milner, Henry (1998), 'The Case for Proportional Representation in Canada', *Inroads* 7:52–8.

Mozaffar, Shaheen (1997), 'Democratization, Institutional Choice, and the Political Management of Ethnic Conflict: Africa in Comparative Perspective', American Political Science Association annual meeting, Washington, DC, 28–31 August.

Nealon, Ted (1997), *Nealon's Guide to the 28th Dáil and Seanad: Election '97*, Dublin: Gill & Macmillan.

Niemi, Richard G., Guy Whitten and Mark Franklin (1992), 'Constituency Characteristics, Individual Characteristics and Tactical Voting in the 1987 British General Election', *British Journal of Political Science* 22:229–54.

Nohlen, Dieter (1984), 'Changes and Choices in Electoral Systems', in Arend Lijphart and Bernard Grofman (eds), *Choosing an Electoral System: Issues and Alternatives*, New York: Praeger.

Nohlen, Dieter (1989), *Wahlrecht und Parteiensystem*, Opladen: Leske & Budrich.

Nohlen, Dieter (1997), 'Electoral Systems in Eastern Europe: Genesis, Critique, Reform', in J. Elklit (ed.), *Electoral Systems for Emerging Democracies: Experiences and Suggestions*, Copenhagen: Danish Ministry of Foreign Affairs.

Norris, Pippa (1985), 'Women's Legislative Participation in Western Europe', *West European Politics* 8:90–101.

Norris, Pippa (1994), 'Labour Party Quotas for Women', in David Broughton, David Farrell, David Denver and Colin Rallings (eds), *British Elections and Parties Yearbook, 1994*, London: Frank Cass.

Norris, Pippa (1995a), 'The Politics of Electoral Reform in Britain', *International Political Science Review* 16:65–78.

Norris, Pippa (1995b), 'Introduction: The Politics of Electoral Reform', *International Political Science Review* 16:3–8.

Norris, Pippa (1996), 'Candidate Recruitment', in Lawrence LeDuc, Richard G. Niemi and Pippa Norris (eds), *Comparative Democratic Elections*, Thousand Oaks, Calif.: Sage.

Norris, Pippa (1999), 'Institutional Explanations for Political Support', in Pippa Norris (ed.), *Critical Citizens: Global Support for Democratic Governance*, Oxford: Oxford University Press.

Norris, Pippa and Ivor Crewe (1994), 'Did the British Marginals Vanish? Proportionality and Exaggeration in the British Electoral System Revisited', *Electoral Studies* 13(3):201–21.

Norton, Philip (1997), 'The case for First-Past-The-Post', *Representation* 34:84–8.

Norton, Philip and D. Wood (1990), 'Constituency Service by Members of Parliament: Does it Contribute to a Personal Vote?', *Parliamentary Affairs* 43:196–208.

Nurmi, Hannu (1997), 'It's Not Just the Lack of Monotonicity', *Representation* 34:48–52.

O'Connell, Declan (1983), 'Proportional Representation and Intra-Party Competition in Tasmania and the Republic of Ireland', *Journal of Commonwealth and Comparative Politics* 21:45–70.

O'Hearn, Denis (1983), 'Catholic Grievances Catholic Nationalism: A Comment', *British Journal of Sociology* 34:438–45.

O'Leary, Cornelius (1979), *Irish Elections, 1918–1977: Parties, Voters and Proportional Representation*, Dublin: Gill & Macmillan.

Orttung, Robert W. (1996), 'Duma Elections Bolster Leftist Opposition', *Transition*, 23 February: 6–11.

Parker, A. J. (1983), 'Localism and Bailiwicks: The Galway West Constituency in the 1977 General Election', *Proceedings of the Royal Irish Academy* 83:C2,17–36.

Peacock, Anthony A. (1998), 'Equal Representation or Guardian Democracy? The Supreme Court's Foray into the Politics of Reapportionment and Its Legacy', in Mark E. Rush (ed.), *Voting Rights and Redistricting in the United States*, Westport, Conn.: Greenwood Press.

Pinto-Duschinsky, Michael (1999), 'Send the Rascals Packing: Defects of Proportional Representation and the Virtues of the Westminster Model', *Representation* 36:117–26.

Plant, Raymond (1991), *The Plant Report: A Working Party on Electoral Reform*, London: *Guardian* Studies, Volume 3.

Poguntke, Thomas (1994), 'Parties in a Legalistic Culture: The Case of Germany', in Richard S. Katz and Peter Mair (eds), *How Parties Organize: Change and Adaptation in Party Organizations in Western Democracies*, London: Sage.

Powell, G. Bingham (1999), 'Westminster Model versus PR: Normative and Empirical Evidence', *Representation* 36:127–32.

Proportional Representation Society (1919), *Sligo Municipal Elections, 1919: The First Town Council in the United Kingdom Elected by Proportional Representation*, London: Proportional Representation Society (PR Pamphlet No. 41).

Pulzer, Peter (1983), 'Germany', in Vernon Bogdanor and David Butler (eds), *Democracy and Elections: Electoral Systems and Their Political Consequences*, Cambridge: Cambridge University Press.

Punnett, R. M. (1991), 'The Alternative Vote Revisited', *Electoral Studies* 10:281–98.

Rae, Douglas (1967), *The Political Consequences of Electoral Laws*, New Haven, Conn.: Yale University Press.

Rallings, Colin (1987), 'The Influence of Election Programs: Britain and Canada, 1945–79', in Ian Budge, David Robertson and D. Hearl (eds), *Ideology, Strategy and Party Change*, Cambridge: Cambridge University Press.

Rangarajan, Mahesh and Vijay Patidar (1997), 'India: First Past the Post on a Grand Scale', in Andrew Reynolds and Ben Reilly (eds), *The International IDEA Handbook of Electoral System Design*, Stockholm: International Institute for Democracy and Electoral Assistance.

Reed, Steven (1994), 'A Path to Reform', *By The Way* 4:32–5.

Reed, Steven (1999), 'Disappointment with Electoral Reform in Japan', photocopy.

Reeve, Andrew and Alan Ware (1992), *Electoral Systems: A Comparative and Theoretical Introduction*, London: Routledge.

Reilly, Ben (1997a), 'The Alternative Vote and Ethnic Accommodation: New Evidence from Papua New Guinea', *Electoral Studies* 16:1–12.

Reilly, Ben (1997b), 'The Plant Report and the Supplementary Vote: Not So Unique After All', *Representation* 34:95–102.

Reilly, Ben (1997c), 'Preferential Voting and Political Engineering: A Comparative Study', *Journal of Commonwealth and Comparative Politics* 35:1–19.

Reilly, Ben and Andrew Reynolds (1999), 'Electoral Systems and Conflict in Divided Societies', *Papers on International Conflict Resolution* No. 2, Washington, DC: National Academy Press.

Representation (1996), Special Issue on 'Mixed Electoral Systems', Vol. 33.

Reynolds, Andrew (1994), 'The Consequences of South Africa's PR Electoral System', *Representation* 32:57–60.

Reynolds, Andrew (1999), *Electoral Systems and Democratization in Southern Africa*, Oxford: Oxford University Press.

Reynolds, Andrew and J. Elklit (1997), 'Jordan: Electoral System in the Aras World', in Andrew Reynolds and Ben Reilly (eds), *The International IDEA Handbook of Electoral System Design*, Stockholm: International Institute for Democracy and Electoral Assistance.

Reynolds, Andrew and Ben Reilly (eds) (1997), *The International IDEA Handbook of Electoral System Design*, Stockholm: International Institute for Democracy and Electoral Assistance.

Riker, William H. (1986), 'Duverger's Law Revisited', in Bernard Grofman and Arend Lijphart (eds), *Electoral Laws and Their Political Consequences*, New York: Agathon Press.

Ritchie, Rob and Steven Hill (1998), 'This Time Let the Voters Decide: The PR Movement in the United States', *Inroads* 7:100–8.

Ritchie, Rob and Steven Hill (1999), *Reflecting All of Us: The Case for Proportional Representation*. Boston, Mass.: Beacon Press.

Roberts, Geoffrey K. (1975), 'The Federal Republic of Germany', in S. E. Finer (ed.), *Adversary Politics and Electoral Reform*, London: Anthony Wigram.

Roberts, Geoffrey K. (1977), 'Point of Departure? The Blake Report on Electoral Reform', *Government and Opposition* 12:42–59.

Roberts, Geoffrey, K. (1988), 'The "Second Vote" Campaign Strategy of the West German Free Democratic Party', *European Journal of Political Research* 16:317–37.

Robson, Christopher and Brendan Walsh (1974), 'The Importance of Positional Voting Bias in the Irish General Election of 1973', *Political Studies* 22:191–203.

Roche, Richard (1982), 'The High Cost of Complaining Irish Style', *Journal of Irish Business and Administrative Research* 4:98–108.

Rose, Richard (1980), *Do Parties Make a Difference?*, Chatham, NJ: Chatham House.

Rose, Richard and Doh Chull Shin (1999), 'Democratization Backwards: The Problem of Third Wave Democracies', *Studies in Public Policy* 314, Glasgow: Centre for the Study of Public Policy.

Rossiter, D. J., R. J. Johnston and C. J. Pattie (1999a), *The Boundary Commissions: Redrawing the UK's Map of Parliamentary Constituencies*, Manchester: Manchester University Press.

Rossiter, D. J., R. J. Johnston, Charles Pattie, Danny Dorling, Iain MacAllister and Helena Tunstall (1999b), 'Changing Biases in the Operation of the UK's Electoral System, 1950–97', *British Journal of Politics and International Relations* 1:133–64.

RTÉ (1997), *Election 1997: Results and Analysis*, Dublin: RTÉ.

Rule, Wilma (1987), 'Electoral Systems, Contextual Factors and Women's Opportunity for Election in Twenty-Three Democracies', *Western Political Quarterly* 40:477–98.

Rule, Wilma (1994), 'Women's Underrepresentation and Electoral Systems', *PS: Political Science and Politics* 27:689–92.

Rule, Wilma (1996), 'Response to Wolfgang Hirczy', *PS: Political Science and Politics* 29:143.

Rush, Mark E. (1993), *Does Redistricting Make a Difference? Partisan Representation and Electoral Behavior*, Baltimore, Md: Johns Hopkins University Press.

Sartori, Giovanni (1986), 'The Influence of Electoral Systems: Faulty Laws or Faulty Method?', in Bernard Grofman and Arend Lijphart (eds), *Electoral Laws and Their Political Consequences*, New York: Agathon Press.

Sartori, Giovanni (1997), *Comparative Constitutional Engineering: An*

Inquiry into Structures, Incentives and Outcomes. 2nd edn, London: Macmillan.

Scarrow, Susan (2000), 'Germany: The Mixed-Member System as a Political Compromise', in Matthew S. Shugart and Martin P. Wattenberg (eds), *Mixed-Member Electoral Systems: The Best of Both Worlds?*, Oxford: Oxford University Press.

Schlesinger, Joseph A. and Mildred S. Schlesinger (1990), 'The Reaffirmation of a Multi-Party System in France', *American Political Science Review* 84:1077–101.

Schlesinger, Joseph A. and Mildred S. Schlesinger (1995), 'French Parties and the Legislative Elections of 1993', *Party Politics* 1:369–80.

Schmitt, David E. (1973), *The Irony of Irish Democracy: The Impact of Political Culture on Administrative and Democratic Political Development in Ireland*, Lexington, Mass.: Lexington Books.

Schoen, Harald (1999), 'Split-Ticket Voting in German Federal Elections, 1953–90: An Example of Sophisticated Balloting?', *Electoral Studies* 18:473–96.

Shiratori, Rei (1995), 'The Politics of Electoral Reform in Japan', *International Political Science Review* 16:79–94.

Shugart, Matthew S. (1999), 'The Jenkins Paradox: A Complex System, Yet Only a Timid Step Towards PR', *Representation* 36:143–7.

Shugart, Matthew S. (2000), ' "Extreme" Electoral Systems and the Appeal of the Mixed-Member Alternative', in Matthew S. Shugart and Martin P. Wattenberg (eds), *Mixed-Member Electoral Systems: The Best of Both Worlds?*, Oxford: Oxford University Press.

Shugart, Matthew S. and Martin P. Wattenberg (2000a), 'Mixed-Member Electoral Systems: A Definition and Typology', in Matthew S. Shugart and Martin P. Wattenberg (eds), *Mixed-Member Electoral Systems: The Best of Both Worlds?*, Oxford: Oxford University Press.

Shugart, Matthew S. and Martin P. Wattenberg (2000b), 'Are Mixed-Member Systems the Best of Both Worlds?', in Matthew S. Shugart and Martin P. Wattenberg (eds), *Mixed-Member Electoral Systems: The Best of Both Worlds?*, Oxford: Oxford University Press.

Sinnott, Richard (1993), 'The Electoral System', in John Coakley and Michael Gallagher (eds), *Politics in the Republic of Ireland*, 2nd edn, Dublin: Folens/PSAI Press.

Sinnott, Richard (1995), *Irish Voters Decide: Voting Behaviour in Elections and Referendums Since 1918*, Manchester: Manchester University Press.

Sinnott, Richard (1999), 'The Electoral System', in John Coakley and Michael Gallagher (eds), *Politics in the Republic of Ireland*, 3rd edn, London: Routledge.

Studlar, Donley T. (1998), 'Will Canada Consider Electoral System Reform? Women and Aboriginals Should', *Inroads* 7:52–8.

Studlar, Donley T. and Ian McAllister (1998), 'Candidate Gender and Voting in the 1997 British General Election: Did Labour Quotas Matter?', *Journal of Legislative Studies* 4:72–91.

Studlar, Donley T. and Susan Welch (1991), 'Does District Magnitude

Matter? Women Candidates in London Local Elections', *Western Political Quarterly* 44:457–66.

Taagepera, Rein (1996), 'STV in Transitional Estonia', *Representation* 34:29–36.

Taagepera, Rein (1997), 'The Tailor of Marrakesh: Western Electoral Systems Advice to Emerging Democracies', in J. Elklit (ed.), *Electoral Systems for Emerging Democracies*, Copenhagen: Danish Ministry of Foreign Affairs.

Taagepera, Rein (1998), 'How Electoral Systems Matter for Democratization', *Democratization* 5:68–91.

Taagepera, Rein and Matthew S. Shugart (1989), *Seats and Votes: The Effects and Determinants of Electoral Systems*, New Haven, Conn.: Yale University Press.

Taylor, P. J. and R. J. Johnston (1979), *Geography of Elections*, London: Penguin.

Valen, Henry (1994), 'List Alliances: An Experiment in Political Representation', in M. Kent Jennings and Thomas E. Mann (eds), *Elections at Home and Abroad: Essays in Honor of Warren E. Miller*, Ann Arbor, Mich.: University of Michigan Press.

Vowles, Jack (1995), 'The Politics of Electoral Reform in New Zealand', *International Political Science Review* 16:95–115.

Vowles, Jack (1999), 'Rascals and PR: How Pinto-Duschinsky Stacked the Decks', *Representation* 36:137–42.

Vowles, Jack, Susan Banducci and Jeffrey Karp (1998a), 'Electoral System Opinion in New Zealand' (http://www2.waikato.ac.nz/politics/nzes/july_report.html).

Vowles, Jack, Peter Aimer, Susan Banducci and Jeffrey Karp (eds) (1998b), *Voters' Victory? New Zealand's First Election Under Proportional Representation*, Auckland: Auckland University Press.

Wattenberg, Martin P. (1998), *The Decline of American Political Parties, 1952–1992*, 5th edn, Cambridge, Mass.: Harvard University Press.

Weaver, Kent (1998), 'MMP is Too Much of Some Good Things', *Inroads* 7:59–64.

Weaver, Leon (1986), 'The Rise, Decline and Resurrection of Proportional Representation in Local Governments in the United States', in Bernard Grofman and Arend Lijphart (eds), *Electoral Laws and their Political Consequences*, New York: Agathon Press.

Welch, Susan and Donley T. Studlar (1990), 'Multi-Member Districts and the Representation of Women: Evidence from Britain and the United States', *Journal of Politics* 52:391–412.

Whiteley, Paul and Patrick Seyd (1999), 'Discipline in the British Conservative Party: The Attitudes of Party Activists Toward the Role of Their Member of Parliament', in Shaun Bowler, David Farrell and Richard Katz (eds), *Party Discipline and Parliamentary Government*, Columbus, Ohio: Ohio State University Press.

Whyte, John (1983), 'How Much Discrimination Was There under the Unionist Regime, 1921–68?', in Tom Gallagher and James O'Connell (eds), *Contemporary Irish Studies*, Manchester: Manchester University Press.

Wright, Jack F. H. (1980), *Mirror of the Nation's Mind: Australia's Electoral Experiments*, Sydney: Hale & Iremonger.

Wright, Jack F. H. (1986), 'Australian Experience with Majority-Preferential and Quota-Preferential Systems', in Bernard Grofman and Arend Lijphart (eds), *Electoral Laws and Their Political Consequences*, New York: Agathon Press.

Zanella, Remo (1990), 'The Maltese Electoral System and its Distorting Effects', *Electoral Studies* 9:205–15.

Index